The Austrian School and Modern Economics: Essays in Reassessment

The Austrian School and Modern Economics: Essays in Reassessment

Nicolai J. Foss

HANDELSHØJSKOLENS FORLAG
Distribution: Munksgaard International Publishers Ltd
Copenhagen

Printed in Denmark by Reproset, Copenhagen
Set in Plantin by ABK-Sats, Copenhagen
Cover designed by Kontrapunkt Design
Book designed by Jørn Ekstrøm

ISBN 87-16-13235-1

Series A
Copenhagen Studies in Economics and Management, No. 4

Preface

The essays in this book are the results of a continuing interest in the economics of the Austrian School, particularly in the economics of Friedrich von Hayek and Ludwig von Mises. Most of them have not been published previously. The oldest essay dates back to 1989, while the most recent was written in 1993.

Many people have made comments on the essays. I would particularly like to mention and thank Thráinn Eggertson, Jesper Jespersen, Christian Knudsen, Carsten A. Koch, Murray Rothbard, and Ulrich Witt. John Murphy skillfully edited the text.

Some of the material in chapter 8 appears in an article in *The Review of Austrian Economics 7* ("Theories of the Firm: the Austrians as Precursors and Critics of Contemporary Theory"), and some of the material in chapters 4 and 6 was originally published in *Økonomi og Politik* (1990 and 1991) and *Rivista Internazionale di Scienze Sociali* (1993). Permission to reprint this material is gratefully acknowledged. Chapter 9 builds on work co-authored with Professor Christian Knudsen, Copenhagen Business School, and his permission to include much of our joint product here is also gratefully acknowledged. Finally, I would like to thank Lauge Stetting, the manager of Handelshøjskolens Forlag, who initially suggested that I published my essays on Austrian economics and has been very supportive throughout.

Nikolai J. Foss
Copenhagen, May 11, 1994

Contents

1: Introduction to the Essays

Although the essays in this book were largely written independently, there is a common overall theme to them. This theme is that the Austrians – and in particular Ludwig von Mises and Friedrich von Hayek – anticipated a number of important developments in modern economics. By "modern" I refer here to economics since about the beginning of the 1970s. Thus, Hayek's work on business cycle theory in a number of ways anticipated modern new classical macroeconomics (chapter 3), and his work on intertemporal equilibrium anticipated modern notions (chapter 2); Mises had a number of deep insights in the area of property rights economics (chapter 5); and both Mises and Hayek may be seen as in many ways anticipating central aspects of the modern theory of economic organization (chapters 4,5,6,8). Finally, there are a number of affinities between the process approach to understanding market activities that Hayek and Mises pioneered and the modern evolutionary economics approach of, most prominently, Richard Nelson and Sidney Winter (chapters 6 and 7).

Undoubtedly, some of these insights may be traced back to some extent to the older Austrians, primarily the three founding fathers of the school, Carl Menger, Friedrich von Wieser and Eugen von Böhm-Bawerk. For example, it really is no coincidence that it is Hayek, an Austrian economist familiar with Böhm-Bawerkian capital theory, who first introduces the notion of intertemporal equilibrium. It is perhaps not so very large a step from time-dimensioned Böhm-Bawerkian capital theory to some notion of intertemporal equilibrium. We should also remember that Böhm-Bawerk wrote on property rights. The process approach to market activities normally thought of as pioneered by Hayek and Mises (for example, Kirzner 1973) can certainly be seen as having its roots in Menger's work (Streissler 1972). Hayek's approach to cultural evolution has a number of central aspects that are anticipated in Menger's thoughts on the same subject.

However, in spite of the fact that much of the work of Hayek and Mises may be traced back to their forebears, theirs are in many respects the most complete Austrian statements of such themes as the business cycle, property rights, the market process as an evolutionary process, and institutions. It is therefore their contributions that most clearly anticipate modern neo-institutionalist and evolutionary thought.

As the above assertions indicate, I see the Austrians as anticipating relatively divergent strands in modern economics. For example, Hayek is – via his introduction in 1928 of the notion of intertemporal equilibrium – a part of the history of general equilibrium theory, but he is clearly also a precursor of modern neo-institutionalist thought and evolutionary thought. This seeming inconsistency is accounted for by the fact that Hayek started out as a very orthodox equilibrium theorist but later on -realizing a number of deep difficulties with equilibrium theory – turned towards the interdisciplinary studies for which he is best known today (Foss 1995). Chapters 2 and 3 detail Hayek's early phase as an equilibrium theorist while other essays discuss his later works.

As the above also indicates, I see the Austrian School of the 1920s and 1930s as a very progressive intellectual force at that time. And, controversially, I think that it was so important and so progressive that it should be considered at least on a par with the Walrasianism that spread from the Continent to the Anglo-Saxon world at the same period. Even more controversially, I suggest that had the Austrian insights emerging in these two decades not been swept so decisively away by the Keynesian tide and the emerging Walrasianism, economic theory would have progressed faster than it has done, and done so in a sounder way. For example, the importance of property rights and asymmetric information would not have had to wait until the late 1960s for their rediscovery but would have been recognized in the economic mainstream much earlier. As a consequence, institutions would not have had to await the 1980s until they entered the agenda of economists. The stability of equilibrium (or coordination) problem would have occupied center stage, instead of being constantly suppressed. The economics of socialism would definitely have followed a different path, etc. That the favorable assessment of the Austrians of the interwar period that this counterfactual claim implies does not to the same extent carry over to their (mostly) American heirs is argued in chapter 9.

The philosopher P.F. Strawson has often been cited for remarking that in order to understand one's philosophical forebears one should reformulate their thoughts in one's own contemporary terms. I feel very much the same way with regard to economics, and that is one reason why I have called this book "The Austrian School and Modern Economics"; not only because I see the Austrians as anticipating a number of important contemporary themes in economics, but also because I have tried to dress their arguments in contemporary garb, particularly economics of the neo-institutionalist and evolutionary variety (chapters 4 to 9). That does not mean that I attempt to present a unified and consistent attempt to tell the doctrinal history of neo-institutionalist and evolutionary thought in terms of the economics of the Austrian school. It is rather some episodes from the history of the Austrian school that are central, as interpreted through the use of modern economic thinking.

Crucial to my reading of primarily Mises and Hayek's contributions is their emphasis on problems of intertemporal trade, their view of the future as inherently uncertain, their conception of the market as an ongoing evolutionary process, and their conception of institutions and organizations as designed or undesigned entities for adapting to the economic problems implied by change. To be sure, these themes emerged rather *gradually* throughout the 1920s and 1930s in the writings of Mises and Hayek; for example, Hayek was in his early career strongly influenced by Walrasianism (so that he for example did not conceive of the future as inherently uncertain). In other words, my reading of Mises and Hayek is to some extent a rational reconstruction in the light of recent neo-institutionalist and evolutionary thought.

All the same, I think this is a rather unusual approach to the economics of the Austrian School. Recent years have seen a burst of scholarship on the history of the Austrian School, particularly on Carl Menger, Hayek and Mises. Much of this has been inspired by the 1974 conferment of the Nobel Prize on Hayek, the revival of classical liberalism in the 1980s, and the expansion – or revitalization – of Austrian economics, primarily in the United States from the middle of the 1970s. However, most of the recent Hayek and Mises scholarship has emerged from a group of mainly American Austrians who see themselves as the true heirs of Hayek and particularly of Mises, and who are mostly strongly critical of mainstream economics.

It seems to me, however, that Mises and Hayek had a number of interesting points that probably cannot be wholly captured within the theorizing of the modern Austro-American school, but should rather be interpreted in the context of more or less mainstream economics (such as property rights economics) and the new heterodoxy of neo-institutionalist and evolutionary thought. Although there can be little doubt that Hayek and Mises pioneered a process approach to market activities in which the entrepreneur is central (today primarily associated with the work of Israel Kirzner), they also anticipated insights associated with recent neo-institutionalist and evolutionary thought rather than with neo-Austrian thought. Furthermore, in contrast to many of Mises and Hayek's faithful followers, I like mainstream economics, although I emphasize the benefits of a fruitful dialogue between heterodox economic traditions -such as the modern Austro-American school – and the mainstream (see chapter 9).

Because of the particular Austrians I have chosen to focus on, and because of the way I have treated their work, the reader will find little or nothing about such modern Austrian controversial subjects as to whether the market process is inherently equilibrating or disequilibrating, what Shackle's work implies for Austrian economics, whether Austrian methodology should be oriented in an ultrarationalist or a hermeneutic direction, the possible differences between a Misesian and a Hayekian approach to Austrian economics, etc. Some of these themes are admirably treated in Karen Vaughn's (1994) forthcoming book, "Austrian Economics in America: the Migration of a Tradition".

Finally, an important motivation behind publishing these essays is that many of them discuss the economics of Ludwig von Mises just as much as the economics of Friedrich von Hayek (the two first essays are however almost solely occupied with Hayek's economics). After long neglect, Hayek finally became enrolled in the super league of modern economists. His 1974 Nobel Prize was the outward manifestation of this; the fact that his work has become a standard reference in the theory of economic organization, comparative systems, theory of efficient markets etc., is the more internal one.

The same honors and recognition were never quite bestowed on Mises, although he became a Distinguished Fellow of the American Economic Association, received some honorary doctorates, and had two Festschriften published in his honor. That Mises was partially ignored was a result of him being considered "difficult", "doctrinaire", "extremist" etc. I have always felt that Mises' work is just as fundamental and trail-blazing as Hayek's work and that he was never given the credit and recognition which he truly deserved. After all, Hayek's Nobel Prize winning work on business cycle theory and the economics of socialism was built on Misesian foundations. In the hope that this book may represent a tiny step towards a reevaluation of his scholarship, I dedicate it to the memory of Ludwig von Mises.

2: Intertemporal Coordination of Economic Activities: the Early Debate between Hayek and Keyes

1. Introduction

> "Hayek's economic writings...are almost unknown to the modern student; it is hardly remembered that there was a time when the new theories of Hayek were the principal rival of the new theories of Keynes. Which was right, Keynes or Hayek?" (Hicks 1967: 203).

Within the economics profession, Friedrich von Hayek acquired the reputation of being perhaps the strongest critic of Keynes and Keynesian economics. Against the background of his "Campaign Against Keynesian Inflation" (1978: 91), and his assessment of Keynes' "General Theory" as a modern John Law's "tract of the times" (1978: 286), this seems indeed to be a quite reasonable judgment.

However, if we step six decades back in time, another picture emerges. Specifically, if we take a look at the assessments that prominent economists of the 1930s (such as Shackle 1933; Robertson 1934; Durbin 1935) made of the relationship between the work of Keynes and that of Hayek, surprisingly we seem to be faced with a remarkable agreement based on strong analytical similarities. For Keynes and Hayek were both seen to have a "...common starting point in the work of Wicksell" (Shackle 1933: 27). And that starting point was clearly something that separated them from the majority of contemporary British theorists of the business cycle (such as Arthur Pigou, Ralph Hawtrey and Dennis Robertson). Keynes himself could only contribute to the strength of such an assessment for in a passage in the "Treatise" he refers approvingly to the "Neo-Wicksell School" – that is, Ludwig von Mises, Hans Neisser and Hayek – whose work was supposedly "...fairly close to the theory of this Treatise" (1930: 199).[1]

However, when contemporary commentators saw similarities between

[1] This endorsement is somewhat surprising, since Keynes in a review in 1914 in Economic Journal had treated Mises' "Theorie des Geldes und Umlaufsmittels" (1912) rather harshly (Keynes 1914).

Hayek and Keynes, they were referring, of course, to Keynes' "Treatise", not to his later "General Theory". And although a few eclectics (such as Durbin 1935) heroically tried to combine Hayek's (1935a) Böhm-Bawerkian set-up with Keynes' (1930) optimum portfolio approach, it became increasingly clear – not the least in Keynes' own mind – that "...Wicksell plus Keynes said one thing, Wicksell plus Hayek said quite another" (Hicks 1967: 204). The seeming similarities quickly dwindled.

It was on the initiative of Lionel Robbins that in February 1931, Hayek held four lectures at the London School of Economics. In November this year they were published in book form under the title "Prices and Production" (henceforth "PP"). This book, it is generally agreed, is *the* classical statement of the Austrian theory of the business cycle.[2] Hayek's lectures induced a turbulent debate among Anglo-Saxon economists, with the young turks at London School of Economics strongly on Hayek's side,[3] and Cambridge economists on the attacking side (Sraffa 1932; Robinson 1933). There was much more involved than institutional rivalry and London School of Economics laisser-faire versus Cambridge policy activism. A large part of the economic profession seems to have preferred Hayek's short and rigorous analysis to Keynes' monumental two-volume "Treatise", not to speak of Dennis Robertson's complicated savings-investments analysis or Ralph Hawtrey's idiosyncratic cycle theory based on investments in inventory. Hayek's theory was seen as having larger explanatory power, while in addition it better satisfied criteria such as rigor and clarity.

The majority of British reviews were, however, negative. For example, Ralph Hawtrey saw PP as "difficult and obscure", primarily because Hayek had entangled his argument "...with the intolerably cumbersome theory of capital derived from Jevons and Böhm-Bawerk" (Hawtrey 1932: 125). But in the United States, Alvin Hansen, in a largely positive review, observed that PP was

> "...the only book of recent years which at all approaches Keynes' *A Treatise on Money* in the impetus it has given to

[2] Assuredly, Hayek was not the only contributor to the Austrian theory of the business cycle. In numerous publications, largely in German, Hans Neisser, Fritz Machlup, Gottfried Haberler, Ludwig Lachmann, Eric Schiff, Wilhelm Röpke and Richard Strigl elaborated the theory, in addition, of course, to Ludwig von Mises (who is the real "inventor" of the theory).

[3] At least initially. The "turks" included Robbins, Lerner, Hicks, Shackle, Benham, Durbin and Kaldor. Lachmann (1982: 630) recalls that when he arrived at the London School of Economics in the spring of 1933 "all important economists there were Hayekians". A curious aspect of all this was the conversion of many economists associated with the Labour Party (such as Evan Durbin, Hugh Gaitskell, Eric Roll and others) to Hayek's theory of the business cycle.

> the renewed interest and discussion of business cycle theory" (1933: 332).

It is not difficult to confirm Hansen's evaluation: there was a quite widespread agreement at the time that the avant-garde in the effort to explain the business cycle was represented by "A Treatise on Money" and by PP.

In this context, we should remember that the most prestigious field of research in economics circa 1930 was business cycle theorizing, as a glance at, for instance, the list of contributors to the 1933 Spiethoff Festschrift ("Die Ställung und der nächste Zukunft der Konjunkturforschung") will confirm. So the drama on the dominant theoretical stage was being played out between Keynes and Hayek. The drama continued, in a sense, until the death of Hayek in 1992, since Hayek was to the end in strong opposition to the ideas of Keynes. But it was just as much Keynes' ethics and epistemology, he later criticized; the strictly economic debate was largely over with Keynes and Hayek's debate over international economics shortly before the end of the Second World War (Hayek 1943; Keynes 1944).

This chapter is about the first act in the drama, the exchange between Hayek and Keynes in the pages of the London School of Economics household journal, Economica. This took place in 1931 and 1932 in the form of a two-part review by Hayek (1931a, 1932a) of Keynes' "Treatise", a response by Keynes (1931), and an answer from Hayek (1931b). The contribution to the enormous amount of doctrinal scholarship on Keynes and the steadily growing Hayek scholarship represented by this essay has to do not only with a detailed discussion of that particular exchange. I am also trying to place the exchange in the context of the broader work of the two dramatis personae (section 2 and 3), and I am attempting to provide a distinct perspective on it. Specifically, I see the early debate between Hayek and Keynes as first and foremost about the intertemporal coordination of economic activities (section 4). Using Leijonhufvud's (1981) terminology, the debate between Hayek and Keynes represented a debate within "The Wicksell Connection".[4] Furthermore, the debate anticipated a number of themes that became important in later debates between Keynes and his critics.

In the context of the themes of this book, a reason for discussing the de-

[4] The only contribution I am aware of that extensively discusses the early exchange between Hayek and Keynes is Dostaler (1991). The present chapter differs in many respects from Dostaler's paper. For a thorough discussion of the debate between Hayek and Sraffa, which took place almost at the same time as the Hayek-Keynes debate, see Lawlor and Horn (1992).

bate in a relatively detailed way is that it clearly brings out how strongly the young Hayek was influenced by general equilibrium theory, and how much he tended to interpret that theory as having descriptive significance. In being so strongly influenced by general equilibrium theory, Hayek seems to have occupied a relatively unique position among the Austrians of that time[5]. But, ironically, he was also the Austrian who was later to accomplish the most effective break with general equilibrium theory. It is these circumstances that account for the paradoxical fact that both new classical and evolutionary economists may count Hayek among their intellectual forebears.

It is certainly undeniable that deep differences between Hayek and Keynes were present (probably already at the beginning of the 1930s) in a number of other dimensions such as epistemology and ethics. But these differences have, I feel, a rather limited bearing on the issues under consideration here, so I have chosen to disregard them in what follows. In other words, I see the early debate between Keynes and Hayek as a strictly economic one.

2. "Prices and Production": Combining Walras, Wicksell and Böhm-Bawerk

2.1. The Methodic Problems of Business Cycle Research

Hayek's London School of Economics lectures were the theoretical expression of the heuristic and methodological program for business cycle research which he had formulated in his 1929 Habilitationsschrift, "Geldtheorie und Konjunkturtheorie" (1933a). This book was essentially a contribution to the contemporary Continental discussions of the scope and method of business cycle research which blossomed particularly in the late 1920s and the early 1930s (Lõwe 1926; Lutz 1932). Retrospectively, two problem areas stand out as especially vital and prominent in these debates:

1) the epistemological status of empirically oriented business cycle research – a problem that derived from the Methodenstreit, and, more relevant in the present context;
2) the possibilities of applying existing equilibrium theory to an explanation of the business cycle.

[5] Professor Ulrich Witt has suggested to me that Hayek's strong early equilibrium orientation was due to Friedrich Wieser being his teacher. Wieser was the most equilibrium oriented of the older Austrians.

Whereas an empirically oriented business cycle analyst, such as the American W.C. Mitchell, explicitly refused to be interested in how "...the fact of cyclical fluctuations...can be reconciled with the general theory of equilibrium" (1927: 462), this theme had at least since Böhm-Bawerk's (1898) assertion of an "organische" relation between the theory of value and business cycle theory, been a relatively prominent theme in Continental discussions. In these discussions, we confront a very distinct conception of the apparent tension between the theory of value and business cycle theory, one that was not at all to the same extent characteristic of contemporary Anglo-Saxon discussion. Löwe's (1926: 193) assertion that, "Wer am statischen System festhält, muss das Konjunkturproblem preisgeben", defines the one extreme of the discussion.

2.2. Problems with the Walrasian Model

Hayek was in broad agreement with the predominant reluctance to associate observed business cycle phenomena with a continuum of equilibria. As he explained it, the main problem with the theory of value – "...most perfectly expressed by the Lausanne School of theoretical economics" (1933a: 42) – was that no changes in data in isolation

> "...could adequately explain, within the framework of this theoretical system, why a general disproportionality between supply and demand should arise" (ibid.).

This was because the theory of value was founded on the assumption that "...prices supply an automatic mechanism for equilibrating supply and demand" (ibid.). It is not particularly difficult to establish evidence for the proposition that Hayek not only implicitly took for granted the existence, uniqueness and stability of equilibrium of the Walrasian model. Many contemporary economists routinely did this, but Hayek also associated this model with very high velocities of price adjustment (see for example, Hayek 1933a: 77,183,197). This implied that a Walrasian economy could not exhibit that "discrepancy between supply and demand", whose existence empirical business cycle research had established. In other words, the theory of value was threatened by an empirical anomaly. Certainly, Hayek did not exclude the conceptual possibility of fluctuations in a system characterized by continuous equilibrating response to, for example, stochastically determined states of nature.[6] What he claimed was rather that the business cycle as an interesting theoretical problem had to be understood in terms of "...developments leading away from equilibrium...without any changes in data"(ibid.: 55). And to rationalize such developments was precisely the theoretical problem.

On the other hand, it was integral to Hayek's program for business cycle research to apply the theory of value to the "more complicated dynamic phenomena" (1933b: 135). There was then an internal theoretical problem in Hayek's approach to the scope and method of business cycle research. The way he "saved" "the unquestionable methods of equilibrium theory"(1933a: 57) began from the fact that since the Walrasian model has no room for disequilibrium phenomena, their presence in the real world has to be rationalized in terms of some factors that do not exist in the pure Walrasian model. These factors are money and credit.[7] The presence of credit, in particular,

> "...does away with the rigid interdependence and self-sufficiency of the "closed" system of equilibrium, and makes possible movements which could be excluded from the latter"(ibid.: 44).

In other words, theories of the business cycle had to be monetary – as a purely logical matter. Hayek considered Wicksell's cumulative process, and particularly Mises' (1912: 396-404) introduction of real effects in the Wicksellian process, to be an excellent starting point. Wicksell had not thought of his cumulative process as an explanation of the business cycle. And through a series of restrictive assumptions (1936: 136-138),[8] he had in fact effectively closed off the possibility of monetary changes having any impact on real quantities; they were the same ex post as they were ex ante.

Hayek's (and of course also Mises') work on the business cycle can be understood as an immanent critique of Wicksell. More precisely, it is an attempt to clarify and try to answer the following problem: what happens to quantities in a Wicksellian cumulative process, when Wicksell's restric-

[6] As represented by, for example, Moore's (1929) attempts to fit American time series to a Walrasian "moving equilibrium".

[7] That Hayek had failed to provide an adequate integration of value theory and monetary theory, because he had not specified behavioral relations for a monetary economy, was pointed out by Sraffa (1932) and Hicks (1933). To Hayek, the differentia of a monetary economy is primarily that is an inflationary divergence from a nonmonetary economy.

[8] Such as a fixed one-year period of production and a one-stage structure of production: "We neglect the fact that capital changes hands before it has completed the full circle" (Wicksell 1936: 128). To Hayek and Mises this "fact" was on the contrary quite essential.

tive assumptions are weakened? According to Hayek, the analysis of this had to take place within the boundaries of a Böhm-Bawerkian general equilibrium system, utilizing "the methods of static analysis, for these are the only instruments available to economic theory" (Hayek 1933a: 197).

2.3. "Prices and Production"

It was in PP that Hayek's program for business cycle research found its theoretical formulation; it was here that the above-mentioned conceptual experiment was actually carried out. Hayek had a very clear grasp of the distinction (which is usually attributed to Wicksell and Ragnar Frisch) between "impulses" and "propagation mechanisms"; between what initiates the cycle and what allows it to continue. This distinction marks off his work on the business cycle in the sense that while Hayek (1933a), in addition to programmatic matters concentrated on a discussion of "the *monetary causes* which *start* the cyclical fluctuations", PP concentrated on "the *successive changes in the real structure of production* which constitute those fluctuations" (1933a: 17).

Hayek's starting-point was Böhm-Bawerk's stationary general equilibrium from "Positive Theory" (1891: 403-424), and he basically adopted all Böhm's underlying assumptions.[9] Following Böhm, Hayek illustrated a capital-using economy as organized in multiple, successive stages of production in a triangular graphical construction (PP: 39), the so-called "Hayekian triangle". The structure of production – or, if you like, the Leontieff input-coefficient matrix – is triangular, and the top of the triangle defines the first application of nonproduced inputs (labor and land) to the production of capital goods. So capital goods are seen by Hayek as "saved up labor and saved up land in combination". Moving down the triangle – under the continuous application of nonproduced inputs – they emerge as consumer goods at the base of the triangle (compare Böhm-Bawerk 1891: 106).

This is, at the same time, a snapshot representation of the overall productive activities of society and one of the intertemporal allocation of resources, given technology and preferences. And in the context of the model, the area of the triangle represents the total mass of capital goods, while the ratio between this area and the output of consumers' goods (both

[9] Such as perfect competition, flow input/point output technology, the produced outputs are not inputs etc. Hayek supplied Böhm-Bawerk's real model with a credit market, making the loan rate of interest an endogenous variable (in addition to the wage rate, the rate of profit, and the period of production). During the nineteen-thirties, Hayek increasingly distanced himself from Böhm-Bawerk's theory of capital, culminating with his "Pure Theory of Capital" (1941).

measured in value terms) represents the capital intensity of the societal process of production (in Hayek's terminology, it equals the average period of production). In stationary equilibrium, factor payments and profit rates ("price margins") must be the same over all stages of production. Furthermore, profit rates must be equal to the loan rate at the credit market for monetary equilibrium to apply. This set-up is now applied by Hayek in two different scenarios.

2.4. The Savings Scenario

In the first one – which I shall call "the savings scenario" – Hayek describes a fully coordinated system response to a change in the intertemporal preferences of households. The rational response in the case of an increase in the propensity to save is an increase in the average period of production, implying larger real consumption in the new corresponding stationary equilibrium. Furthermore, consistent with the Wicksell effect, real wages increase and profit rates drop. Böhm-Bawerk (1891: 104-118) and Wicksell had, of course, conducted similar experiments, although on a more aggregate level and in comparative static terms. As Hill (1933: 607) noted, "The economics of transitions finds no place in [Böhm's] system". Hayek had more to say. Compared to his mentors, his analytical innovation was the application of the analytical apparatus he had introduced in 1928, namely intertemporal equilibrium, to a quasi-sequential analysis of the price and quantity effects of a change in intertemporal preferences.[10] In analyzing the relative price and quantity effects of a change in intertemporal preferences, Hayek may be seen as giving the Wicksell-effect a more microeconomic and dynamic underpinning.

Thus, the traverse between alternative stationary equilibria is investigated using perfect foresight intertemporal equilibrium (see Hayek 1932b: 245). This allows Hayek to portray the intertemporal invisible hand (to borrow Garrison's (1985) felicitous phrase) as working effortlessly through a complicated sequence of changes in "price margins", relative prices and quantities (PP: 69 85). Since Hayek's Böhm-Bawerkian set-up is characterized by full resource utilization, resources are bid away from stages of production temporally close to final consumption and towards stages temporally far away from final production, implying an increase in the average period of production. Temporary differences in profitability

[10] For a (neo-Ricardian) discussion of Hayek's role as innovator of the notion of intertemporal equilibrium, see Milgate (1979).

between production in different stages of production induce entrepreneurs to carry out those changes in quantities that are consistent with the change in the intertemporal preferences of households.

Hayek emphasizes that the change to more capital-intensive ("roundabout") investment projects that follows a drop in the loan rate of interest is not only a consequence of the circumstance that the interest elasticity of the discounted present value is higher for long projects than it is for short ones. It also a result of the drop in the interest rate *in itself* signalling a change in the returns that accrue to (temporally) different investment projects (Hayek 1932a: 23). In other words, Hayek implicitly assumes that entrepreneurs understand the economic theory describing the system; that is, possess a correct model of the world.

Under the traverse to the new stationary equilibrium, the plans of savers and investors are continuously consistent: the saving of households goes on "...continuously, exactly as they can be used for building up the new processes of production" (PP: 50), and households bear the diminished consumption possibilities until more productive processes "mature" with a greater real output. There are no difficulties of adjustment; the system is continuously on its factor-price frontier (or wage-interest curve) and in monetary equilibrium. That is to say, for all the combinations of the loan rate of interest and real wage that the system travels through, the rate of profit and the loan rate of interest are equal. Monetary equilibrium implies what Hayek calls "neutral money", and can be described as the situation in which "...relative prices would be formed, as if they were influenced only by the "real" factors which are taken into account in equilibrium economics" (PP: 130) (compare Wicksell 1936: 103). As this indicates, Hayek had no distinct conception of a monetary economy; an economy in which money is "neutral" is an economy without money (cf. Sraffa 1932).

In fact, Hayek compares the final stationary equilibrium as identical to the one that would have resulted if "...the savings were made in kind instead of in money" (PP: 50). It is basically Böhm-Bawerk's idea of the subsistence fund and "echte Sparmitteln" that raises its head here. Under a neutral money regime, Hayek had earlier explained, one is "justified" in assuming that "...the price which entrepreneurs expect to result from a change in demand...will more or less coincide with the equilibrium price" (1933a: 69). In modern terminology, a neutral money regime is one in which rational expectations are good approximations to economic reality.

2.5. The Crisis Scenario

This savings scenario is merely a benchmark for Hayek's theory of the *crisis*; that is, the analysis of the effects of "...disturbances of the intertemporal price system which are without any economic function" (1928: 99). Any divergence from monetary equilibrium/neutral money implies such "disturbances". Consistent with, for example, Spiethoff or Pigou's real business cycle theories, Hayek views entrepreneurial forecast errors as a necessary part of any theory of the business cycle. The problem with those real business-cycle theories that highlighted such errors was, however, their appeal to entrepreneurial irrationality and their inability to explain why movements in prices and interest rates could not compensate for instability caused by wrong entrepreneurial decisions (Hayek 1933a: 181-186). However, application of what would today be called "noisy" price and interest rate signals – noise being caused by "disturbing monetary influences" – could handle this problem. Hayek explained:

> "...it may be that the prices existing when they [entrepreneurs] made their decisions and on which they had to base their views about the future have created expectations which must necessarily be disappointed" (1933b: 141).

The relevant price signal here is the observable loan rate of interest, which is taken by Hayekian entrepreneurs to be a reliable proxy for the unobservable natural rate (1933b: 141). In other words, the loan rate of interest is taken to reliably summarize information about the intertemporal preferences of households and the physical rates of transformation of firms. A divergence between the loan rate of interest and the natural rate implies dissemination of misinformation concerning real underlying determinants. Since entrepreneurial expectations are based on entrepreneurs' sets of information, the divergence between the rates of interest has the effect of creating "...expectations concerning the future behavior of some members of society which are entirely unfounded" (1933b: 145).

Entrepreneurs receiving "false" signals undertake the reallocations in the production structure that are consistent with a change in the planned future demands of households. Initially, the dynamics are identical to Hayek's benchmark, the savings scenario: entrepreneurs start more capital-intensive, more time-consuming investment projects; resources are bid away from production temporally close to consumption towards production temporally far away from production etc. But contrary to the savings scenario, the intertemporal preferences of households are unchanged. Combined with increasing (nominal) factor payments from the added credit creation (Hayek 1932b: 242), this implies excess demand on the market for consumer goods (i.e. "forced saving"). At the same time firms have an excess demand for capital goods and labor services for the longer investment projects. At some point during all this, prices of consumer goods will have risen so much that production, in stages of production temporally close to final consumption, increases in relative profitability.[11] This is the upper turning point of the cycle, in which investments in the more "roundabout" projects cease; "Work on the new Cunarder will be suspended", as Dennis Robertson (1934: 87) said.

The structure of production undershoots in a cyclical adjustment, that is to say the average period of production is shorter than in the initial equilibrium, since the profit rates that are temporarily in existence at the time of the upper turning-point of the cycle in stages temporarily close to final consumption are higher than in the initial equilibrium. Not all labor will be absorbed in the new shorter projects since the amount of capital, because of specificity and complementarity among capital goods, places restrictions on the demand for labor ("classical unemployment"). Because of production lags, it takes time before complementary capital goods come forward, and, because of inflexibility of the technology, labor will "...find employment only as the new shorter processes are approaching completion" (PP: 93).

On Hayek's perfect competition labor market, the real wage will however fall under the average product of labor, and it is probably through the changes in the functional distribution of incomes that follow this that the recovery, about which Hayek has little to say, begins. Expansive economic policies can only make things worse by amplifying the distortions in the structure of production, and the policy recommendation is therefore, passively, to let time

> "...affect a permanent cure by the slow process of adapting the structure of production to the means available for capital purposes" (PP: 99).

The only way in which cycles may be avoided is through total fixation of "the effective amount of money", MV, implying continuous monetary

[11] As Durbin (1935) pointed out, Hayek unfortunately never specifies the lag structure of this complicated process. One of the major research efforts of the Stockholm School was in contrast to provide a precise description of the events that followed an initial savings-investment discrepancy.

equilibrium and secular deflation. Because of unpredictable changes in the velocity of money, this is, however, not possible, and Hayek concludes pessimistically and Schumpeter-like that crises are the price we pay for technological progress (PP: Lecture IV).

Summing up, we may say that for Hayek, intertemporal coordination problems in a monetary market economy is the very stuff out of which business cycle theories are made. But Hayek focused this general insight and gave it a distinctly Austrian interpretation (with a nod to Walras and Pareto). Specifically, he saw the theory of intertemporal allocation as represented by Austrian capital theory as necessary for any sound understanding of the business cycle. It allowed him to give a disaggregated and explicitly microeconomic account of price and quantity trajectories in a business cycle, giving full room for all relevant intertemporal market forces. This was the perspective from which he attacked Keynes.

3. The Debate

3.1. Keynes' "Treatise"

On an overall level, Keynes' "Treatise" had the same purpose as the contemporary contributions of Hayek, Robertson and Hawtrey: to identify the causes of "the credit cycle" and the banking policy that could sustain monetary equilibrium, by which Keynes – and Hayek, Hawtrey and Robertson – understood full employment savings-investment equilibrium. Keynes' "novel means of approach to the fundamental problems of monetary theory" (1930: V) consisted in an application of Wicksellian doctrine, which marks the debut of this monetary tradition in English monetary theory (Marshall does not seem to have known Wicksell's works). As Keynes saw it, the task of monetary theory was to supplement the quantity theory in the sense of providing a stability theory, that is, an examination of the causal process "...by which the price level is determined, and the method of transition from one position of equilibrium to another" (1930: 133).

The formalism Keynes utilized to explicate his dynamic quantity theory of money were the "Fundamental Equations". They implied that the price level would fluctuate around a quantity, E – O (total income minus total output), and that the fluctuations would depend on the size of "windfall profits". These profits were determined by differences between savings and investments which, in their turn, were determined by differences between the loan rate of interest and the natural rate. "Windfall profits" constituted the "mainspring of change" of the business cycle, since they influenced the production levels of firms and their factor demands. In the Marshallian tradition they were defined as the difference between an output unit's "demand price" and its "supply price". In this way, the theory of the business cycle became reduced to the study of divergence in price and cost, specifically and "operationally" to the study of differences between price and cost indices.

3.2. Hayek's Review

The usual evaluation in the Keynes literature has been that Hayek's (1931a, 1932a) two-part, 42-page, review of the "Treatise" is primarily characterized by a stubborn and ultimately unproductive attempt to clarify terminological differences of rather limited general interest.[12] An examination of Hayek's review indicates, however, that much more was involved than mere terminology. All of Hayek's objections to Keynes' analysis have to do with the theory of capital and interest, and with Keynes' overly aggregative style of theorizing. As I shall argue, these two levels are closely related. And as I shall then proceed to argue, more than purely technical differences between PP and the "Treatise" were involved in the Hayek-Keynes debate. For example, the contours of Keynes' later break with the "ancient ceremony" of the neoclassical theory of interest begin to take shape, and Hayek's partial recognition of this represents one of the first and most clever critiques of Keynes' heresy.

If we distance ourselves from the near orgy of terminological discussion that does in fact characterize Hayek's review, his primary objection emerges as the following one: Keynes has overlooked "...those fundamental theorems of "real" economics", which must serve as the basis for any "successful" theory of the business cycle (1931a: 270). As Hayek goes on to make clear, these theorems refer to the Böhm-Bawerkian theory of capital (p.279). Although he enthusiastically endorses the Wicksellian distinction between the loan rate of interest and the natural rate, Keynes has nevertheless ignored the Böhm-Bawerkian underpinnings of Wicksell's theory (ibid.: 274). This critique amounts to more than simply criticizing Keynes for not working with Hayek's own analytical framework.

What Hayek really makes clear is Keynes' incomplete understanding of Wicksellian doctrine. For example, of Wicksell's three conditions for monetary equilibrium, Keynes only focuses on two conditions: that the loan

[12] For example, this is largely Patinkin's (1976: 56-58) evaluation.

rate of interest corresponds to the natural rate when savings equal investments, and when price stability obtains (Keynes 1930: 139) (i.e., Wicksell's second and third conditions). Wicksell's first condition, that the loan rate corresponds to the marginal productivity of extending the average period of production, is not brought into the analysis. Or in other words: the natural rate of interest does not exist as a *separate* analytical entity in the "Treatise".[13]

3.3. Keynes' Suppression of Critical Relative Prices

Hayek seems, then, to have been the first economist to point to that problem which should later on be so important in Keynes' discussions with Dennis Robertson in particular after the publication of "The General Theory"; that the rate of interest in Keynes' work is without any anchor in real determinants. That the "Treatise", as "The General Theory" later on, puts forward a dynamic theory of movements around some level of interest, rather than a theory about this level itself, is indicated by Keynes' response to Hayek's critique. Keynes explains that he has defined the natural rate as that rate at which there is savings-investments equilibrium, "...after taking account of the psychology of the market" – a "short period natural rate" as distinct from "...that envisaged by Dr. Hayek...the "long period natural rate"" (1931: 395).

Closely akin to Hayek's point that Keynes has not really understood the Böhm-Bawerkian underpinning of the distinction between the two rates of interest is another – and quite crucial – point to which he returns again and again. This is that Keynes, by neglecting the Austrian disaggregated conception of the productive activities of society, and instead choosing to theorize with a much more aggregative set-up, has managed to suppress critical relative prices. As Hayek says: "Mr. Keynes' aggregates conceal the most fundamental mechanisms of change" (1931a: 277). Consistent with his starting point in value theory, these mechanisms refer to relative prices. Had Keynes chosen a lower level of aggregation he would, in fact, have arrived at other theoretical results, since he would then have brought all relevant relative prices into full play.

The problems with Keynes' excessive level of aggregation, and particularly with his concentration on total profits as the "mainspring of change" of the business cycle, relate fundamentally to his simplistic conception of the productive activities of society as organized in only one stage of pro-

[13] For example, Keynes analyzes "the credit cycle" as initiated by "a new technical discovery", without bringing in changes in the natural rate of interest at all (1930: chapter 18).

duction. This is what Hayek means when he observes that Keynes "...-treats the whole process of the current production of consumption goods as an integral whole" (ibid.: 274). The profit of this stage of production therefore becomes identical to total profits. Furthermore, since Keynes assumes "the structure of goods" to be "relatively rigid" (ibid.), his analysis can only produce trivial quantity theoretical conclusions. It cannot explain the complicated price and quantity effects of "a monetary disequilibrium on real investment" (1932a: 40), as Hayek's PP analysis purportedly can. This is because Keynes does not allow the period of production to vary under the impact of monetary disturbances (Wicksell had done the same thing).

The upshot of all this is that Keynes' aggregate perspective blinds him to the changes in profitability between different, more or less capital-intensive, projects that follow monetary disturbances or variations in the intertemporal preferences of households.[14] An understanding of these effects can only be achieved through

> "...a close analysis of the factors determining the relative prices of capital goods in the different successive stages of production...But this is excluded from the outset if only total profits are made the aim of the investigation" (1931a: 277).

Once more it is clear that Hayek attacks Keynes from his own Austrian perspective; however, Hayek seems to have a point whose validity is independent of this particular perspective. He essentially criticizes Keynes for suppressing the relative price between consumer goods and investment goods, or, more trivially, of overlooking that under conditions of full resource utilization, investment and consumption must vary inversely in the short run. In Hayek's own analysis, this relative price is the central one.

In Keynes' discussion of "the credit cycle" (1930: chapter 18), for example, it is never brought systematically into the discussion. Keynes starts the business cycle with "a new technical discovery" which causes a movement of resources from the production of consumption goods to the production of investment goods. Prices of consumer goods rise, exactly as they do in Hayek's analysis (that is, "forced saving" is also a part of the "Treatise" analysis). In Hayek's scheme of things, this marks the beginning of the downturn; however, Keynes thinks the contrary: "The upward phase of the credit cycle will have made its appearance" (1930: 283). For

[14] Hayek made exactly the same points in his critique of Ralph Hawtrey's theory of the trade cycle (Hayek 1932c).

"windfall profits" in the production of consumer goods stimulate their production as well as the production of investment goods, and the boom period only fades when these above-normal profits are eliminated by a larger supply of consumer goods. It is not only that this Marshallian way of thinking is wholly alien to Hayek's Austrian and Walrasian approach, it is also that Keynes is wholly blind to the fact

> "that the...stimulus to investment, which makes it exceed current saving, may cause a disequilibrium in the real structure of production, which...must lead to a reaction" (1932a: 40).

Keynes has overlooked the fact that the resources needed for the expansion of production of consumer goods have to come from the investment goods sector; the two sectors cannot both be expanded. However, Keynes may have started his analysis from a situation of less than full utilization of resources, Hayek observes at the of his review, but this is inconsistent with the discussion of "The Fundamental Equations" (1930: chapter 10) in which full resource utilization is assumed. And it is furthermore methodologically suspect, since Keynes will then have assumed what he set out to explain. All in all, Keynes' "Treatise" represents neither an adequate explanation of "the more deep-seated causes of depression" (Hayek 1932a: 44) nor "the initial disequilibrium".[15]

3.4. Keynes' Response

Hayek's review of the "Treatise" came in two sections. However, Keynes did not await the publication of the second part, but wrote a response (Keynes 1931) to the first part of Hayek's review in which he argued that Hayek had completely misunderstood him.[16] Furthermore, breaking with

[15] An analytical starting-point in a situation with less than full utilization of resources was, however, routine for many of Keynes and Hayek's contemporaries. This is because it allowed them to account for a central stylized fact of the business cycle, namely that sectoral movements of output are positively correlated. Hayek, who in the debate with Keynes was more formally analytical than informally realistic, insisted however on beginning analytically "..where general economic theory stops...at a condition of equilibrium when no unused resources exist" (PP: 34). But he also went so far as to indicate that his own analysis of "the initial disequilibrium" was a complementary part of a more encompassing theory of the business cycle, Keynes' analysis of "the secondary deflation" (1932: 44) being the second part (see Robertson (1934) for a similar point).

[16] The editor of Keynes' "Collected Writings", Moggridge, tells us that Keynes was "very unhappy" with Hayek's review, for "..his copies is among the most heavily annotated of the surviving copies of his journals...Keynes summed up his reaction by writing: "Hayek has not read my book with the measure of "good will" which an author is entitled to expect of a reader. Until he can do so, he will not see what I mean or whether I am right. He evidently has a passion which leads him to pick on me, but I am left wondering what this passion is" (Keynes 1973: 243).

the usually cordial tone in English economic debate he began a vitriolic attack on PP, which Keynes saw as "...one of the most frightful muddles, with scarcely a sound proposition in it", and as an extraordinary example of how "...starting with a mistake, a remorseless logician can end up in bedlam" (1931: 394).

In spite of such attacks, Keynes admits that "...I do not myself propound any satisfactory theory of capital and interest", and, specifically, that "a clear account" of the factors determining the natural rate of interest is not present in the "Treatise". However, "Later on, I will endeavor to make good this deficiency" (1931: 394). This was precisely what Keynes "later on", in "The General Theory", did *not* do. Although there are in fact numerous insights in the theory of capital and investment in "The General Theory", it is surely difficult to associate it with any distinct theory of capital. Keynes is content with making "Sundry Observations on the Nature of Capital" (chapter 16). It may have been the case that Keynes, after the debate with Hayek, and possibly also under the impact of the rather inconclusive nature of the debates on capital theory in the 1930's, was strengthened in that (Marshallian) conception for which Hayek criticized him: that for the explanation of short-run monetary dynamics, a distinct theory of capital was simply not necessary. Keynes admits in his response to Hayek, to be sure, that it is "...very possible...that the ideas Böhm-Bawerk was driving at lie at the heart of the problem" (1931: 394). But in "The General Theory" he mocks Austrian capital theory and trivializes the Austrian concept of "roundaboutness", noting that it is no more significant in relation to the productive activities of society than the fact that these are "smelly" or "risky" (1936: 215). Surely that does not indicate any reorientation in the theory of capital on the part of Keynes.

In his response to Hayek, Keynes is mostly on the offensive. He briefly paraphrases Hayek's argument that a monetary change is a necessary and sufficient condition for a divergence between savings and investments (PP: 23), emphasizing that his own analysis is "quite different" from Hayek's analysis here, since

> "...in my view, saving and investment...can get out of gear without any change on the part of the banking system from "neutrality" as defined by Dr. Hayek, merely as a result of the public changing their rate of saving or the entrepreneurs changing their rate of investment, there being no automatic mechanism in the economic system...to keep the two rates equal" (1931: 393).

Furthermore, it is central to Hayek that saving always "finds its way into investment"; his savings scenario is the theoretical expression of this. For Keynes, in contrast, it is "fundamental...to deny this" (p.391). In his "Rejoinder" to Keynes, Hayek is baffled: to him the rate of interest is that "automatic mechanism", which brings savings and investments into equilibrium. And Keynes' suppression of the interest mechanism -precisely an example of Keynes' neglect of "the fundamental non-monetary problems of capitalistic production" (1931b: 401) – can with equal justice be extended to a broader proposition: that there is no "automatic mechanism in the economic system to adapt production to any other shift in demand" (ibid.) – which is obviously false. Clearly, the Hayek-Keynes debate at this stage is about more than a "true" Wicksellian, Hayek, criticizing an able but incomplete application of Wicksellian doctrine, that of Keynes, from a purely technical and terminological perspective. There seems to be something deeper involved; what is it that underlay the controversy?

4. Perspective on the Debate

4.1. Shackle's Interpretation

It was one of Hayek's London School of Economics students, George Shackle, who saw the problem of the *intertemporal coordination of economic activities* as underlying the debate. "The chief point at issue", explained Shackle, was whether an increase in the propensity to save would "...stimulate a shift of productive effort from consumers' goods to intermediate products [capital goods]" (1933: 27). Shackle's point allows us to obtain a better understanding of Hayek's seemingly purely technical objections to Keynes' argument, and his attempt to clarify which of Keynes' assumptions had allowed him to suppress important intertemporal market forces. We have seen that Hayek did this from an essentially Böhm-Bawerkian position; however, this is not just a matter of this perspective on capital theory forming the basis for Hayek's own theory.

4.2. The Austrian Theory of Capital as a Meta-perspective

It also seems to reflect Hayek's not wholly explicit belief that the Böhm-Bawerkian theory of capital constitutes a sort of *meta-perspective*. It is an overarching perspective precisely because it is formulated in disaggregated terms,[17] and brings the interest mechanism into full play. It therefore allows consideration of all relevant intertemporal market forces. And it is on the basis of this perspective that Hayek thinks he is able to point out where Keynes' level of aggregation, and lack of understanding of the real determinants of the rate of interest and also its role as the determinant of intertemporal allocation, have allowed him to suppress critical market forces. The obvious implication is then that *if* Keynes had considered all relevant market forces, he would have arrived at quite different conclusions. Let us examine that assertion, starting with a brief look at Keynes' own pronouncements on the subject of intertemporal coordination.

4.3. Intertemporal Coordination

This focus leads us to the famous story in the "Treatise" about the miserable banana growers, which is clearly an anticipation of the paradox of saving of "The General Theory". With this story, Keynes sought to dramatically illustrate that "The performance of the act of saving is in itself no guarantee that the stock of capital goods will be correspondingly increased" (1930: 175). In an idyllic society of fully employed banana growers, a Hayekian savings campaign suddenly begins. The campaign results in falling banana demand, falling prices, and, since the wage rate is fixed, losses and dismissals. This will, however, not better the position of the banana producers since the demand will fall pari passu with the costs of production (that is, wages). As long as planned savings exceed planned investments (which are assumed to be unchanged), banana producers will experience losses, and the process will not stop until either all the banana growers are dead or the savings campaign is cancelled.

Hayek's comment on this gloomy scenario is that it seems to him that Keynes has entirely neglected "the part played by the rate of interest", since he assumes that after production of consumer goods has been unprofitable, "...some other openings for investment which are now more profitable will not be found" (1932: 31). Keynes has suppressed the allocative function of the rate of interest and the relative price between consumption goods and investment goods, and it this essentially arbitrary suppression which allows Keynes to produce his dire conclusions. This point is applicable to "The General Theory" a fortiori. For in terms of the intertemporal coordination of economic activities, "The General Theory" represents "...a natural evolution in a line of thought which I [Keynes]

[17] Although concepts such as "the average period of production" are surely aggregate ones.

have been pursuing for several years" (1936: XXI-XXII). Here, Keynes increased the scale of aggregation and conceptualized all relevant causal connections between capital goods, their prices, and the expectations of their return in two aggregated variables, namely the marginal efficiency of capital and "the state of long term expectation", respectively.

4.4 "The General Theory"

Keynes' remarks on intertemporal coordination in "The General Theory" (1936; mostly in chapters 12 and 16), are almost all focused on what he perceives as a permanent lack of intertemporal coordination. In strong contrast with Hayek's analysis, Keynes never really views intertemporal preferences as relevant parameters or exogenous variables. Implicitly, changes in the preferred intertemporal pattern of consumption are never reflected in the realized pattern. In particular, entrepreneurial expectations are not allowed to mediate between intertemporal consumption patterns and intertemporal investment decisions in any coordinating way (cf. also Garrison 1985). This derives from Keynes' view of our inability to know the future, his emphasis on the lack of an economic rationale for most forward markets in a monetary production economy, and his insistence on separating the rate of interest ("virtually, a *current* phenomenon") from the intertemporal preferences of households.

Of course, there *are* intertemporal connections in Keynes' theorizing, though not ones that act to coordinate plans: the marginal efficiency of capital and the state of long term expectation. The uncertainty that Keynesian entrepreneurs confront regarding the nature and time of that future consumption which, in Hayek's scheme of things is made possible through additional savings, is really tantamount in Keynes' theory to the total absence of this consumption. As Keynes puts it: "Every weakening of the propensity to consume regarded as permanent habit must weaken the demand for capital as well as the demand for consumption" (1936: 106). To be sure, Keynesian entrepreneurs do in fact consider any such "weakening" as "permanent habit".

It was on this basis that Keynes attacked older economists – though including Hayek, his junior by 16 years – for "...fallaciously supposing that there is a nexus which unites decisions to abstain from present consumption with decisions to provide for future consumption" (1936: 210). And it also explains why Keynes treated Austrian capital theory so harshly in "The General Theory". Keynes understood that there was a connection between the Austrian concept of "roundaboutness" and intertemporal coordination. In a discussion of "the optimum amount of roundaboutness", he emphasizes that "In optimum conditions...production should be so organized as to produce in the most efficient manner compatible with the delivery at the dates at which consumers' demand is expected to become effective" (1936: 215). However, Keynes concluded that such "optimum conditions" – as portrayed in PP's savings scenario – presupposed a condition which he denied generally (ever?) obtained: the existence of a nexus between intertemporal preferences and intertemporal production plans.

4.5. Hayek's Implicit Assumptions

Hayek, of course, had a radically different conception of this. It is important to emphasize that the savings scenario in PP is not merely a Gedankenexperiment conducted in total abstraction. On the contrary, the savings scenario applies to the real world (see in particular Hayek (1933b: 143-144), which implies that important policy conclusions (such as the recommendation that money be kept "neutral") can be derived from it. Hayek's mentors had been much more guarded, never investing their analyses with such realistic interpretations. Wicksell, for example, emphasized that full coordination of savings and investment decisions outside of stationary equilibrium required an entrepreneurial "adaptability and degree of foresight" which was "far from existing in reality" (1934: 191). And Böhm-Bawerk explained that entrepreneurial efforts to match the savings plans of households with corresponding investments were not so much a matter of "positive information" as one of "a process of testing, guessing and experimenting", often involving "misapplied productive forces" (1901: 68).

Today, we realize that Hayek's very strong conclusions were conditional on a set of similarly strong implicit assumptions. Much is known today about the connections between, for example, transaction costs, closed markets (including forward markets), and speculative behavior. And while we may know relatively much about the existence and uniqueness of equilibrium, we still know relatively little about the general issue of stability, and even less about adjustment velocities and their determinants. We should not really blame Hayek for this – that would be ahistorical – but we should note that in his analysis he implicitly took all this as unproblematic, and based his policy recommendations on that. Piero Sraffa (among other critics) glimpsed the nature of these implicit assumptions when he criticized Hayek for not having any conception of disequilibrium in a barter economy, and emphasized that intertemporal coordination was not less problematical in a nonmonetary than in a monetary economy: "With or without money, if saving and investment have not been planned to match, an increase of saving must prove to a large extent 'abortive'" (1932: 52). Finally, Sraffa highlighted the lack of attention paid to institutions in Hayek's analysis: "There are no debts, no money contracts, no wage-agreements, no sticky prices in his supposition" (ibid.: 43).

Although Keynes and Hayek in their debate were seemingly discussing the same models, they phrased their comments and responses in terms of widely divergent analytical frameworks, employing widely divergent (implicit and explicit) assumptions. Hayek's point, that the costs of aggregation are the potentially important causal relations that are thus suppressed, is correct and acquired prominence in later debates. Applied to Keynes' work it indicates that his level of aggregation suppressed something that any theory of capital should address: that capital is not a mass of Samuelsonian "shmoo" but an amorphous mass of widely different assets. However, some of the previous arguments should cast doubt on the specific content Hayek invested in his point about aggregation, and particularly as he applied it to the early work of Keynes.

4.6. Keynes and Intertemporal Coordination: Epistemics and the Interest Mechanism

In fact, Keynes did not completely suppress and neglect all intertemporal market forces through an excessive level of aggregation as Hayek suggested. Already in the "Treatise", Keynes had provided reasons why their operation may be muted, reasons that center around 1) knowledge, particularly as it relates to the future, and 2) the speculative aspects of the determination of the rate of interest.

With regard to the knowledge issue, Keynes' discussions of the lack of a rational basis for estimating the yield "ten years hence" on "a railway, a copper mine, a textile factory" etc., in (1936: 149) are too well known to need yet another repetition. It is more interesting that Keynes in his "Treatise" had already emphasized how "accurate forecasting in these matters", such as forecasting the consequences of a change in savings, "...is so difficult and requires so much more information than is usually available that the average behavior of entrepreneurs is in fact mainly governed by current experience supplemented by...broad generalizations" (1930: 160). This is really quite close to the emphasis put in "The General Theory" on "conventions" as a basis for forecasting. So already in the "Treatise", Keynes emphasized the problematical epistemological situation of entrepreneurs with regard to long-term investments. Hayek's entrepreneurs were placed completely differently. In a sarcastic comment on PP's savings scenario, Ellis (1934: 355) observed that what Hayek had portrayed here were entrepreneurs who "...combined the mathematical wizardry of Einstein with a capacity in economic theory equal to Hayek's". In other words, Hayek's entrepreneurs reacted as if they knew the classical theory of interest, and also the Austrian theory of capital.

With regard to the interest issue, the following observations are in order. Other theorists of the business cycle – such as Spiethoff and Pigou – had, prior to Keynes, seen entrepreneurial forecast difficulties as central in any theory of the business cycle. Hayek (1933a: 81) criticized these approaches, arguing that theories that ascribed instability to entrepreneurial forecast errors should also be able to explain why movements in prices and interest rates could not compensate for this instability. Generally, this was something (nonmonetary) theorists had not been able to do.

In the "Treatise" version (or anticipation) of the liquidity preference theory, Keynes offered precisely a theory that could supply the missing component. Hayek did not see this, probably because in his own work he systematically neglected some of the problems that were most central in the work of his British contemporaries such as the general issues of the households' demand for money, speculation on asset markets etc. The central innovation in the "Treatise" may be seen as the rejection of any rigid connection between the prices of consumers' goods and the prices of investment goods.[18] This also implied a rejection of the classical theory of interest. And it was on the basis of this that Keynes insisted that "...saving and investment can get out of gear...without any change from "neutrality" as defined by Dr. Hayek" (1931: 393). Departures from neutrality, that is, changes in MV, was a sufficient but not necessary condition for monetary disequilibrium, and neutrality was no longer sufficient to guarantee intertemporal equilibrium.

According to Keynes, the price level of investment goods is "...that price level at which the desire of the public to hold savings deposits is equal to the amount of savings deposits which the banking system is willing and able to create" (1931: 143). With this insight, Keynes introduced a theory of the speculative demand for money. One consequence is that this made him able to eliminate that confusion between the stock-flow/income-wealth aspects of the demand for money which had plagued Canta-

[18] Keynes' pejorative rejection in "The General Theory" of "a peculiar theory of interest", propagated by the Austrians, according to which "..changes in the rate of interest can be identified with changes in the relative price levels of consumption goods and investment goods" (1936: 192), can therefore be traced back to "Treatise".

brigian monetary theory since Marshall (see Keynes 1931: 140-6, 232). Supplying wealth effects of monetary changes with substitution effects, Keynes ruined the conception of stability that was underneath so much inter-war monetary theory and business cycle theory, including Hayek's: that a fixed quantity of money guarantees monetary equilibrium. This could no longer automatically be the case. For example, portfolio changes could imply changes in interest rates even in the absence of monetary changes. Applied to Hayek's theory, this meant that neutral money did not guarantee intertemporal equilibrium; savings and investment decisions could in fact "get out of gear" even in the absence of departures from neutrality. Alternatively, it was not warranted to conclude that monetary changes would induce a crisis. In essence, Keynes flatly denied that financial markets could be generally relied upon to coordinate savings and investment. Hayek never produced a serious answer to this challenge.

4.7. Different Conceptualizations of Equilibrium and the Function of the Rate of Interest

An implication of this is that Hayek's point about aggregation – although a clever one – as applied to Keynes' work is of relatively little relevance. The sources of disequilibrium which Keynes had identified simply cannot be explicated within Hayek's analytical set-up. This also suggests that Hayek's and Keynes' concepts of equilibria were quite central to their theorizing. Hayek's conception of the rate of interest, as inherently an intertemporal relative price which "...expresses itself in the whole structure of price relationships" (1933a: 207), and his treatment of intertemporal coordination problems in terms of the Austrian theory of capital, were wholly consistent with the concept of intertemporal equilibrium he had pioneered in 1928. In much the same way, Keynes' Marshallian concept of equilibrium – which did not imply intertemporal plan consistency but merely equality between current supply and demand – was wholly consistent with his separation of the rate of interest and intertemporal preferences, and his emphasis on genuine uncertainty and speculative behavior.

It is, furthermore, against this background that the introduction in the 1930s of widely different conceptions of monetary equilibrium should be seen. On the one hand there was Hayek's conception (ultimately derived from Wicksell), according to which monetary equilibrium/neutrality implied that "...a monetary policy is "neutral" in the sense of being equivalent to a nonmonetary economy which differs from it...only by name" (Sraffa 1932: 51). On the other hand, there was the ultimately successful conception, that is, Hicks' (1933, 1935) general equilibrium version of Keynes' (1930) attempt to rationalize a positive marginal utility of money in terms of asset demand under uncertainty. As Hicks explained it:

> "Either we have to give an explanation of the fact that people do hold money when rates of interest are positive or we have to evade the difficulty somehow. It is the great traditional evasions which have led to Velocities of Circulation, Natural Rates of Interest, et id genus omne" (1935: 66).

From this perspective, Hayek's theory was precisely an example of one "- great traditional evasion", and Keynes' (1936) point that the classical theory of interest was fundamentally a theory about a nonmonetary economy is – at least as applied Hayek's theory – completely valid.

5. Conclusion

In the light of modern economics, the conclusion that Keynes ultimately triumphed over Hayek, or that his theories were sounder, is not warranted, however. To be sure, the Keynesian tide effectively eliminated themes such as "forced saving", "neutral money" etc., and relegated them to a theoretical limbo from which they have never returned. Almost at the same time, the increasing dominance of atemporal production function theory in the Clark/Knight tradition eliminated the distinctively Austrian approach to intertemporal coordination.

However, there are not only cycles in economic activities, but also in the popularity of business cycle theories. In that perspective, the new classical economics of Lucas, Sargent et al. may be – at least to older economists – something of a déjà vu. The basic new classical conceptualization of the business cycle as the result of the responses of maximizing locally informed agents to monetary shocks, and emphasizing changes in real capital as a propagation mechanism, is almost entirely Hayekian in spirit (I elaborate on this assertion in the next chapter). And the mainstream of modern economic theory could in many respects be said to be more Hayekian than Keynesian. For example, modern concepts of equilibrium are derived from Hayek's notion of intertemporal equilibrium rather than from Keynes' Marshallian concept of equilibrium. In this connection, much energy has been invested in investigating the nature of the stability- or convergence-to-equilibrium problem whose nature Hayek understood at an early point (Hayek 1933b, 1935b). Furthermore, of course, Hayek's insights in local information and the information-providing role of the price system loom large in modern economics. In short, Hayek's early work certainly deserves a place in the history of general equilibrium theory and its farther reaches. That the same cannot be said about his later (post 1937) work, will be argued in the next chapter.

However, Keynesian type problems have never really lost the attention of the modern economist; in fact, during the last two decades they have increasingly been approached through analytical apparatus that has Hayekian origins such as equilibrium concepts derived from Hayekian intertemporal equilibrium and asymmetric information. And that may make one doubt the relevance of Hick's question, "Which was right, Keynes or Hayek?" (1967: 203). Seen in the light of modern mainstream economics they may both have been "right".

3: Hayek and Lucas on Equilibrium and Knowledge

1. Introduction: Hayek and the New Classicals

It has often been observed that there is a propensity among innovators in economic theory to associate their new thoughts with some alleged forebear. Well-known examples include Keynes on Malthus, Friedman on Hume, and Barro on Ricardo. It would be an interesting, worthwhile but very demanding task to discuss the possible justification for these doctrinal atavisms, their rhetorical function (cf. McCloskey 1985), or whether they have any other social function than to provide grist for the doctrinal historian's mill. Undertaking that task is not the purpose of this chapter. I shall restrict myself to remarking that one of the most innovative economists of the last two decades, Robert E. Lucas, faithfully followed the above-mentioned ancient and established tradition and will examine the justification of his so doing.

During the 1970s, a radical critique of Keynesian macroeconomics and econometric models appeared, associated with economists such as Lucas, Thomas Sargent, Robert Barro, and Neil Wallace. Although it was usually broadly monetarist in policy conclusions, this *new classical* literature nevertheless differed in terms of rigor, degree of formalization, and analytical content.[19] It was more than just a matter of adding the famous "rational expectations" to a basic monetarist set-up; the research style of the new classicals differed, being much more explicitly Walrasian. And whereas monetarists such as Friedman looked to Hume, the English Currency School and American economists such as Clark Warburton for their intellectual forebears, new classical economists have looked elsewhere. The new classical research program had barely been established before Lucas thought he could discern a remarkable similarity between his own monetary theory of the business cycle on the one hand and the theorizing of the pre-Keynesian monetary business cycle theorists on the other hand (Lucas 1975: 202). Specifically, Lucas (1977) – in a programmatic and methodological discussion of new classical macroeconomics – admiringly

[19] I shall neglect the nonmonetarist outgrowths of the new classical economics, such as the work that has emerged during the last decade on real business cycle theory. I also neglect the new classical critique of Keynesian econometrics and the discussion of time inconsistency in public policy.

quoted Hayek's[20] early diagnosis of the main problem of business cycle research:

> "The incorporation of cyclical phenomena into the system of economic equilibrium theory, with which they are in apparent contradiction, remains the crucial problem of Trade Cycle Theory" (Hayek 1933a: 33).

Lucas considered it plausible that modern theorists of the business cycle would find this conceptualization "roughly equivalent to their own" (1977: 216). In accordance with this, Fitoussi and Velupillai (1987: 122) noticed Lucas' adoption of "the methodological implorations of Hayek", and monetarist David Laidler observed that it is Hayek and his mentor, Ludwig von Mises, who should be considered the true "predecessors of Lucas, Sargent and their associates" (1981: 12).

All this raises a number of questions; such as, 1) is Lucas justified in claiming Hayek among his theoretical forebears? and 2) how does Hayek's overall work – not just his early work in business cycle theory – relate to new classical economics and methodology? These are fundamentally the two questions that I shall examine in this chapter. In section 2 I present a comparison between new classical methodological positions and Hayek's early reflections on the scope and method of business cycle research. A result of this discussion is the recognition that Lucas, to some extent, is justified in claiming Hayek among his theoretical forebears. The point should not be neglected, however, that Hayek becomes increasingly skeptical towards equilibrium theory, and does so on grounds that are extremely pertinent to the modern rational expectations method (section 3). In section 4, I discuss some parallels between Hayek's early work in technical economics, his extensive later interdisciplinary contributions and modern neo-institutional theory. To a large extent, it is the same problems that Hayek highlighted in equilibrium theory more than fifty years ago that explain why economics is increasingly taking an institutional turn in recent years – also in its more formalistic, mainstream manifestations.

[20] The correct reference is really Löwe (1926). Hayek (1933a: 33) summarized Löwe's discussion of the conceptual tension between existing equilibrium theory and theories of the business cycle, a discussion begun by Böhm-Bawerk and reflected in a long series of contributions through the nineteen-twenties and 'thirties (e.g. Kuznets 1930).

2. Hayek, Lucas and the Theory of the Business Cycle

As argued elsewhere in this book (chapter 2), Hayek's early work was strongly influenced by general equilibrium theory. As Lucas (1977: 215) did not fail to point out, Hayek made equilibrium theory, and indeed economic theory, synonymous with

> "...the modern theory of the general interdependence of all economic quantities which has been most perfectly expressed by the Lausanne School of theoretical economics" (Hayek 1933a: 42n).

In the same way as Hayek in his early work on business cycle research (such as Hayek 1933a), the new classicals are characterized by a deep methodological awareness and subtlety. In a series of contributions, new classical economists (for example, Lucas 1977, 1980, 1987a; Lucas & Sargent 1979) have explained the choice of a Walrasian basis for business cycle theory in terms of the overall research strategy that characterizes their program: the explanation of the business cycle under the constraint that the two "classical" assumptions be adhered to. These two assumptions are that "...markets clear...and...agents act in their own self-interest" (Lucas & Sargent 1979: 304). In order to focus our discussion, it is necessary to account more precisely for what it is exactly that new classical economists pack into these two assumptions or "classical postulates" (ibid.). In themselves, the two assumptions are almost completely empty. Not even a radical subjectivist Austrian such as Ludwig Lachmann would deny that market clearing, in the sense of temporary demand/supply equilibrium, obtains sometimes on many markets, and that people in fact usually act "in their own self-interest".

Broadly characterized, the new classical standard set-up is a Walrasian economy that follows a multivariate stochastic process and is continuously in equilibrium. Agents are locally informed but hold Muth-rational expectations. Adding various accelerator, or time-to-build effects, to this set-up, makes it possible to spread the effects of a monetary shock over several periods, simulating the characteristic covariation between aggregate variables – "Mitchell's discoveries", as Lucas (1980) says – which is a business cycle. Starting with a stochastic Walrasian set-up, where "...prices and quantities are taken to be always in equilibrium" (Lucas 1980: 287), makes new classical economics conform to the classical postulate, that "markets clear". New classical economists do not see any inconsistency between this equilibrium approach and existing empirical evidence, for "...simply to look at any economic time series and conclude that it is a disequilibrium phenomenon...[is]...a meaningless observation" (Lucas and Sargent 1979: 305). Furthermore, excess demands cannot be associated with any "observed magnitudes". This means that they do not have any "observational role" (Lucas 1980: 287). The strongly anti-Keynesian content in this should be obvious.

Implied in the second classical postulate, that agents act in their own interest, is the proposition that all opportunities for trade are continuously exploited. Furthermore, rationality is extended to expectations so that the second classical postulate, in the context of new classical temporary equilibrium models, implies that subjectively held probability distributions for prices cannot diverge systematically from the (objective) distribution implied by the equilibrium of the model (Lucas 1980: 285). Muth (1961) called this principle "rational expectations".

It is in the context of the above basic themes: the relation between theory and empirical evidence, equilibrium, knowledge and expectations, that I shall discuss similarities and differences between Hayek and the new classicals in the rest of this chapter. I shall largely disregard other relevant considerations such as the relation between the new classicals' quantity theory approach and Hayek's Wicksellian approach, which implied a strong rejection of naïve versions of the quantity theory as an explanation of the business cycle. With regard to Hayek's early work on the business cycle, I shall focus mostly on the similarities between this work and that of the new classical school.

The contribution in which Hayek is most explicit about the scope and method of business cycle research, his Habilitationsschrift, "Monetary Theory and the Trade Cycle" (1933a), seems to support the assertions of Lucas et al. We have already seen that Hayek in this early contribution insisted on a Walrasian foundation for business cycle theory. Empirical business cycle researchers, such as Mitchell (1927), found it generally counterproductive or at least uninteresting to "...determine how the fact of cyclical fluctuations...can be reconciled with the general theory of equilibrium" (ibid: 462). Hayek, in contrast, maintained that business cycle theory

> "...must be deduced with unexceptionable logic from the fundamental notions of the theoretical system...it must explain by a purely deductive method those phenomena with

all their peculiarities which we observe in the actual cycles" (1933a: 32-33).[21]

Specifically, it was fundamental to Hayek's conception of equilibrium theory that a *nonmonetary* Walrasian economy could be taken to be continuously in equilibrium. As he says: "a change in data...directly and immediately, leads to a change in [prices]" (p.77); he talks about "the smooth working of the equilibrating process, as presented in equilibrium theory" (p.197) etc. This indicates that Hayek in his early work took the existence, uniqueness and stability of (Walrasian) equilibrium for granted. That would change, as we will see later on. However, regarding a nonmonetary economy as fundamentally stable was the basis for Hayek's recommendation of the policy of keeping money "neutral" through keeping the stock of money completely fixed (adjusting, however, for changes in the velocity of money). Although new classical macroeconomists would not subscribe to this kind of monetary policy, but prefer a Friedmanite policy of a growth rule for the stock of money, they share a basic conviction with the early Hayek: that the economy in the absence of monetary shocks is fundamentally stable.

In contrast to the majority of his contemporaries (notably Schumpeter), Hayek did not think of a Walrasian economy as stationary. This was of course completely justified, since, for example, an Arrow-Debreu economy is wholly consistent with the existence of fluctuations as time and states of nature are realized.[22] Furthermore, perfect foresight – the deterministic equivalent of rational expectations – characterized the nonmonetary Walrasian economy (1933b: 143-143).[23] In fact, Hayek often seems to suggest that his agents possess correct models of their world (cf. c. 2).

To sum up, we can observe the following striking similarities between the early Hayek and new classical methodological positions: A) the recommendation of intertemporal Walrasian equilibrium (or derived constructs such as temporary equilibrium) as the analytical starting point of business cycle theory, B) a strong emphasis on methodological individualism and

[21] Compare with Lucas: "One exhibits understanding of business cycles by constructing a model in the most literal sense; a fully articulated artificial economy which behaves through time so as to imitate closely the time series behavior of actual economies" (1977: 219).

[22] This is not an ahistorical observation, since Hayek's (1928) introduction (before Lindahl and Hicks) of intertemporal equilibrium underlies his understanding of the consistency between fluctuations and equilibrium. However, Hayek emphasized that such fluctuations were not the ones focused on in business cycle theory, basically because they did not diminish welfare. On the basis of his Marshallian period analysis, Dennis Robertson (1926) made essentially similar points.

[23] For a 1929 version of rational expectations, see Hayek (1933a: 69-70). Anticipating modern critique of the rational expectations hypothesis, Ellis (1934: 355) observed that Hayek's agents "combined the mathematical wizardry of Einstein with a capacity in economic theory equal to Hayek's".

subjectivism, that is the explanation of economic phenomena in terms of "the logic of economic action" (Hayek 1933a: 30), starting from insight in "...the situations people finds themselves in...as they themselves see them" (Lucas 1987a: 57). This deductive and individualistic starting point explains Hayek and Lucas' shared aversion towards aggregate theory (Hayek 1935a: 1-32; Lucas 1980), and C) finally, we may notice a similarity that has to do with investing perfect foresight/rational expectations and market clearing with realistic significance so that they are more than merely heuristic constructions (Hayek 1933b: 143-144; Lucas 1987b).

If we shift our attention to Hayek's business cycle *theory*, as distinct from his reflections on *method*, the claims put forward by Lucas et al., seem to gain in strength. As in Lucas' (1975) monetary theory of the business cycle, Hayek's (1935a) analysis begins in a competitive set-up with maximizing, locally informed agents, with monetary shocks as the "impulses" that initiate the cycle, and with intersectoral changes in the structure of capital as the propagation mechanism that spreads the effects of a monetary shock through several periods. And misinformation transmitted through the price system plays a role in Hayek's theory that is equally as important as it is in Lucas' theory.

Any theory of the business cycle, Hayek explains, must incorporate "the assumption that entrepreneurs have committed errors" (1933b: 141). In a dynamic economy, changes in underlying data will, of course, cause such errors. But a theory of the business cycle cannot be constructed on this basis since changes in "data" will "net out" on an aggregate level (compare Lucas 1977: 228). What should be addressed is why "entrepreneurs should all *simultaneously* make mistakes in the *same* direction" (1933b: 141 my emphasis). "Noisy" price signals offer a solution: "...it may be that the prices existing when they [entrepreneurs] made their decisions and on which they had to base their views about the future have created expectations which must necessarily be disappointed" (1933b: 141). The relevant price signal in Hayek's story is the observable loan rate of interest, which is taken by agents to be a reliable proxy for the natural rate of interest. In Hayek's set-up, unanticipated and monetarily induced divergence between the loan rate and the natural rate cause investment projects that are not consistent with resource scarcities and intertemporal preferences, and which will therefore ultimately fail (see chapter 2 for a fuller statement of the theory).[24] This is a crisis.

[24] Such obvious overall similarities should not disguise deep theory-specific differences. It is quite significant that it is the rate of interest that occupies center stage in Hayek's story, which makes his theory part of "the Wicksell connection" (Leijonhufvud 1981), whereas the sophisticated monetarism of the new classicals makes them belong to the quantity theoretical approach.

The assertions of Lucas et al., that Hayek was an important precursor of new classical economics, seems then to be well validated on a methodological as well as on a theoretical level. But this should not divert attention away from the fact that it is only Hayek's *early* work that can be invoked as really anticipating new classical economics. This is because Hayek, during the 1930s, becomes increasingly skeptical towards equilibrium theory. Fundamentally, his skepticism relates to the difficulties of applying (static) equilibrium theory to the understanding of a (dynamic) reality. That, of course, was not an uncommon recognition at that time but, as I shall argue, Hayek reacted in a way that differs from the way his fellow economists reacted. In short, Hayek's later (post-war) work on cultural evolution has a direct lineage leading back to the problems that troubled him in the 1930s.

3. Equilibrium and Coordination

3.1. Equilibrium Concepts and Business Cycle Theory

Central to the efforts of pre-Keynesian monetary, capital and business cycle theorists was the attempt to develop theoretical frameworks that would allow them to eliminate that tension between static equilibrium theory and dynamic reality which so many of them were aware of. Quite naturally, this tension presented itself with particular force to theorists of the business cycle. Practically all those economists who came up with new equilibrium concepts during the inter-war period were occupied with explaining the business cycle as a major part of their research efforts (for example Robertson 1926; Hicks 1933). These efforts gave birth to, for instance, Hayek's (1928) concept of intertemporal equilibrium, and the Swedish (Lindahl, Myrdal et al.) and Marshallian (Robertson) period analyses.

In an extensive attack on Keynesian theory, Lucas and Sargent (1979) expressed their admiration for these efforts and contrasted them favorably with the work of Keynes. According to Lucas and Sargent, pre-Keynesian theorists did not – in contrast to Keynes – see any need for "...a special branch of economics, with its own special postulates, designed to explain the business cycle" (p.304). Economists such as Hayek and his contemporaries followed essentially the same research strategy as the new classicals do: the logical time of analytical models can be reconciled with historical time through associating existing time series with a continuum of equilibria.

It is precisely here that the new classical doctrinal history seriously misrepresents pre-Keynesian theorists in general and Hayek in particular. Let us focus on a representative example, John Hicks who directly proclaimed that the theory of the business cycle "falls outside equilibrium theory" (1933: 35). Such remarks – typical of the theorists of the period – did not indicate an emerging alliance with atheoretical business cycle researchers such as Mitchell. They reflected rather the awareness of the subtle problems and dilemmas that related to the application of equilibrium theory to the understanding of cycles in monetary economies.

In particular, remarks such as Hicks' demonstrate that pre-Keynesian theorists in fact rejected the association of observed business cycles, and their representation in times series, with a continuum of equilibria. Hayek was particularly explicit about the character of the dilemma that confronted the theorist of the business cycle. In a critique of nonmonetary theories of the business cycle (Spiethoff, Schumpeter, Pigou and others), Hayek pointed out that these theories confronted a severe theoretical difficulty:

> "This difficulty arises because, in stating the effects of... [a real shock]...they have to make use of the logic of equilibrium theory. Yet this logic...can do no more than demonstrate that such disturbances can come only from outside....and that the economic system always reacts to such changes by its well-known methods of adaptation, i.e. by the formation of a new equilibrium" (1933a: 43).

In other words, equilibrium theory confronted a serious Kuhnian anomaly: given Hayek's strict conception of equilibrium theory (cf. section 2), this theory could not rationalize those *observed* "developments leading *away* from equilibrium" (1933a: 55) which characterized the business cycle. This is what Hayek meant when he argued that there was "an apparent contradiction" between business cycle phenomena and equilibrium theory (cf. section 1). In fact, Hayek (1933a) – from which Lucas so enthusiastically quoted – is really one extensive proclamation of the *inability* of existing equilibrium theory to rationalize the business cycle. Of course, this did not lead Hayek to a historicist or institutionalist rejection of neoclassical economics (as was the case with Löwe, Mitchell and Kuznets). Rather, equilibrium theory should be further developed.

Employing a well-known kind of argument, Hayek (1933a) argued that since the Walrasian model could not be made to convincingly mimic the business cycle, the existence of business cycles in the real world had to be caused by something that did not exist in this model, that is, money and credit. Walrasian theory in isolation was not sufficient for a theoretical understanding of the business cycle – monetary theory had to be factored in (also the conclusion of Hicks 1933). Or, in other words, pre-Keynesian theorists did in fact argue for the need for "a special branch of economics...designed to explain the business cycle".

3.2. Beginning Doubts about Equilibrium Theory

A large part of Hayek's early work consisted in attempts to develop analytical tools that could meet the challenges which the empirical phenomenon of the business cycle posed for economic theory. Thus, Hayek's 1928 introduction of intertemporal equilibrium was essentially an attempt to offer an apparatus that could handle those causal processes that were the domain of the theory of capital and the theory of the business cycle. His later work on the theory of capital (Hayek 1941) should probably also be seen in this light. It became clear to Hayek, however, that intertemporal equilibrium had applicational as well as conceptual problems. How could one, for example, analyze dynamic, sequential processes in a monetary economy, characterized by uncertainty and incomplete information etc., – such as the business cycle – with an analytical construction that incorporated perfect foresight?[25] How could the coordination problems characteristic of the cycle be analyzed by the help of such an instrument? Only in the same – very restricted – way as it has been argued that the Arrow-Debreu model may cast light over Keynesian type problems by completely ruling out such problems (Hahn 1973).

Rather than attempting to eliminate this problem through developing new analytical concepts – as Lindahl may be argued to have done with his innovation of temporary equilibrium – Hayek focused on even deeper problems in economic theory. However, the assumption of perfect foresight continued to loom large in his thinking as the defining characteristic of equilibrium. This assumption was generally thought to be necessary for the application of equilibrium analysis (cf. Hicks 1933); however, the conditions that must obtain for perfect foresight to be a good approximation were not clarified (in addition, the assumption seemed to introduce logical problems, on which see Morgenstern 1935). Hayek seems to have been one of the first economists to point out that

[25] Further complications related to the problems of incorporating a monetary medium in intertemporal equilibrium. As contemporary critique (such as Hicks 1933) indicated, Hayek was essentially up against the problems of incorporating money in general equilibrium.

> "The only way in which such foresight...is conceivable is that all...prices are actually fixed simultaneously in advance on some single market, where not only present but also all future commodities...are traded" (1935e: 96n).

In other words: perfect foresight could no longer be postulated as descriptively correct in the absence of a quite special kind of market organization, that is, the clearing of all forward markets by the use of the services of the auctioneer. At approximately the same time as Hayek began to raise doubts concerning the standard assumptions of equilibrium theory, he became involved in the socialist calculation debate. His well-known position – brilliantly summarized in Hayek (1945) – was that because of the idiosyncratic nature of local, economically relevant, knowledge, decentralization using markets and extensive property rights did the job of making use of all the information much better than central planning (more on which in the following chapter).

3.3. "Economics and Knowledge"

All this seems to reflect Hayek's growing awareness of the importance of the epistemic aspects in economic theory. And it was this that made him rediscover that coordination problem,[26] which was central to Adam Smith but subsequently became suppressed through assumptions such as perfect foresight/full knowledge: how can a multitude of agents, each one of them involved in a complex and expanding division of labor, successfully coordinate their actions, when each agent possesses only local and idiosyncratic knowledge? Hayek's first comprehensive discussion of "Smith's problem" appears in his 1937 article, "Economics and Knowledge".

In the introductory section of this article, Hayek explains that he will examine:

> "...the role which assumptions and propositions about the knowledge possessed by the different members of society play in economic analysis...[and]...the question to what extent formal economic analysis conveys any knowledge about what happens in the real world" (1937: 33).

[26] Caldwell (1988) essentially argues that Hayek's involvement in the socialist calculation debate was the crucial event behind his realization of the importance of the coordination problem, while Foss (1995) argues that his work on business cycle theory was equally important here.

It is obvious that Hayek is focusing here on two different epistemic levels: the knowledge of the analyzed agents and the knowledge of the analyzing economist, respectively. The logic behind this dichotomization is that it is only to the extent that the tautologies of economic theory can be supplemented by "definite statements about how knowledge is acquired and communicated" (ibid.), that economists are justified in putting forward nontrivial propositions about causal relations in the economic sphere.[27]

Hayek makes this claim more specific by identifying a (further) dichotomy between equilibrium for a single agent and equilibrium in a system of interdependent agents. For an individual agent, equilibrium poses no special problems: actions are qua actions always based on plans, and plans are based on subjective perceptions of what exists objectively. In terms of these perceptions, equilibrium for a single agent can be said to exist a priori, Hayek argues. That follows from "the pure logic of choice", by which he presumably means Mises' praxeology. Now, that claim may in itself be problematic, but Hayek ignores this to the benefit of something else. For the problems, he says, only arise when we wish to establish a correspondence between the equilibrium of a single agent and equilibrium in a system of interdependent agents. To say something about social processes by focusing on the logic with which we understand the actions of a single agent is not in general a permissible principle of composition. But why is that? Since every agent can be taken to be in equilibrium at any time, why is equilibrium in a system of interdependent agents not established at the same time?

Hayek dissects this objection, arguing that it is only meaningful to talk about equilibrium (that is, consistency of plans) in a system of interdependent agents, if these agents all share the same perception of objective reality. Importantly, this reality includes the actions and plans of other agents. Standard equilibrium theory disregards this difficulty, Hayek claims, since it assumes as a matter of routine that the same knowledge of the objective reality is given to all agents. To claim that the logic of choice with which we understand the actions of individual agents can lead to propositions about social processes is necessarily tantamount to assuming that all

[27] This position is usually interpreted as a tacit attack on Mises, since – so the story goes – Mises had argued that all economic propositions could be derived on a purely a priori. That this is a misrepresentation of Mises, and that Hayek's positions is not necessarily a break with Mises, is indicated by the fact that Mises did not claim that all of economics could be derived in a purely rationalistic manner. Usually, one had to add "auxiliary hypotheses" which were contingent, not a priori true. That he definitely said that praxeology could be conceived in a purely rationalistic manner is a separate issue.

agents possess the same knowledge, and "The statement that, if people know everything they are in equilibrium is true simply because that is how we define equilibrium" (1937: 46).

The problem is that assumptions of full information, perfect foresight etc., "...do not get us any nearer an explanation of when and how such a state will come about" (1937: 46). In other words, "pure equilibrium analysis" cannot say anything about disequilibrium or convergence towards equilibrium. Propositions about this must necessarily be empirical propositions; specifically, they must be "propositions about the acquisition of knowledge" (p.33). And it is only by focusing on such propositions, that is to say, by theorizing learning processes, that economic theory will be able to solve the problem why agents "should ever be right" (p.34), that is implement consistent plans: "...if we want to make the assertion that...people will approach [equilibrium], we must explain by what process they will acquire the necessary knowledge" (p.46).

The only justification for being interested in such coordinated states is "the supposed existence of a tendency towards equilibrium", and although Hayek does not doubt that such a "tendency" is an empirical fact, the failure to rationalize this theoretically in the economics of his day worries him. To sidestep or not take into account learning processes – as Lucas explicitly does (1987b: 218) – is implicitly to assume that "Smith's problem" has been solved. In modern terminology, the problem Hayek highlighted – approximately at the same time as Wald and von Neumann – was the stability problem. And he also implicitly put forward a strong critique of the representative agent models, now so much in fashion in macroeconomics (Kirman 1992), not least under the impact of new classical theorizing: if we only focus on a representative agent and therefore only apply "the pure logic of choice", all interesting coordination problems are suppressed.

Furthermore, Hayek identified a number of deep problems that still have not been satisfactorily resolved: if there is no explicit coordinator of economic activities, then how can individual agents hope to exploit all potential possibilities of utility-increasing trade, when they themselves have to discover which goods can be traded, where they can be traded, when, with whom, at what prices etc. (cf. Fisher 1983)? To postulate – as the new classicals do – that individual rationality implies continuous absence of possibilities for utility-increasing trade would, for Hayek, amount to an illegitimate identification of individual and systemic rationality, and fundamentally beg the very question he addressed in "Economics and Knowledge". Which brings us back to rational expectations; for Hayek's distinction between individual equilibrium and equilibrium for a system of interdependent agents has significance in this context, too.[28]

3.4. Hayek, Knowledge and Rational Expectations

Hayek (1937) suggested as a heuristic principle that the evaluation of assumptions in economic theory generally should be based on whether a given assumption was "justified" in the sense that it could "...be regarded as likely to be true, and it must be possible, at least in principle, to demonstrate that it is true in particular cases" (p.37). Applying this principle, we recognize that economic agents – "at least in principle" – are able to maximize utility, since this activity involves purely individual decisions. The formation of rational expectations equilibrium forecasts demands, however, knowledge of the parameters of equilibrium distributions of endogenous variables, and this assumption cannot in general "...be regarded as likely to be true in the context of decentralized competitive markets" (Frydman 1984: 111). As a quite extensive literature on convergence to rational expectations equilibrium indicates, Hayek's distinction between individual equilibrium and equilibrium in a multi-agent economy is indeed quite fundamental (see also Machlup 1983; Arrow 1987b).

A further look at Hayek's (1937, 1945) reflections on the role of knowledge in economic analysis may further underline the basic methodological and epistemic differences between Hayek and the new classicals. Underlying Hayek's (1937) discussion of learning processes was what he saw as "a problem of *the division of knowledge*" (p.50), or, as modern Austrians say, the fact that "different men know different things". Given this division, the central problem of economics was to explain how results (in casu: equilibrium) could be brought about through "...the spontaneous interaction of a number of people, each possessing only bits of knowledge" (p.49-50): results that could only be brought about by comprehensive planning if the planner possessed the whole societal stock of knowledge (which, and this is the point, "no single person can possess" (p.54)). This may be seen like an early version of a methodological stance today primarily associated with Hayek (and Karl Popper): that the primary domain of applicability of the social sciences is the *unintended* consequences of *intentional* human action. Market phenomena, for example, are "invisible hand-explananda" (cf. Ullman-Margalitt 1978).

[28] Another modern connotation to Hayek's distinction is the Sonnenschein-Debreu result on the weak restrictions that individual behavior places on aggregate excess demands.

Of course, Hayek's insights in local information have naturally acquired prominence in the more microeconomic part of new classical economics in particular. The crucial distinction between the epistemic situation of Hayekian and new classical agents, respectively, does not really relate to the issue of local information *per se*. Rather, it is that Hayekian agents do not know "the structure of the relevant system describing the economy" (Muth 1961: 5). Already in (1933a), Hayek emphasizes that economic agents generally will not possess theoretical/scientific knowledge about the functioning of the economy. As he puts it: "...production is governed by prices, independently of any knowledge of the whole process on the part of individual producers" (p.84). And in "The Use of Knowledge in Society" (1945), Hayek makes an explicit distinction between scientific knowledge ("in the sense of knowledge of general rules", p.80) and "knowledge of the particular circumstances of time and place".

In our context, this taxonomy implies a crucial distinction between "the predictions of the relevant economic theory" (Muth 1961: 3) and local knowledge. Hayek's distinction between scientific and practical knowledge (as it really is) – which every student of the history of philosophy will recognize – is essentially an application of invisible-hand reasoning: the economic system "works", and this does not in principle require anybody having scientific knowledge about precisely why this is so. That does not mean, of course, that the "why" – that is to say the nature of the invisible-hand process which aggregates individual actions into an overall (beneficial) unintended outcome – is uninteresting.

On the contrary, the understanding of this process is quite essential; as Franklin Fisher (1983) has argued, constructing a satisfactory stability theory is necessary for equilibrium analysis to be applicable. To postulate that agents possess knowledge of "the structure of the relevant system describing the economy" is therefore tantamount to a neglect of Hayek's taxonomy of knowledge, and it is also tantamount to neglecting a not yet (fully) understood aspect of economic reality (stability, learning processes etc.,). And most importantly, perhaps: it is to leave very little room for the primary explanandum of the social sciences, the unintended consequences of human action. As Arrow (1987b) observes in a similar context: "If every agent has a complete model of the economy, the hand running the economy is very visible indeed" (p.208). In other words: with such a wide-ranging specification of the epistemic powers of individual agents, market phenomena are not explained with the use of the notion of the invisible hand, but in essence in a fully intentional way.

4. Concluding Comments: towards a Neo-institutional Economic Theory

As Hayek argued in "Economics and Knowledge", the theory of equilibrium, or "the pure logic of choice", is an exercise in means-ends logic. And this logic does not incorporate any causal "statements about how knowledge is acquired and communicated" (p.53); it is therefore insufficient for understanding processes of change in general and the problem of stability in particular. At a given point of time, agents make decisions that can be understood in terms of application of the pure logic of choice. Often decisions will not be consistent so that price/quantity feedback results. But as Kirzner (1979) explains, for Hayek there is "...nothing in the logic governing the set of choices made by market participants at one date to account for the set of choices they make at future dates" (ibid.: 27). In other words: if we, as Hayek does, associate rationality with the pure logic of choice exclusively, learning (including the set-up of *new* means-ends structures) cannot be a rational activity. Of course, the same criticism may be levelled against Mises' praxeological conception of human action, which is also a conceptualization entirely in terms of a logically coherent means-ends structure (Lachmann 1951). Kirzner's (1979) theory of the entrepreneur represents an Austrian attempt to eliminate the problem by broadening the scope of rationality to also include entrepreneurial awareness of new opportunities for trade. But what about Hayek?

If we only stick to Hayek's work in technical economics, we must conclude that he leaves the problem unresolved. But extending the focus to his later interdisciplinary work in political philosophy, jurisprudence etc., allows us to construct an argument that Hayek in fact has a sort of theory that unites allocation and learning. And it is a theory that is distinct from, though not necessarily opposed to, Kirzner's neo-Austrian theory.

An organizing theme in Hayek's extensive post-war work is his opposition to what he identifies as an essentially Cartesian conception of rationality, that is to say, the conception of rationality as being solely a matter of a logical deduction from explicit and given premises. In contrast to this, Hayek identifies – and endorses – a long philosophical tradition, primarily associated with Scottish Enlightenment philosophers such as David Hume, Adam Ferguson and Adam Smith, in which rationality meant "...the capacity to recognize truth when one meets it, rather than a capacity of deductive reasoning from explicit premises" (Hayek 1967: 84). In others words, rationality should be identified with learning as well as with rule-following behavior, a position that strongly contrasts with his earlier positions (for example, in Hayek 1937). What this amounts to is a rejection of the conception of rationality represented by the strict situational logic of "the pure logic of choice" in which the individual is merely a "zero" (in Popper's terminology), and adopting a much more historical view of the individual agent.

Although action in such a conception is no longer purely a matter of an individual "zero" being subsumed under "the logic of the situation", external influences are still important: action may be constrained and partly determined by norms, institutions etc. Furthermore, much behavior may be governed by largely tacit rules. However, such social formations as rules, norms and institutions can be explained historically – but informed by economic theory – in terms of the earlier actions of other agents, coupled with various evolutionary and invisible-hand explanations (Ullman-Margalitt 1978). Such "institutional individualism" is one way in which the demands placed on individual agents' epistemic powers can be relaxed and made more realistic: rules, norms, institutions etc., bring stability and foresight into the social landscape. This indicates that Hayek's (post-war) interest in social institutions as well as his theory of cultural evolution may be seen as attempts to provide an institutionally oriented answer to the coordination problem he had highlighted in 1937. The institutional set-up of society assists the formation of coordinated states, what Hayek in later contributions calls "spontaneous orders" (Hayek 1973).

The interest in conceptualizing the economy as a dynamic process, the focus on the epistemic powers of agents and the emphasis put on undesigned social institutions which we have seen emerge from the work of Hayek (from 1937 on) are precisely paradigmatic characteristics of a new and expanding economic approach, often identified as "neo-institutional" (Langlois 1986a). I shall have much more to say about these similarities in the rest of this book. But economists in the neoclassical mainstream, too, are increasingly directing their theoretical focus towards social institutions, as witness, for example, the recent neoclassically oriented burst of activity on the theory of the firm and contracts. The institutional agenda is no longer defined by "classical" (Veblen-type) institutionalists. This "institutional turn" has brought with it a strong stimulus to economists' interest in the Smith-Menger-Hayek theme of institutions as spontaneous non-planned formations. One reflection of this is the extensive modern work in game theory associated with names such as Robert Sugden (1986), Andrew Schotter (1981) and others.

This increasing interest in social institutions cannot be found in the new classical program. A central heuristic theme in new classical economics is the insistence that all economic phenomena be reduced to fundamental data, that is, technology and preferences. This implies that "free parameters", i.e., social entities that are not explained by the use of rational choice theory, should be avoided in all social scientific explanations. Such reductionism may on the face of it seem to exclude utilizing institutional constraints for the explanation of individual action. As Lucas however admits (in the introduction to his 1981 book): "At some level of detail, social conventions and institutional structure affect these patterns [of observed behavior]". But, he continues, such social formations

> "...do not simply come out of the blue, arbitrarily imposing themselves on individual actors. On the contrary, institutions and customs are *designed* precisely in order to aid in matching preferences and opportunities satisfactorily" (p.4; my emphasis).

In other words, Lucas seems to insist on explaining *every* social phenomenon intentionally, that is, as consciously designed. In a later contribution, Lucas (1987b) relaxes this extreme position somewhat, but maintains that to the extent that economists focus on the study of efficient equilibria, there is no need for an independent economic study of institutional formation and change (ibid.: 218). An implication that emerges from Hayek's (1937) interest in the societal coordination problem and his later interdisciplinary work is, however, precisely that it is from the starting point of the fact that the social world is not in continuous efficient equilibrium that we must begin our search for the raison d'être of social institutions. An adequate understanding of institutions seems therefore difficult to obtain within the new classical research program. In the rest of this book, I shall be concerned with an examination of the relations between the work of Hayek and Mises and modern institutional and evolutionary economics, broadly conceived. I shall continue chronologically, and discuss the socialist calculation debate, arguably one of the events that led Hayek away from equilibrium theory.

4: Economics and Socialism: the Austrians Revisited

1. Introduction

The last few years have been years of intellectual reorientation among a great number of Western intellectuals, largely caused by the worldwide collapse of centrally planned economic systems. This intellectual reorientation also applies to economists. Take Frank Hahn (1990), for instance, who, in a rare excursion into political economy, observes how his reflections "...bear a close family resemblance to propositions found in Hayek's "Road to Serfdom" (1944), a book which in my youth I detested" (p.142). For, as Hahn remarks, "...recent work on agency and information has strengthened rather than weakened the force of Hayek's arguments" (ibid.). Similarly, we find the English Marxist economist, Andrew Gamble (1985/1986), praising Ludwig von Mises' (1920) "closely reasoned argument" against socialism as well as Hayek's contributions to the economics of socialism, partly as a result of which "Many socialists have become unsure about the feasibility of socialism" (p.365). On a more specific level, we find Paul Samuelson (1983) concluding that Schumpeter was "...uncharacteristically naive in awarding Lange and Lerner victory over Ludwig von Mises on the issue of whether rational economic calculation would be possible under socialism" (p.176).[29]

What are the reasons for this sudden prominence of Austrian arguments, put forward in the context of a debate that took place more than fifty years ago? Some of the explanation is of course to be found in the rather sudden collapse – following many years of stagnation, to be sure – of centrally planned economies, which led to a search for more encompassing economic explanations for it. In such an interpretation, it is quite natural if the Austrian root-and-branch argument against full-scale socialism should have received increased attention.

[29] All this may be seen to reflect a rather long lag of theorizing behind empirical evidence. For listen to Leon Trotsky, the man behind history's first attempt at real comprehensive central planning, the Soviet war communism, describing the experience of this experiment: "How did we start? We began...in economic policy by breaking with the bourgeois past firmly and without compromise. Earlier there was a market – we liquidate it, free trade – we liquidate it , competition – we abolish it, commercial calculation – we abolish it. What to have instead? The central, solemn, sacred, Supreme Economic Council for National Economy that allocates everything, organizes everything, cares for everything: where should machines go, where raw materials, where the finished products – this all will be decided and allocated from a single center, through its authorized organs. This plan of ours failed" (quoted in Szamuely 1974: 94). Should have the made the economists think, shouldn't it?

Another possible explanation is the increasing revisionism that has taken place since the end of the 1970s within the historiography of comparative systems (Vaughn 1980; Nelson 1981; Nelson and Winter 1982: chapter 15; Lavoie 1981, 1985, 1986; Steele 1981; Keizer 1987, 1989; Murrell 1983; Kirzner 1988; Rothbard 1991; Ebeling 1993). What is noteworthy about this new revisionism is that it has largely emerged from the fortresses of heterodoxy, specifically from Austrian and evolutionary economists.

The long dominant interpretation of what happened in *the socialist calculation debate* of the 1920s and 1930s has in contrast been put forward by neoclassical economists. It has often been said that the victors write the history, and those who were at least claimed to have won the calculation debate were primarily neoclassically oriented economists with a formalist bent, such as Oskar Lange or Abba Lerner.

It is the historiography of this debate which I shall briefly consider in this chapter. And I shall go a little further and indicate how insights from modern economics of both the neo-institutionalist and the evolutionary variety may be argued to have strengthened Austrian arguments originally put forward in the context of the calculation debate by Mises and Hayek. I therefore implicitly agree with at least some of the above-mentioned revisionists in seeing these arguments as largely inexpressible within a pure neoclassical framework. Where I differ from them, however, is in interpreting the Austrian arguments more in terms of neo-institutionalism and evolutionary theory than in terms of the Austrian market process approach (for that interpretation, see in particular Lavoie 1985; Kirzner 1988). However, the two interpretations may turn out to be largely complementary, both capturing aspects of what Mises and Hayek said during the debate.

2. The New Revisionism in the Historiography of Comparative Systems

2.1. The Contours of the New Revisionism

In general, the last two decades have marked an increased interest in that debate on comparative systems which, according to Don Lavoie (1985), should be considered the most important one: here called "the socialist calculation debate". This debate was played out at different tempi and in different phases over more than twenty years, involving numerous important economists. The main actors were, on the anti-socialist side, Mises,

Hayek and Lionel Robbins and, on the socialist side, Oskar Lange, Abba Lerner, Maurice Dobb, Henry Dickinson and Fred Taylor.[30]

The general tendency of this increased interest is – as already indicated – clearly revisionist. It is argued, in short, that a precise exegesis of the original Austrian arguments reveals something quite different from the standard account of these arguments. Don Lavoie (1985) in particular has attempted to trace the emergence of the standard account to quite fundamental – paradigmatic, really – differences between the parties of the calculation debate. The neoclassical market socialists did not understand the specifically Austrian perspective from which they were criticized by Mises, Hayek and Robbins.

On the other hand, the Austrians themselves did not really understand that they were – in terms of fundamental theoretical outlook – quite different from their opponents. As Kirzner (1988) argues, it was largely as a result of the calculation debate that the Austrians understood that they were a school apart. It was only as a consequence of the debate that the Austrians realized that they differed fundamentally from the formalist general equilibrium approach of their opponents. In this connection, Richard Nelson (1981) noted that

> "It is interesting that von Mises...and Hayek...pose their arguments in a form much more distant from that of contemporary welfare economics than does Lange" (p. 95n).

It has often been argued (fx Koopmans 1957: 42) that the calculation debate helped crystallize Walrasianism into the dominant approach to neoclassical economics, particularly in regard to welfare economics; what is new is the above-mentioned neo-Austrian claim that the debate in fact did a similar thing to the Austrian school. And what is also new is the claim that the debate was not over with the alleged victory of the market socialists.

2.2. The Standard Account

From around the time Abram Bergson wrote his authoritative survey essay, "Socialist Economics" (1948), and until the new revisionism, a cer-

[30] The central contributions are: Mises (1920, 1936), Hayek (1935b&c, 1940, 1945), and Taylor (1928), Dickinson (1933), Lange (1936/1937), Lerner (1944). Hoff (1948) is an early and comprehensive survey, largely on the side of the Austrians. It should be mentioned that it really is something of a rational reconstruction to talk about a debate at all, since most of the presumed debate took place among the socialist economists, and since Mises – to the extent that he was mentioned – was made appear ridiculous, and Hayek and Robbins were largely neglected.

tain interpretation – a "standard account" – was generally accepted. It was held that the themes and divergence of the calculation debate on a theoretical level had essentially been debated conclusively – and that the debate had ended with the Austrians' defeat. Schumpeter (1942: 185) summarized the emerging consensus when he observed that "...as a matter of blueprint logic, it is undeniable that the socialist blueprint is drawn at a higher level of rationality".

Armed with the theoretical state of the art of their day, market socialist contributions in particular had conclusively demonstrated the theoretical possibility of a rational allocation of resources in a socialist economy. What was left were more trivial elaborations of planning technology, i.e. "planometrics" (Wilczynski 1970) or "mechanisms for resource allocation" (Hurwicz 1971, 1973).

The more specific contours of the standard account have been comprehensively identified by Lavoie (1985); briefly, they are as follows. Before 1920 the economic content of schemes for central planning was orthodox Marxism, which implied central planning on the basis of units of labor value and "liquidation" of money, prices, and the profit motive. As David Ramsay Steele observes, almost "any active socialist" at that time would have known, "almost by heart", the famous passage from "Anti-Dühring" in which Engels explains how

> "Society can calculate how many hours of labor are contained in a steam-engine, a bushel of wheat of the last harvest, or a hundred square yards of cloth of a certain quality...People will be able to manage everything very simply, without the intervention of much-vaunted "value"" (quoted in Steele 1981: 12).

As an explicit reaction to such schemes, Mises (1920) put forward what was essentially a twin argument. He argued that, first, in the absence of prices which reflected real scarcities, and, second, also emerged from the interaction among multiple holders of ownership rights to goods,[31] rational economic "calculation" was impossible:

[31] Notice this separation. The necessity of a price system for rational allocation had already been argued by Gossen in 1855, and was later restated by Friedrich von Wieser, Max Weber, Boris Brutzkus, Pareto, Walras (Ménard 1990), Pierson, Barone and many others before Mises (see Ebeling (1993) for a scholarly discussion of a number of Mises' less well-known predecessors). In other words, in 1920 this point was not a new one, as Lange (1936/1937) noticed. What was new, however, was Mises' emphasis on property rights. And it was this argument that was misunderstood and interpreted as essentially an institutionalist argument by Lange (1936/1937). More about this later.

> "Where there is no free market, there is no pricing mechanism; without a pricing mechanism, there is no economic calculation...we have the spectacle of a socialist economic order floundering in the ocean of possible and conceivable economic combinations without the compass of economic calculation...Socialism is the abolition of rational economy" (Mises 1920: 110-111).

In the absence of prices, decision makers have no relevant indicators for the relative economic importance of factor services in their alternative uses. And that is why socialism in an economic sense is "a system of groping about in the dark" (Mises 1949: 700).

After the initial shock waves had subsided, Mises' point about the necessity of a price system for "rational calculation" was incorporated in Walrasian planning models. These theoretical efforts involved the polemic point – which is usually repeated in the standard account – that Mises' assertion of the "impossibility" of socialist allocation had in a sense already been proven fallacious. This is, so the argument goes, because Barone in 1908 (and also Pareto prior to this) had demonstrated "the formal similarity" between the allocation problem in a private enterprise economy and a socialist economy. These allocation problems were structurally similar, Barone had argued that since a Walrasian equation system could be taken as describing them both, this in its turn implied that the same principles of optimal allocation of resources could be applied. Specifically, a socialist economy could achieve efficiency in the sense of Pareto optimality.

While Barone (1908) was satisfied with merely pointing out this "formal similarity", Dickinson (1933) went much further. He seemed to believe that letting the planning authorities write down a set of Walrasian equations and solve them, the corresponding system could be practically accomplished. Inside the "glass walls" of socialism, Dickinson thought, planning authorities would have direct and unproblematic access to production technologies and presumably also to individual preferences and endowments.

Under the impact of the discovery of the theoretical possibility of efficiency under socialism, Hayek and Robbins retreated – the standard account claims – from Mises' untenable postulate of "impossibility". Instead they put forward the essentially practical – nontheoretical – objection that solving the "millions of equations" of the market socialist-planning model would be outside contemporary computational capacity (Robbins 1934: 151; Hayek 1935c: 156). In fact, Barone (1908: 71) made the same point much earlier. Leonid Hurwicz (1973) summarized Hayek and Robbins' position:

> "It should be recalled that one of Hayek's...chief points...was that the number of variables and equations would be "at least in the hundreds of thousands" and the required equation solving "a task which, with any of the means known at present, could not be carried out in a lifetime. And yet these decisions would...have to be made continuously" (p.5).

Now, as Lange's (1936/1937) famous contribution made clear, even these calculational problems could be eliminated under socialism, since his reasoning made clear that it was not at all necessary for the planning authorities to have direct access to, for example, the technologies of individual firms. This is one of the reasons why Lange's article long was considered the definitive answer to the Austrian challenge (Bergson 1948). In Lange's scheme, planning authorities are not required to solve enormous equation systems on the basis of detailed knowledge about technology, preferences and endowments, as Dickinson had suggested; they "merely" have to find market-clearing prices on markets for real capital through something like a Walrasian tatonnement mechanism (inspired by Taylor 1928).[32]

This procedure takes place under the assumption that managers minimize factor costs, implying efficient use of resources, and produce until marginal costs are equal to prices, implying efficient size of productive units. In other words, it leads to the same resource allocation as under the standard perfect competition model with the implied beneficial welfare effects. The only difference from the standard set-up is that ownership titles to capital goods are not exclusive and tradable, and that the planning authorities appropriate capital rents.

Although Lange's contribution, according to the standard account, constituted a satisfactory response to Mises' challenge on a theoretical level (cf. Nove and Nuti 1972b: 12), the market socialists were very well aware that as a "practical" planning scheme, Lange's idea was less successful. And in fact, Lange has very little specific to say about the trial and

[32] Lange's scheme is not completely identical to Walras' tatonnement, since he allows for some trading at false prices. Lange (1936/1937) took the stability of the trading process as unproblematic, completely side-stepping the problem of endogenously generated changes in the parameters of the systems. Research in mechanisms for resource allocation (see Hurwicz (1973) for an excellent, though probably somewhat outdated overview) has clarified that very strong restrictions have to be imposed on the iterative procedure for convergence to equilibrium.

error procedure through which equilibrium prices can presumably be found. Much of the literature on market socialism which has taken its lead from Lange has, in fact, been taken up with specifying this procedure, under the restriction that a minimum of information be transferred from local producers to central planning authorities (Hurwicz 1984). The "practical" lesson taught by Hayek, relating to "...the difficulty of placing all the relevant information in the hands of a single agency because it is dispersed throughout the economy" (Hurwicz 1973: 5), has not been forgotten, to be sure.

The design of operational market socialist planning schemes has, however, turned out to be harder than initially envisaged (by, for example, Koopmans 1951). And it is under the impression of such difficulties that Hurwicz (1973) ends his survey of the literature by noting that we should look at these models as "...somewhat like synthetic chemicals: even if not usable for practical purposes, they can be studied in a pure form and so contribute to our understanding of the difficulties and potentialities of design" (p.27). That does not, however, detract from the fact that such models constitute the definitive answer to Mises' postulate of the theoretical impossibility of "rational" allocation in a socialist order. In the following section, I shall briefly discuss some of the objections that have been raised against the standard account from the new revisionism (Vaughn 1980; Lavoie 1981, 1985; Steele 1981; Nelson 1981; Murrell 1983; Kirzner 1988).

2.3. The Standard Account Versus the New Revisionism

One of the central points in this revisionism is that the calculation debate was characterized by much conceptual and theoretical confusion between the antagonists. This confusion basically derived from the paradigmatic differences between the positions from which the antagonists debated. Furthermore, the standard account has narrowly adopted the point of view of only the socialist side in the debate. The most obvious example is the interpretation of what Mises actually meant when he said that socialism was "impossible". In fact, Mises has been interpreted as simply unscholarly (Nove and Nuti 1972b: 12), since Barone "already in 1908" had established the theoretical possibility of efficiency under socialism.

However, neither Mises, Hayek nor Robbins ever claimed that market-socialist models were inconsistent given their assumptions. What they argued was that the internal logic of such models was not sufficient to establish the practical possibility of efficiency under socialism simply because these models did not capture a sufficient part of essential aspects of the real world (Hayek 1940). They were flatly inapplicable. This objection may be argued to be "practical" – and I shall argue that it is more than that – but it is not trivial.

This may be seen as a controversy over the legitimate domain of applicability of neoclassical economics. However, it is argued by the new revisionism that more was at stake: the methodological, conceptual and theoretical differences of the debate all had their roots in unrecognized paradigmatic differences between the parties. Specifically, the debate involved at least three economic approaches: Marxism, Austrian economics and Walrasian economics. Furthermore, it took place in at least three phases. The first phase is marked by Mises' attack on central European Marxists. The second relates to the emergence of Walrasianism as the foundation for market socialism and the Austrian critique of this. And the third phase relates primarily to Hayek's critique of the later Walrasian market socialist models. Let us briefly consider these episodes seriatim, in order to underscore the proposition that deep-rooted differences were indeed involved.

Mises' (1920) attack on the classical Marxist planning ideal basically derived from a specific conviction: that all the economic institutions of capitalism are necessary for what he calls, somewhat ambiguously, "rational calculation".[33] Of these institutions, property rights are the most important; they are "...the fundamental institution of the market economy. It is the institution whose presence characterizes the market economy as such" (Mises 1949: 678). So for a market economy to have a meaningful existence, not only are the price system and money needed, but also exclusive and tradable ownership rights to capital assets. However, Mises' neoclassical opponents effectively separated the point about property rights from the point about prices. And while they conceded the last point, they ridiculed the first one (Lange 1936/1937: 62), chiding Mises for adopting what seemed to be an atheoretical institutionalist position. The reason for this is obvious: conceding Mises' point about property rights would mean abandoning the socialist ideal.

Summarizing the first phase of the calculation debate, it is evident that Mises was not defeated. Rather, the fact that his insight as to the necessity of pricing was admitted in socialist planning schemes should be considered a victory. Mises did not fail to notice this (Mises 1949) but argued that the market-socialist response was incomplete. There can be no "playing market", such as the market socialists attempt, since the economic institutions of capitalism are inseparable; the markets and prices of Lange et

[33] The notion of "rational calculation" is ambiguous in Mises' writings because it here relates both to calculation by individual entrepreneurs and to social efficiency.

al., are not "real" prices, because they have not emerged from the rival interplay of multiple owners of titles to property rights. This does not bring us much further, however. For what does it mean exactly, to say that prices and markets are "real"? Although I shall have more to say about this in the next chapter, it should be mentioned at once that property rights' insights were strong in Mises' thinking. And these insights underlie his objection to the kinds of markets envisaged by the market socialists. As he says:

> "...it is not possible to divorce the market and its functions in regard to the formation of prices from the working of a society which is based on private property in the means of production" (1936: 137).

More precisely, exclusive and tradable rights to capital assets are required for efficiency, which is a tendency under the capitalist order, since here such ownership rights underlie "the ceaseless search on the part of capitalists and entrepreneurs to maximize their profits" (ibid.: 138).

The second phase of the debate is identified with Hayek and Robbins attacking the early Walrasian planning schemes. According to the standard account, Mises "...in his powerful attack...tends to spoil his case by the implicit assumption that capitalism and optimum resource allocation go together...[and]...imply that a socialist economy could not function at all" (Nove and Nuti 1972b: 12). Unlike Mises, Hayek and Robbins admitted the logical consistency of Walrasian market-socialist models. Hence, it is asserted, they accepted the theoretical possibility of socialism. If true, this would be a major retreat from Mises' position. However, the new revisionism argues against this interpretation. On the basis of a close analysis of the original Austrian contributions, and armed with the modern Austrian understanding of the market as a process of entrepreneurial discovery, the new revisionism argues that:

1) the fact that Hayek admitted the logical consistency of market socialist models does not imply that he regarded them as relevant answers to Mises' challenge. As Hayek put it, the market socialists demonstrated an "excessive preoccupation with problems of the pure theory of stationary equilibrium", which blinded them towards understanding how entrepreneurs handled "adjustments to the daily changing conditions in different places and different industries" (Hayek 1940: 188). Surely, these "adjustments" were not necessarily best handled through a centralized tatonnement procedure,

2) Mises had in fact anticipated later market socialist developments and rejected them (see Mises' critique of "The Artificial Market as the Solution of the Problem of Economic Calculation" (1936 [1922]: 119-123). Therefore, Hayek's later contributions do not mark a retreat from Mises' position,

3) Hayek's objections were anything but trivial. And it was precisely during the confrontation with formalist, Walrasian market socialism that Hayek developed his view of the market as the procedure for the discovery and coordination of knowledge (Kirzner 1988: 7).[34]

As indicated by these three points, the Austrian critique of Walrasian market socialism really had a broader scope. As the new revisionism interprets the story, the Austrians revolted against the emerging lock-in of unlimited rationality and equilibrium as the dominant economic tools. Specifically, the Austrians criticized 1) the static nature of Walrasian models, 2) the epistemological assumptions of these models such as the one that all relevant knowledge is given to agents, and 3) the conceptualization of economic behavior as merely maximizing given prices. The Austrians wished to have such static assumptions replaced by a process perspective that could give due attention to the entrepreneurial *discovery* of the presumed "data".

It should be admitted, I think, that the Austrians and their opponents did, in fact, reason within relatively divergent frameworks. However, it must be understood that conceptualizing the Austrian position in the calculation debate in terms of the perspective of the modern neo-Austrian school is largely a retrospective rationalization. It is, I think, not until Hayek's 1937 article, "Economics and Knowledge", that there can be said to have been any Austrian awareness of having fundamentally diverged from the Walrasianism of their opponents. What Hayek did in this justly celebrated article was to argue that what should be clarified was the problem of how agents could obtain such information so that they were able to implement equilibrium plans. The market socialists' Walrasian models implicitly presumed that this problem had already been solved.

What Hayek took steps towards in 1937 was the establishment of the modern Austrian perspective of the market process as a process in the entrepreneurial discovery of opportunities for trade – which is precisely the lens through which most of the new revisionists perceive the calculation debate. Three years later, we indeed find Hayek adopting this discovery perspective in a critique of market socialism:

[34] For some critical comments on this interpretation, see Foss (1995).

> "What is forgotten [by the market socialists] is that the method which under given conditions is the cheapest is a thing which has to be discovered, and to be discovered anew, sometimes almost from day to day, by the entrepreneur, and that, in spite of the strong inducement, it is by no means the established entrepreneur, the man in charge of the existing plant, who will discover what is the best method" (1940: 196).

In other words, the discovery of the best productive techniques is not a static parametric optimization problem which can be easily ascertained and solved by local producers once the benevolent Langean planning authorities have issued the right prices. Rather, this discovery is fundamentally an entrepreneurial problem. What prices offer here is a reduction of the enormous number of technically possible ways to produce goods to a handful of potentially profitable ways. But prices do not bring full determinacy. And without an adequate underlying property rights structure it is unlikely that much will be discovered. For example, Lange's planning authorities do not have strong incentives to participate efficiently in the discovery process.

Since prices are continually in flux, only some of the productive techniques chosen ex ante will be profitable ex post. Guided by expectations of profit, entrepreneurs will bid resource prices up and down, and it is this active process which directs the market in an equilibrating direction. The rationality of the system does not really hinge on the decisions of the individual entrepreneur/producer; rather, it is the whole process of active rivalry that imparts rationality to the system. It is something like this argument that Lavoie (1985) is driving at when he observes that

> "...the key point of the calculation argument is that the required knowledge of objective production possibilities would be unavailable without the competitive market process" (p.102).

Clearly, this is an evolutionary conception of market activity; the variation and selection mechanisms of the market are needed to generate new production possibilities and sort among them. And as I shall argue later on, this conception converges with modern developments in evolutionary economics (such as Nelson and Winter 1982). In the next section, I shall, however, continue to discuss what was really at stake in the calculation debate. I shall argue that how the parties conceived of the economic discipline – its domain of application and how it should develop – was a crucial factor.

3. Formalism, Institutions and the Austrians

Before Mises wrote his 1920 article, economic approaches to the economics of socialism were largely institutionalist and historicist in the sense that the universality of basic economic categories (rationality, incentives – even scarcity) was denied. In this context, Mises' article and the context in which it appeared could be viewed as yet another episode of the Methodenstreit. Although Mises' point about the necessity of pricing could be seen as simply an application of basic microeconomic theory, at a different level it can be seen as emerging from that position which Menger had defended during the Methodenstreit: that the universal fact of rational action under scarcity implies necessary and systematic relations which are invariable relative to spatiotemporal characteristics, and which therefore must also hold under socialism.

In such an interpretation, there is no sharp distinction between Mises-as-methodologist and Mises-as-theorist. However, a division between these two roles was exactly what Oskar Lange tried to impute to Mises when he argued that according to Mises

> "...the economic principles of choice between different alternatives are applicable only to a special institutional set-up, i.e., to a society which recognizes private ownership of the means of production. It has been maintained...that all economic laws have only historico-relative validity. But it is most surprising to find this institutionalist view supported by a prominent member of the Austrian school, which did so much to emphasize the universal validity of the fundamental principles of economic theory" (1936/1937: 62)

That would be "most surprising", indeed, if it were true. To interpret Mises' argument as a denial of "the fundamental principles of economic theory" is to misrepresent him completely: what Mises consistently argued throughout his whole career was that choice-theoretical principles can be applied to action in any society.

Lange's misrepresentations were perhaps not so much an attempt to tease Mises as expressing a tendency that became general and dominant in economics at approximately the time Lange wrote his article. Under the impact of the emerging Walrasian revolution, economists were increasingly directed away from gaining a realistic understanding, though informed by theory, of real institutions. A transformation of how economists viewed their science accompanied this: neoclassical economists increasingly began to let their conceptualizations be wholly limited by what analytical armory was present. In the context of economic policy, such an attitude easily leads to what Schumpeter called "the Ricardian vice", that is, the tendency to jump directly from very abstract models to policy implications. Clearly, Lange is a practitioner of this vice: he does not hesitate to jump from abstract propositions about a model without, for example, transaction costs, uncertainty and intertemporal trade to claiming this model to be of direct applicability.[35] For the Austrians, by contrast, conceptualizations of problems indicated gaps to be filled in existing theory. For instance, as we saw in chapter 3, it was conceptualizations of the actual market process as a process of learning that led Hayek (1937) to doubt the validity of the equilibrium approach.

In a fascinating contribution, Ludwig Lachmann (1973) discussed the above neoclassical stance, and isolated one of its attributes which he called "formalism": "...a style of thought according to which abstract entities are treated as though they were real" (p.9). In other words, "formalism" implies what philosophers call "the fallacy of conceptual realism". That fallacy may or may not be more prevalent among neoclassical economists than among economists in general; what is relevant here is that it was very clearly present in the thinking of the market socialists and particularly in the economics of Oskar Lange.

Lange (1936/1937) defines his task in the following way:

> "It is...the purpose of the present essay to elucidate the way in which the allocation of resources is effected by trial and error on a competitive market, and to find out whether a similar trial and error procedure is not possible in a socialist economy" (p.65).

[35] For a relevant distinction between a "normative" and a "descriptive" strand in the evolution of general equilibrium theory, see Ingrao and Israel (1990). Clearly, Lange belongs to the normative strand, as Walras himself did, and as the modern work on "computable general equilibrium" associated with Herbert Scarf does.

He then undertakes an exercise in Walrasian price adjustment, that is, a tatonnement process, essentially making use of the purely imaginary construction of the auctioneer. Using this mind construct is, of course, not illegitimate per se, provided its imaginary character is kept in mind. But the dominating impression conveyed by Lange's discussion is that Walrasian tatonnement very closely mimics – is "something similar" to – what takes place on real markets (1936/1937: section 2).

In his thinking, there seems to be a strong tendency towards understanding conceptual constructions as very "verisimilar" projections of real actors and real phenomena. His polemic against Hayek and Robbins' "millions of equations" argument seems to indicate this:

> "Professor Hayek and Professor Robbins themselves "solve" at least hundreds of equations daily, for instance, in buying a newspaper or in deciding to take a meal in a restaurant, and presumably they do not use determinants or Jacobians for that purpose" (1936/1937: 88).

With such a formalistic understanding of price formation, it is surely not surprising that Lange could answer his question "whether a similar trial and error procedure is not possible in a socialist economy" in the affirmative. Mises may (again) have been too general in his characterization when he argued that mathematical economists "...deal with equilibrium as if it were a real entity and not a limiting notion, a mere mental tool" (1949: 251). But such a remark is quite understandable in the light of Lange's formalist discussion. And it is also quite understandable that Mises noticed that "...it is hardly possible to construe the market process in a more erroneous way" (ibid.: 354) than done by the market socialists.

A few years before Lange (1936/1937) accused Mises of institutionalism, Hayek was criticized by Piero Sraffa (1932) for wholly neglecting the role of institutions in his theorizing and for having theorized on an excessively abstract level. In the midst of the 1930s, the Austrians were then in the strange position of being simultaneously accused of being atheoretical institutionalists and of being excessively abstract. In fact, they were neither. Since Menger, one of the prime motivations for the Austrian developments in value theory had been to understand real institutions, their raison d'être and functioning. It has become customary to think of the Austrians as aloof apriorists almost solely engaged in spinning out the logical and rather trivial implications of a few self-evident propositions.

This means that the Austrian quality of the Mengerian emphasis on the importance of real institutions and the need to explain them, of Mises' work, in particular on monetary and credit institutions, and of Hayek's very encompassing theory of cultural evolution has been largely forgotten. And while the Austrians saw economic categories as necessary shorthands for understanding the laws of the market, they also recognized that these can only be fully applied in historic research and forecasting when they are supplemented by "verstehende" insight in the structures of meaning through which the economizing actions of real economic agents manifest themselves (cf. Mises 1949: 59-64; Hayek 1952: chapter 3). The Austrians were never "against" historical and institutional research per se. For example, Menger's 1871 contribution contains a largely historical chapter on the evolution of a monetary medium.[36] Mises – the foremost proponent of an apriorist methodology – started out as an economic historian, and his main treatise on socialism is packed with historical detail (Mises 1936). Furthermore, he was instrumental in setting up the first Austrian institute of empirical business cycle research, with Hayek serving as its first director. What the Austrians said was that institutional and historical analysis should and, for basic epistemological reasons, could not stand alone, but ought to be conducted with the use of theoretical concepts.

This is the historical and methodological light in which the Austrian arguments in the calculation debate should be seen. And it was because the Austrians' formalist opponents had little understanding of the role that the investigation of institutions played for the Austrians, that they could misconstrue their (particularly Mises') complex property rights-based argument as atheoretical institutionalism. In some important dimensions, then, what really clashed in the calculation debate were basic outlooks on the scope and method of economics. To use terminology from the evolutionary theorists, Richard Nelson and Sidney Winter (1982), the Austrians – common opinion notwithstanding – did not only conduct "formal" theory. Their theorizing was also "appreciative"; that is to say, a matter of letting real institutions and processes significantly influence theorizing. For example, in the preceding chapter we saw Hayek growing increasingly skeptical towards equilibrium theory because of its inability to handle processes of change. In the context of the socialist calculation debate, the Austrians saw change and property rights as features of the real world that simply could not be excluded from any sensible discussion of comparative systems.

[36] However, Menger's account is not intended as an accurate historical portrayal, but rather as an exercise in "conjectural history"; that is, he gives a plausible account of the historical forces that could conceptually have produced a monetary medium.

4. Property Rights, Selection and Capital Markets

Mises' complex comparative institutional arguments during the calculation debate anticipated themes that did not acquire prominence until the property rights approach of the 1960s. Specifically, Mises' proposition, that only a system where ownership rights to capital goods are exclusive and tradable allows "rational calculation", anticipated property rights insights into the functioning of capital markets and how they monitor managers' shirking (Alchian 1965, 1969; Manne 1965; De Alessi 1969, 1980, 1983). However, Mises' insights went unrecognized. To a large extent, this has to do with his often implicit theorizing – in the sense that he did not always fully spell out all the assumptions underlying his analysis, smuggled new ones in etc. But it has also to do with his opponents' neoclassical, formalist bent which led to the rejection of property rights based arguments as atheoretical institutionalism. The partial exception to this was Dickinson (1937) who in a review of Mises' "Socialism" noted that

> "The full establishment of the author's thesis would seem to require a careful analysis of the concepts of exchange and of the market, and of the extent to which these essentially *economic* phenomena are necessarily linked to particular *institutional* forms of entrepreneurship and of private property in the means of productions" (p.96).

Notice that although he understands its importance for Mises' work, Dickinson insists on thinking of property as an essentially noneconomic category.

However, arguments that anticipated neo-institutionalist thought of the property rights variety were not the only ones employed by the Austrians which differed from the Walrasianism of their opponents. As emphatically argued by the new revisionism, it was during the course of the calculation debate that the specifically Austrian perspective on competition as an entrepreneurial process of discovery of opportunities for trade emerged. This is quite close to the truth, I think, but something is omitted; the arguments of the modern Austrians do not capture all aspects of the Misesian and Hayekian arguments of the calculation debate. As I later clarify, we get additional assistance in interpreting Hayek and Mises if we also include the work of modern evolutionary theorists such as Richard Nelson and Sidney Winter (1982) (in addition to property rights insights). Although Nelson and Winter's intellectual debt is primarily to Joseph Schumpeter and Herbert Simon, their work is in some ways quite related to the modern Austrian work of, say, Israel Kirzner (1973). The most obvious basic similarity is that both approaches conceive of the market as essentially a discovery procedure.

In Mises' work, property rights based arguments are mixed inseparably with his view of the market as a discovery procedure/selection forum. This becomes clear if we consider his description of "the problem of economic calculation". Human action, Mises proclaims in dramatic Heraclitean terms, "...is one of the agencies bringing about change. It is an element of cosmic activity and becoming" (1949: 18). And it is such change which explains why "...the problem of economic calculation is of economic dynamics; it is no problem of economic statics" (1936: 121). Although Mises does not really clarify what he means by "change", we should (as argued in a more detailed way in chapter 6) associate it with unanticipated change, since this is the kind of change that makes a difference for economic organization. Although anticipated change will have economic effects through changing relative prices, it will in general leave economic organization unaffected. For example, anticipated change may be incorporated in contracting. Intuitively, the implication is that various kinds of economic organization derive their efficiency attributes from their ability to handle unanticipated change.

The economic problem of society is therefore not one of static optimal allocation within given means-ends structures, as it is in Lange's stationary state (Hayek 1945). The economic problem arises because of the very phenomena suppressed by Lange: uncertainty, unpredictable change, intertemporal trade, and transaction costs. So the economic problem is largely a matter of efficient adaptation to unanticipated change, implying "...dissolving, extending, transforming, and limiting existing undertakings, and establishing new undertakings" (Mises 1936: 215). Such actions are based on "speculative anticipations" (ibid.: 205) and bring the entrepreneur in focus. In Mises' thinking it is the entrepreneur who creates the data of the market, to the benefit of those individuals who do not possess entrepreneurial competence. This implies that his function is universally necessary for rational allocation; he "...fulfills a task which must be performed even in a socialist community" (ibid.: 213). In terms of Kirzner's (1973) work on entrepreneurship, the services of the entrepreneur are necessary for any society, since economic opportunities have to be *discovered*. The issue of discovery of profitable opportunities, implying the formation of new firms and change in existing ones, is completely suppressed in Lange's scheme of things.

In Mises' works the role of the entrepreneur and that of the capitalist overlap[37]; the capitalist/entrepreneur is not only a Kirznerian alert discoverer of hitherto unexploited opportunities for trade; he is also a (Knightian) bearer of that uncertainty which has to be borne by someone. But "...the capitalist does not just invest his capital in those undertakings which offer high interest or high profit; he attempts rather to strike a balance between his desire for profit and his estimate of the risk of loss" (1936: 122). Since such incentives are absent in a socialist economy, there will a premium on "audacity, carelessness and unreasonable optimism" (1949: 709). Evidence for Mises' views here are, for example, Bauer's (1978) discussion of investment-driven business cycles in centrally planned economies, because of the "investment hunger" of socialist managers, and Kornai's (1980) discussion of "the soft budget constraint", according to which the central planning authorities act as insurance institutions, taking over the moral hazard of individual managers.

As the above indicates, Mises' property rights arguments are all formulated in the context of a process view of the market which has a distinctly evolutionary character. The emphasis that Mises puts on change and differential firm growth illustrates this. Furthermore, although Mises clearly anticipated a number of insights from agency theory, he did not say that managers only differ in terms of how efficiently they pursue their principals' interests, as is customary in agency. In a number of dimensions, entrepreneurs' and managers' talents differ; there is an asymmetrical distribution of entrepreneurial competence (cf. Manne 1965; Lucas 1978). It is the market which selects among entrepreneurial ventures:

> "The more successfully [an entrepreneur] speculates, the more means of production are at his disposal, the greater becomes his influence on the business of society. The less successfully he speculates, the smaller becomes his property, the less becomes his influence in business. If he loses everything by speculation he disappears from the ranks of those who are called to the direction of economic affairs" (1936: 182).

Clearly, this is a kind of selection argument formulated in terms of differential growth rates of firms. And as in evolutionary theory in general, it is the rationality of the system as a whole that is important, rather than the

[37] I owe this point to Murray Rothbard.

rationality of individual market participants (cf. Alchian 1950). As Mises puts it, entrepreneurs

> "...earn profit not because they are clever in performing their tasks, but because they are more clever or less clumsy than other people are. They are not infallible and often blunder" (Mises 1974: 114).

That is, "Even in a world of stupid men there would still be profits" (Alchian 1950: 20).

As in recent applications of evolutionary arguments to comparative systems (Pelikan 1988), Mises' places the financial and capital markets centrally in his attempt to explain the forces of selection that operate in a capitalist economy:

> "Under capitalism, the capitalist decides to whom he will entrust his own capital. The beliefs of the managers of joint stock companies regarding the future prospects of their undertakings and the hopes of project-makers regarding the profitability of their plans are not in any way decisive. The mechanism of the money market and the capital market decides. This indeed is its main task: to serve the economic system as a whole, to judge the profitability of alternative openings and not blindly to follow what the managers of particular concerns, limited by the narrow horizon of their own undertakings, are tempted to propose" (1936: 121-122).

It is the crucial importance of these markets which explains why Mises can argue that if they are eliminated, as they are under socialism, "...one does not preserve any part of the market" (1949: 709). This is fundamentally what Mises means by saying that socialism is "impossible". Although the utility functions of managers in state owned and privately owned firms may contain the same arguments, probably even weighted the same way, managers in privately owned firms are ultimately kept (at least within bounds) in check through capital market discipline. No such discipline exists in Lange's market-socialist scheme (Nutter 1967); he merely assumes continuous incentive compatibility between socialist managers and the planning authorities. But that compatibility – if it can be achieved – is precisely what should be explained.

5. Evolution and Knowledge

In the above sections, I have interpreted Mises and to some extent also Hayek's property rights-based arguments as an attempt to steer a course between the Scylla of atheoretical institutionalism and the Charybdis of Walrasian formalism (cf. Lavoie 1986). A recent example of a similar undertaking is the evolutionary work of Nelson and Winter (1982): to be sure, theirs is a formal economic theory, yet they manage to incorporate disequilibrium, process and entrepreneurship in the formal apparatus. Their intellectual debt is to that economic tradition "...where competition was viewed as a dynamic process, involving uncertainty, struggle and disequilibrium, not as a tranquil equilibrium" (1982: 164). Schumpeter, and, to some extent, Alfred Marshall, are the prime patron saints here; however, it could as well have been Mises and Hayek. Firms – which in a Hayekian manner are seen as evolved entities consisting of behavioral rules – grow or decay on the basis of how well they cope with unanticipated change, and it is this evolutionary process which imparts rationality to the system as a whole, much in the way Mises conceived of the market process.

On the level of the individual agent, bounded rationality (in the sense of Herbert Simon 1976) and tacit knowledge (in the sense of Polanyi 1958) are seen as crucial. And it is fundamentally this which underlies Nelson and Winter's view of the market as a discovery procedure and their coming out in favor of the private enterprise system[38]: "Arguments for private enterprise must take the form that, given man's limitations, patched up private enterprise is as good an organizational solution as can be devised" (Nelson 1981: 95). We should note that Nelson and Winter's emphasis on Simonian bounded rationality does not actually amount to the same thing as the modern Austrian emphasis on incomplete knowledge (Kirzner 1973). Whereas Simon tends to ascribe the limitations of rationality to the mind's inability to process vast amounts of given knowledge, the Austrian emphasis is on the lack of all the relevant knowledge, and the need for an entrepreneurial market process to cope with this knowledge problem.[39]

[38] However, Nelson and Winter would not accept Hayek and Mises' libertarian policy views. See the policy chapters of their 1982 book.

[39] However, Mises seems to have had a notion of bounded rationality at the back of his mind when he described the problems that would meet the planner who confronted "..the embarrassing multitude of producers' goods and the infinite variety of procedures that can be resorted to for manufacturing definite consumers' goods" (1949: 698; see also the example on page 699). This may be interpreted as a purely computational problem, one that may be overcome with the development of computers that can relax the bounds on the planner's rationality. To have put forward a merely computational argument was precisely how the Austrians were interpreted by their opponents according to Lavoie (1985).

However, although the epistemic positions are conceptually distinct, the views about competition that emerge from these positions are very complementary, indeed. And they are both very far from the standard view and assessment of competition.

As Richard Nelson (1981) noticed, arguments for the superiority of the decentralized private enterprise system usually fall within the category of "appreciative theory", not within the category of "formal theory". The Smithian pin factory, Hayek's "telecommunications system" metaphor of the price system (Hayek 1945), and the Schumpeterian heroic entrepreneur are standard in informal discussions in comparative systems. A little more specifically, arguments for private enterprise usually take the form of highlighting the system's 1) administrative parsimony (Hayek 1945), 2) its responsiveness to change (Mises 1936; Hayek 1945), and 3) its innovativeness (Pelikan 1988) (Nelson 1981). While agency theory, property rights theory, and the literature on mechanism design give some insight into the first issue, the remaining two are not easily addressed by mainstream theory.

As Nelson observed, the three arguments above have "...a strong common premise linking them, and separating them from contemporary welfare economics" (1981: 95). This common premise is the recognition – explicit or implicit – that "man's data processing capacity, his ability to understand complex or novel situations, and his ability to gain agreement are bounded" (ibid.), and that theorizing about comparative systems should not neglect this. One of Nelson's (1981) main points is that modern welfare economics is at best an incomplete basis for evaluating and comparing economic systems since it is derived from a theoretical structure that cannot accommodate bounded rationality. As Nelson argues, the Austrians understood this, while their Walrasian market-socialist opponents did not. However, because of the unformalized nature of the arguments above, they should "...be regarded as prejudices and not soundly based on any analytical structure" (ibid.: 109). That is a bit strange coming from Richard Nelson since it could be argued that he, along with Sidney Winter, has in fact succeeded in constructing a formalized theory that may lend support to at least one Austrian "prejudice": the beneficial effects of the discovery procedure of the market. As they say, in their view,

> "...the market system is (in part) a device for conducting and evaluating experiments in economic behavior and organization. The meaning and merit of competition must be appraised accordingly" (p.277).

One of the merits of the capitalist market system is that it can cope with *tacit* knowledge, a point which was suggested by Hayek in the calculation debate. A substantial part of Nelson and Winter's work has been occupied with clarifying the assumptions on technology that characterize neoclassical theory (see also Winter 1982). One of the main problems with these assumptions is that the role of tacit knowledge, how it is stored and developed in firms, is neglected when, in reality, productive activities are best understood as the result of largely tacit and extremely firm-specific routines. In a critique of the early market socialism presumption that all relevant productive knowledge could be concentrated in the hands of the planning authorities, Hayek emphasized that

> "It is hardly necessary to emphasize that this is an absurd idea even in so far as that knowledge is concerned which can properly be said to "exist" at any moment of time. But much of the knowledge that is actually utilized is by no means "in existence" in this ready-made form. Most of it consists in a technique of thought which enables the individual engineer to find new solutions rapidly as soon as he is confronted with a new set of circumstances" (1935c: 155).

In other words, the epistemic problem in socialist economic organization is not really that only individual firms know about their own productive technologies. This issue may conceptually be handled through various incentive schemes. And neither is it a matter of enormous amounts of knowledge having to be transferred between the center and individual producers. Rather, the problem is that much of the relevant economic knowledge is tacit. This implies that it is "...knowledge of the kind which *by its nature* cannot enter into statistics" (Hayek 1945: 83), and that it "...cannot possibly be called scientific in the sense of knowledge of general rules" (ibid.: 80). In other words, entrepreneurs and producers know more than they can communicate (to the planning authorities).

The capitalist market system can cope with such knowledge – its efficient functioning does not require it to be articulated – while socialist economic organization probably cannot (see Pelikan 1988). For example, the iterative procedures through which a price vector is found in market socialist models essentially requires that productive knowledge be articulated. This is so, because producers during the dialogue with the center have to respond with which levels and kinds of output they can produce using which inputs, given prices and the condition that they maximize profits. It is completely unlikely that managers will in fact be able to do this – and even if they could, it would probably be quite inefficient. As Nelson and Winter observe:

> "The economic theorist's abstract account of business decision making is not to be confused with the businessman's skills...Clear articulation of his methods may be valueless, or even counterproductive for the businessman (1982: 92),[40]

and

> "...it is quite inappropriate to conceive of firm behavior in terms of deliberate choice from a broad menu of alternatives that some external observer considers to be "available" opportunities for the organization. The menu is not broad, but narrow and idiosyncratic; it is built into firm routines, and most of the "choosing" is also accomplished automatically by those routines" (ibid.: 134).

If these conceptualizations of the nature of productive knowledge in firms are accepted and taken as descriptively correct, we must flatly reject Lange's assertion that "The administrators of a socialist economy will have exactly the same knowledge, or lack of knowledge, of the production functions as the capitalist entrepreneurs have" (1936/1937: 61) as a formalist (in the above sense) excess and a "pretense of knowledge" (Hayek 1974).

Although modern economists recognize the naïvety of Lange's market socialist scheme, they have not (yet) recognized such arguments from tacit knowledge. Thus, Grossman and Stiglitz (1976: 251-252) argue that the socialist calculation debate comes down to a distinction between economies where "prices and hence allocations are the outcome of a competitive arbitrage process which will, of necessity, be imperfect because of the costs of arbitrage" on the one hand, and economies in which prices and allocations are outcomes of centralized allocative mechanisms and are imperfect because of "the costs of monitoring bureaucrats". What is forgotten here are that to the agency costs of socialist allocation should also be added the

[40] Chester Barnard (1938) clearly saw the importance of tacit knowledge for understanding the manager's skills: "In the commonsense, everyday, practical knowledge necessary to the practice of the arts, there is much that is not susceptible of verbal statement – it is a matter of know-how. It may be called behavioral knowledge. It is necessary to doing things in concrete situations...It is nowhere more indispensable than in the executive arts" (p.291). Compare this to Hayek (1945).

costs of imperfectly transmitting tacit knowledge. It was the Austrian contention in the calculation debate that these two cost categories far outweighed "the costs of arbitrage" in the capitalist system.

To some extent the Austrians also anticipated Pelikan's (1988) forcefully argued point that the basic comparative systems issue has to do with the allocation of tacit knowledge, or the allocation of "competence", as Pelikan calls it. Since competence is assumed to be unbounded in standard neoclassical economics, this problem cannot arise here. Pelikan's point is then that the allocation of tacit knowledge cannot leave organizational structures unaffected. Among other things, this implies that the separation assumed in standard market socialist schemes between the allocation mechanism and the resources to be allocated breaks down. This is because the competence/tacit knowledge underlying economic rationality is itself scarce and has to be efficiently allocated. But there is nothing else with which to allocate scarce competence than scarce competence itself. In Pelikan's argument, the capitalist system can handle this allocation problem while socialist economic organization cannot. Although the Austrians did not apply Pelikan's clever argument, they reached essentially the same conclusion: that the capitalist market system allocates tacit knowledge in a way that is superior to socialist economic organization.

6. Conclusion

In this chapter I have first given a review of the new – primarily modern Austrian – revisionism in the historiography of comparative systems. Second, I argued that the basic proposition in this revisionism, that the calculation debate marked a clash of widely divergent economic approaches, should be accepted. However, the modern Austrian approach does not capture all aspects of Hayek and Mises' arguments such as the emphasis put by them on property rights and tacit knowledge. Such arguments are better understood in terms of neo-institutionalist theory of the property rights variety and evolutionary theory. I have also argued that what lay beneath the debate was ultimately a clash over the conception of economic theory. This difference relates to whether economic theory should be seen as something that should be developed for the explicit purpose of addressing real institutions, or, on the other hand, whether it should be developed as largely a formalist enterprise in which static and institutionless models are allowed to be the only glasses through which economic reality is perceived.

Recent developments in economic theory seem to have strengthened the Austrian case for the first type of theory. Economics, not even in the economic mainstream, is no longer wholly driven by changes in the basic analytical armory but is also increasingly influenced by conceptualizations of empirical problems which are allowed to gradually change the hard core of the discipline. For example, concepts such as bounded rationality and path dependence are increasingly incorporated into mainstream economics. The differences between mainstream neoclassical economics and the new heterodoxy of neo-institutionalism and evolutionary theory may gradually be vanishing. If that is the case, increasing appreciation of the Austrian insights into the problems of socialist economic organization should be expected to emerge.

5: Precursor of Property Rights Economics: Ludwig von Mises

1. Introduction

The recent (1991, 1993) conferment of the Nobel Prize in economics on Ronald Coase and on Douglass North should further stimulate interest in property rights theory. After all, Coase received the prize for his insights based on property rights into the origins and workings of social institutions – not least in the firm (Coase 1937) – and for the proposition known as the "Coase Theorem" (Coase 1960), often interpreted (perhaps too narrowly) as basically a property rights version of perfect competitive equilibrium. And North received the Prize for his property rights inspired work on economic history and the state.

Property rights theory as a field in economics began in the mid-1960s under the influence of reasoning in Coase's 1960 contribution, "The Problem of Social Cost". Important early contributors were Armen A. Alchian (1965) and Harold Demsetz (1964, 1988a), and later impetus came from the work of the likes of Stephen Cheung (1974, 1992), Yoram Barzel (1974, 1989), Douglass North (1990), Michael Jensen and William Meckling (1976, 1992), Louis De Alessi (1983, 1987), Eirik Furubotn, and Svetozar Pejovich (1972).[41]

During the 1960s, property rights economics joined with theories of decision making under risk and human capital theory to become the most explanatorily potent approach in economics, explanatory success being measured in terms of explanation of the economic rationales of real institutions. Today, many of the original property rights insights are assimilated into theories of the firm, of the incentive liabilities of hierarchies and bureaucracies, of principals and agents, of rent-seeking, of invention and innovation, and they appear in resource economics, in law and economics etc. Indeed, one could argue that it is very much the presence of property rights insights in such diverse theories that makes it reasonable to speak at all of a unified approach -sometimes dubbed "the new institutional economics" (Williamson 1985; Arrow 1987a).

[41] More than two decades old, Furubotn and Pejovich's (1972) survey still makes excellent reading. The best currently available presentation of the property rights approach is Eggertson (1990). The most original contemporary property rights theorist is probably Yoram Barzel; see his (1989). The classic methodological statement is Alessi (1983).

Although it is surely still possible to speak of a distinct property rights school – as witness, for example, Barzel (1989) and North (1990) – there is nevertheless much to be said in favor of the proposition that the approach has become very much a part of contemporary standard theory of allocation. Indeed, to Eggertson (1990: 5) the property rights approach is fundamentally "...a new research program...that is aimed at generalizing microeconomic theory while retaining all the essential elements of the economic approach – stable preferences, the rational choice model, and equilibria".[42]

Given its mainstream character, it is a somewhat surprising fact that those economists who are usually seen as precursors of the property rights approach are (at least in some respects) among the more prominent heretics in the history of economic thought. Following Cheung (1992) and Jensen and Meckling (1992), they include, in this century, Knight (1924), Aaron Director, and Hayek (1945), in addition to Coase, of course.[43] However, these were also extremely respected economists, and the fact that they incorporated embryonic property rights insights in their theorizing indicates that property rights was a subject that was pretty much "in the air" in the inter-war period.[44] Since debates on comparative systems flourished at this time, and since issues such as incentives and property rights obviously are quite central here, it would have been strange, had property rights insights not appeared in the economic discourse at some level. However, the relevant insights were generally poorly articulated, and were eventually suppressed for approximately two decades by the formalistic revolution that followed the Second World War.

In the ensuing pages, I shall argue that a figure who is normally considered a good deal more of a heretic than, say, Knight, namely Ludwig von Mises, should be included among the precursors of the property rights approach. Assuredly, the Austrian school of economics has a history of involvement in the theory of property rights that begins even before Mises began to write. One of the founding fathers of the school, Eugen von Böhm-Bawerk clearly expressed the idea that economic goods are fundamentally bundles of rights (Böhm-Bawerk 1881). And Carl Menger clearly understood the relation between scarcity and property rights, and how changing degrees of scarcity imply (re)definitions of property rights (Men-

[42] For a very different reading of "the new institutional economics", see Langlois (1986), in which Austrian and evolutionary influences are explicitly incorporated.

[43] For an argument that Marx should be considered a precursor of property rights economics, see Pejovich (1982). Of course, classical economists, particularly Adam Smith, also emphasized the role of property rights. However, they did not see property rights as changing endogenously in responses to shocks to preferences and technology, as, for example, Marx clearly did.

[44] I owe this point to Thráinn Eggertson.

ger 1871: 97,100). To Menger property rights are directly derived from the facts of scarcity and human rationality; as he notes

> "...human self-interest finds an incentive to make itself felt, and where the available quantity does not suffice for all, every individual will attempt to secure his own requirements as completely as possible to the exclusion of others...Thus human economy and property have a joint economic origin since both have, as the ultimate reason for their existence, the fact that goods exist whose available quantities are smaller than the requirements of men. Property, therefore, like human economy, is not an arbitrary invention but rather the only practically possible solution of the problem that, in the nature of things, imposed upon us by the disparity between requirements for, and available quantities of, all economic goods" (1871: 97).

Ownership of scarce goods – *economic* goods – should be protected by the legal order (ibid.: 97,100); property rights to economic goods will arise under all conceivable circumstances (p.100), and as regards economic goods it is logically fallacious to think that property rights per se can be disposed of under any kind of social organization. With goods that are not scarce, the situation is, of course, different; here "men are communists" (ibid.). But whether a good is economic or noneconomic is fundamentally a subjective category and may change over time; that is, property rights to goods will be defined when goods that were once noneconomic become economic.

Menger, along with Böhm-Bawerk, is one of the very few economists to discuss property rights before Coase, Alchian and Demsetz in the 1960s laid the foundation for the property rights approach. And in some respects he anticipates modern developments, particularly in the dynamic perspective in which he places the development of property rights (cf. Demsetz 1967). But what Menger's discussion does not incorporate is the crucial division of property rights into rights to use goods, appropriate their benefits and exchange them. And he did not investigate how different constellations of property rights influence allocation. Mises came much closer to such insights; nowhere in Austrian scholarship is property rights doctrine better developed than in Mises' work.

Mises is of course best known for his work in socialist economics and monetary theory, and many of his interpreters – particularly the more sympathetic ones – have pointed out the vital importance of his theorizing on the first topic of the category of property (Vaughn 1980; Murrell 1983; Lavoie 1985; Salerno 1990). However, nobody seems to have explicitly linked Mises to modern insights into property rights economics, or seen him as an important precursor of that approach. To do so is the purpose of this chapter. I shall speculate less, however, on why Mises actually came to formulate his property rights doctrines. The following remarks must suffice at this point.

Mises was a classical liberal, a subjectivist, and an Austrian economist. The importance of his classical liberalism is simply that the concept of right – including all sorts of property rights – is perennially important in classical liberalism (modern classical liberals have in fact tried to reduce all rights to property rights, see for example Buchanan 1975: 10). This does not conflict with Mises' strong utilitarianism, since (property) rights for Mises ultimately derived their justification from their social expediency. Mises' subjectivism should probably also come into an assessment of why he incorporated property rights insights in his work, on the ground that an understanding of goods as bundles of rights is more consonant with a subjectivist stance than identifying goods with their physical characteristics. Finally, Mises' position as a prominent member of the Austrian school may be argued to be important because the Austrians since Menger can be seen as explaining the origins and workings of social institutions with the help of choice theory as an important part of their overall theoretical agenda – rather than simply taking them as exogenous, as the two other neoclassical schools did.

I shall start out by providing a brief summary of the essentials of the property rights approach (section 2); then move on to an examination of Mises' work on property rights in the light of the preceding discussion (section 3), and add some further speculations on the relation between the property rights approach and Austrian economics (section 4).

2. Essentials of the Property Rights Approach

In spite of its complex formulations in more rigorous formulations (such as Debreu 1959), neoclassical economics rests on basically simple propositions such as decreasing marginal productivity, substitutability, maximization of concave utility functions etc. Since approximately the mid-1960s, it has, however, been possible to distinguish (at least) two groups of neoclassical price theorists: those who want to proceed by refining the classic view of the price-mediated exchange economy, and those who want to generalize and extend the neoclassical apparatus. Modern general equilibrium theorists belong to the first category, while property rights theorists belong to the second.

It was the growing dissatisfaction with certain inherent features in the standard general equilibrium framework that led to the revisionist literature focused on property rights. Among the features against which the revisionist literature pressed its claim was the belief that allocation and optimality under standard assumptions are invariable relative to institutions in the standard general equilibrium framework; the market is only one among many potential means of realizing first-best outcomes. But according to property rights theorists this result only holds because of the neglect of transaction costs. What are these transaction costs and what is their relation to property rights?

At some trivial level, one could simply say that transaction costs are what gives rise to all institutional arrangements that differ from the pure price-mediated coordination schemes of the standard general equilibrium model. Less trivially, transaction costs are the costs associated with the definition, the enforcement and the transfer of property rights (Barzel 1989; North 1990).[45] Property rights, in their turn, are the rights of individuals to the use of scarce resources, established and enforced not only by formal legal rules but also by the mores and customs of society (Demsetz 1967). In other words, property rights are assignments of authority over the use of resources (within a class of permissible uses), specifying the rights to physically use, obtain income from and transfer resources (Alchian 1965).

Rights that are exclusive and transferable are private ones; those that are exclusive but cannot be transferred are usufruct rights; and those that are nonexclusive and nontransferable define common ownership with open access (Alessi 1987). Moreover, property rights over a given resource may be divided so that different agents hold different rights to their use. The more carefully defined, enforced and allocated property rights are, the more externalities will be internalized. At the limit, where definition, enforcement and allocation are perfect, there are no externalities at all. Here, the standard general equilibrium model obtains. In this setting it is, however, not possible to give nontrivial economic explanations of the existence of institutions.

[45] Including the costs of searching for contracting partners, concluding contracts and monitoring them (Williamson 1985), monitoring team production (Alchian and Demsetz 1972), inspecting quality (Barzel 1989), deciding on price etc.

Institutions are seen as embodiments of property rights; to understand the behavioral implications of alternative institutions is tantamount to investigating the effects that alternative constraints in the form of property rights have on behavior. The reason institutions are adopted is that they minimize the transaction costs of allocating resources to their most highly valued uses (Demsetz 1967); for example, the firm minimizes the transaction costs of organizing team production relative to the market (Alchian and Demsetz 1972). Markets and market pricing are likewise low-cost arrangements for facilitating specialization and exchange, as well as a means for determining value correctly, minimizing the dissipation of rent, providing incentives and information. Capital markets, for example, price assets, allow managers to specialize in management and monitor them.

It is only when transaction costs and property rights are factored in that efficiency analysis that transcend the Nirvana of the standard general equilibrium model is possible (Demsetz 1969) (that is, efficiency analysis should be "comparative institutional"). This is also a matter of the standard model being totally abstracted from dynamics; assuming a stationary state or essentially similar intertemporal constructions, lends credibility to the disposal of information and transaction costs. But in that case, it is not possible to give efficiency rationales for alternative economic institutions. For example, it is difficult to understand pricing consistently as an information cost-minimizing institution (Hayek 1945).

As Alchian consistently emphasizes, when two or more agents in society want more of the same good, competition is always implied (Alchian and Allen 1964). The rules that restrain competition and resolve conflict are property rights. Market pricing is one such restraining or conflict resolving mechanism, and underlying all pricing are property rights. Therefore, existing property rights determine the allocation of costs and benefits of given actions among the actors and other members of society (Coase 1960) via existing or imputed prices.

Although pricing in principle is only one means of resolving conflict over resource uses, it has some unique properties. For one thing, it is inseparably tied up with private property. Less obviously, it is also the means that minimizes the dissipation of rent among all conceivable (or at least known) ones (Cheung 1974; Barzel 1974). Let us illustrate this by an example from Cheung (1992), and consider rationing by waiting. Under this scheme, at least some rent will be dissipated, since the value of a good won by a queuing competitor will be partly absorbed by his cost of waiting, a cost that represents no value to society. If competition were organized as in a free market with price-mediated transactions, this cost could have been avoided. Allocation in terms of non-price criteria will always encourage competitors to incur costs to gain advantage from such criteria beyond what they would have chosen in a free market.

In the following section, I shall present evidence of the view put forward at the beginning of this chapter, that Ludwig von Mises should be included in the doctrinal history of the property rights approach, and drawing on the discussion above.

3. Mises as a Precursor of Property Rights Economics

During a very long and productive life, Ludwig von Mises touched on almost every conceivable matter of the economics and methodology of his time within a remarkably coherent scheme of thought (cf. Salerno 1990) (most completely presented in Mises 1949). However, Mises' style of presentation, his low level of patience with opponents (imagined and real), as well as his habit of seldom making explicit all the assumptions his analysis required, has often led to his portrayal as someone doctrinaire who was even, in some respects, lacking in scholarship. This last accusation has – in the context of the socialist calculation debate – been effectively dealt with by the revisionism of Vaughn (1980), Nelson (1981), Murrell (1983), Lavoie (1985) and Kirzner (1988).

What emerges from these studies is, as we saw in the preceding chapter, a picture of a scholar who, in the specific context addressed, was consistently misunderstood because his implicit economic framework strongly differed from that of his opponents (such as Lange 1936/1937). More precisely, these studies – particularly Lavoie (1985) and Kirzner (1988) – "read into" Mises' arguments the arguments of the modern Austro-American school (represented by, for instance, Kirzner 1973), which leads to the obvious conclusion that what essentially collided in the calculation debate was a process-oriented perspective, placing primary emphasis on entrepreneurial discovery, on the one hand, and a static general equilibrium perspective on the other hand. In the following, I shall refrain from rehearsing these arguments as well from discussing the calculation debate in greater detail. However, I agree with the revisionist literature that a clash of economic frameworks was indeed involved. But it was more – or at least just as much – a matter of a clash between what were essentially property rights insights and the transaction cost-free general equilibrium model. I briefly made this suggestion in the preceding chapter. In this chapter, I shall elucidate those aspects of Mises' work that qualify him as an important, but neglected, precursor of modern property rights economics.

Underlying Mises' overall perspective on economics and social philosophy is an essentially Smithian view of the beneficial effects of the progressive division of labor (see also Salerno 1990). As he puts it, in somewhat highbrow language:

> "Human society...is the outcome of a purposeful utilization of a universal law determining cosmic becoming, that is, the higher productivity of the division of labor" (Mises 1949: 145).

But the division of labor introduces an "intellectual division of labor" – that is, a knowledge dispersion – and therefore a coordination problem (1936: 101). This coordination problem is handled by various social institutions, including the market, prices, money, property, law, the moral code, marriage and the nuclear family. Social institutions are explicitly seen as requirements of the division of labor (ibid.), and evolve as products of a partly evolutionary, partly conscious process, in which trial and error learning, natural gifts and rational self-interest-seeking combine to produce an efficient result.[46] The origin and the function of social institutions are consistently explained in terms of efficiency. Here lies the fundamental reason behind Mises' opposition to socialism: socialism fundamentally wants to do away with the very institutions necessary to sustain efficiently an elaborate division of labor.

Private property and its contractual embodiments are, of course, such institutions which are "the outgrowth of an age-old evolution" (Mises 1949: 650). Or rather they are the institutions underlying a number of other institutions, and therefore "...the fundamental institutions of the market economy" (p.678). For example, the institution of monogamous marriage is described in the following terms:

> "...marriage...has come into existence entirely as a result of the contractual idea penetrating into this sphere of life...[The rights and duties of marriage] develop from the contractual attitude...modern marriage...is the result of capitalist...development" (1936: 82-83).

[46] For an explicit property rights approach to social evolution, see North (1990).

Mises gives various explanations of the emergence of private property, based on homesteading, on force and theft (1936: 32), and on efficiency. Thus, private property

> "...came into existence when people with their own power and by their own authority appropriated to themselves what had previously not been anybody's property. Again and again proprietors were robbed of their property by expropriation...Virtually every owner is the direct or indirect legal successor of people who acquired ownership either by arbitrary appropriation of ownerless things or by violent spoliation of their predecessors" (1949: 679).

But the explanation of the emergence of private property most consistent with the overall efficiency perspective that informs Mises' view on societal evolution, is one that is closely akin to Demsetz' (1967). A number of examples (1949: 652-653) illustrate Mises' view that private property arises to internalize the externalities (Mises' talks about "external costs") implied by the existence of nonalienable resources with open access. For instance, "If land is not owned by anybody...it is utilized without any regard for the disadvantages resulting" (1949: 652). But if, on the other hand, private ownership of land is "rigidly established", there will be "no question of soil erosion" and "forest devastation" (p.653), a situation characteristic of "...the central and western areas of continental Europe, where the institution of private property had been rigidly established for many centuries" (p.653).

Solutions to externality problems do not in general lie in Pigovian means, then, but in "...reform of the laws concerning liability for damages inflicted and by rescinding the institutional barriers preventing the full operation of private ownership" (Mises 1949: 653). Here, the relevant barriers refer to those that prevent the definition of full ownership, that is, the "...full control of the services that can be derived from a good" (p.678). Implied in this is clearly a view of different specifications of property rights as being explicable in terms of responses to social problems that find their source in scarcity; according to Pejovich (1982), *the* fundamental insight of property rights economics.

Mises understood that property rights may be divided up and that they come in different forms (1936: chapter 1). In his anticipation of property rights doctrine, he placed primary importance on rights to alienate resources and rights to draw income from them. With regard to the last kind of rights, he observed that they were crucial to the efficient working of the economy, largely for reasons of incentives for efficient risk-taking:

> "In an economic system based upon private ownership of the means of production, the speculator is interested in the result of his speculation in the highest possible degree. If it succeeds, then, in the first instance, it is his gain. If it fails, then, he is the first to feel the loss. The speculator works for the community, but he himself feels the success or failure proportionately more than the community" (1936: 182).

One of the (many) reasons why "the artificial market" of market socialism will not work is precisely because the transfer of goods between socialist managers is not equivalent to the transfer of goods in a capitalist economy: under socialism it is not full property rights that are transferred; prices and incentives are accordingly perverse. On property rights grounds, it is inherently wrong to believe that "...the controllers of the different industrial units" in a socialist economy can be instructed "...to act *as if* they were entrepreneurs in a capitalistic state" (1936: 120; see also Mises 1949: 702-705).

One of the areas where Mises perhaps most explicitly anticipates modern theory – specifically the modern work on how financial markets monitor management – is when he points out that for the efficient working of the economy, capital markets are absolutely crucial. It is here that rights to alienate resources become really crucial. Capital markets alone ensure that, what Mises calls "the calculation problem", can be solved in a dynamic economy through "...dissolving, extending, transforming, and limiting existing undertakings, and establishing new undertaking" (1936: 215). Only unhampered capital markets and markets for corporate control can perform the two crucial tasks of monitoring management – solving the principal-agent problem between owners and managers – and pricing assets correctly. Or as Mises summarizes it:

> "Under Capitalism, the capitalist decides to whom he will entrust *his own* capital. The beliefs of the managers of joint stock companies regarding the future prospects of their undertakings and the hopes of project-makers regarding the profitability of their plans are not in any way decisive. The mechanism of the money market and the capital market decides. This indeed is its task: to serve the económic system

> as a whole, to judge the profitability of alternative openings and not blindly to follow what the managers of particular concerns, limited by the narrow horizon of their own undertakings, are tempted to propose" (1936: 122).

Contrast this with Lange's (1938: 110) assertion about "...private corporation executives, who practically are responsible to nobody". Modern theory would be more on Mises' side than on Lange's.

One of the most expanding areas in the theory of economic organization, and an outgrowth of property rights economics, is principal-agent theory. As already indicated, Mises anticipated several insights from this theory, arguing, for example, that it did not follow that under socialism, individual managers (agents) would act in the interest of the principals, that is, the planning authorities. Furthermore, Mises also had an awareness of the problem of risk allocation between principals and agents: under socialism, managers would be either inefficiently risk-averse or risk-loving, in the face of career concerns and/the presence of an institution (the planning authorities) that could act as an insurance institution and take over the moral hazard of individual managers (Mises 1936: 122). Furthermore, socialist economic organization would supply a number of opportunities for rent-seekers (Mises 1936, 1945, 1949). That is, socialism would, in modern terminology (Milgrom 1988), provide a number of targets for influence activities and be associated with high levels of influence costs.

The market socialists, in contrast, had no grasp of the principal-agent problem, or, if they had, assumed it away; as has often been pointed out, Lange (1938) implicitly assumed continuous incentive compatibility between the individual managers and the planning authorities. One of the primary virtues of the market system organized on the basis of private ownership, as Mises saw it, was that it strongly mitigated potential principal-agent problems. In the capitalist economy, the

> "operations of the market do not stop at the doors of a big business concern...[They] permeate all its departments and branches...It joins together utmost centralization of the whole concern with almost complete autonomy of the parts, it brings into agreement full responsibility of the central management with a high degree of interest and incentive of the subordinate managers" (1945: 47).

Breaking the corporation up into separate profit centers is the way that top management monitors subordinate managers. And, anticipating Fama (1980), Mises (1920: 35; 1945: 42-47) points to the existence of career concerns as important forces mitigating managers' shirking.

Several other observations are in order. Mises' point about the necessity of market pricing on the basis of the exchange of titles to property rights to capital assets for overall efficiency (Mises 1920, 1936, 1949) is akin to the Cheung/Barzel proposition about the minimization of rent dissipation under pricing (Cheung 1974; Barzel 1974). Although Mises primarily emphasizes the information providing function of cardinal money prices, it is surely important to his argument that prices perform this function best when they are the result of the exchange of full property rights to assets. In terms of the Cheung/Barzel proposition, Mises can be interpreted as saying that the "artificial market" of the market socialists, which is not based on such exchange, will lead to inefficient dissipation of rent (in addition to other, information-based types of misallocation).

It is also in his commentaries on the economic organization of socialism that Mises most explicitly anticipates the methodological basis of property rights economics, that is to say, comparative institutionalism. It is apparent already from Mises' (1920) opening salvo in the debate over later Austrian contributions, and until Hayek's "Use of Knowledge" article (Hayek 1945), that what really irritated the Austrians was their socialist opponents' use of unrealistic and unattainable social ideals – Nirvanas – as standards of comparison. Naturally, by such standards, capitalism would appear inefficient and wasteful. As the first economists to insist that socialist economic organization too should be approached with the tools of economic analysis, and that idealized, institutionless models should be banned as standards of comparison, the Austrians – and particularly Mises – may be said to be the first economists consistently pursuing comparative institutionalism.

The reasons why models such as Oskar Lange's (1938) market socialism did not conform to the dictates of a program of comparative institutionalism are at least three in number. First, the socialist economists neglected the role of incentives (Mises 1936; Hayek 1940), Second, they made unrealistic assumptions about the amounts of knowledge that agents can posses (particularly the planning authorities). And third, they formulated their reasoning within static models that obscured all significant economic problems. Or, in a more compact formulation, basing theorizing on the economics of the stationary state, market socialists were able to suppress the knowledge and incentive problems of real economies.

According to recent revisionism in the historiography of the calculation debate (Lavoie 1985; Kirzner 1988), it was the realization of this which made the Austrians understand how far apart they were from the Walrasian approach, and which really ignited the development of the distinct Austrian approach. This interpretation may raise some difficulties since interpreting Mises in terms of the basically neoclassical property rights approach conflicts with the entrepreneurial and process oriented approach in, for example, Mises (1949) In the following section, I shall briefly discuss this and other interpretative problems.

4. Austrian Economics and the Property Rights Approach

Given the later history of the Austrian school, and the eagerness with which modern Austrians often want to dissociate themselves from mainstream economics, it is quite noteworthy that, as late as 1933, Mises could see no essential differences between the three existing marginalist schools[47]:

> "We usually speak of the Austrian and the Anglo-American Schools and the School of Lausanne...[However] these three schools of thought differ only in their mode of expressing the same fundamental idea and...they are divided more by their terminology and by peculiarities of presentation than by the substance of their teachings" (Mises (1933), 1960: 214).

However, as a result of the socialist calculation debate, the Austrians understood that since their beginning, the three schools had been far apart. Or so the, not implausible, story goes (Kirzner 1988). Assuredly, it cannot be denied that there were indeed deep differences between the Walrasian framework of the market socialists and Austrian theorizing (Murrel 1983). But this does not necessarily imply a fundamental divide between generalized neoclassical economics – that is, property rights eco-

[47] This is not only noteworthy but also surprising. For in 1932, Hans Mayer had published a long essay on the differences between "functional" and "causal-genetic" theories of the market, associating the first group with the Lausanne School and the second with Austrian theorizing (Mayer 1932). Mises must surely have known this contribution, and it is hard to believe that he disagreed with its message (in spite of his and Mayer's difficult relation).

nomics – and Austrian economics. In the following I shall argue why this is the case.

The most trivial reason is simply that the categories of property, and their allocative implications as analyzed by property rights economics, are also relevant in the kind of dynamic setting envisaged by the Austrians. There is no conflict between the various *concepts* of property and Austrian economics. Where the theories may differ lies in how fundamental ideas and concepts are *focused*; that is, whether property rights insights are focused in terms of equilibrium or process methodology.

Underlying Mises' work is, of course, a fundamentally dynamic view of the economic process (see also Nelson 1981). As he says, "...the problem of economic calculation is of economic dynamics; it is no problem of economic statics" (1936: 121). And Hayek later on supported Mises when he observed that "economic problems arise always and only in consequence of change" (1945: 82). As Mises (1936: 105) recognizes, in an essentially changeless stationary state – what he (1949) calls "the evenly rotating economy" – the political authorities can implement the existing allocation as their plan and everything will continue the way it was before. Here, "The essential function of economic calculation has *by hypothesis* already been performed" (1936: 120). The lesson to be drawn from this Misesian insight is the general one that it is only when economic change is introduced that economic organization is determinate. This can be interpreted in different ways.

One is the general (neo-)Austrian one that we need the entrepreneurial process of discovery of opportunities for exchange to cope with the knowledge problems that economic change introduces (Kirzner 1973). And this process performs most efficiently when fueled by well-defined and protected private property rights that provide appropriate incentives for entrepreneurial alertness. It is not really that people do the job best when motivated by adequate incentives, as in standard property rights and agency theory; it is rather that they will not know what the right thing to do is if not given incentives to *discover* this.

This is an important insight. But a more specific and perhaps more pertinent interpretation is to view the Misesian insight as anticipating the point that in the absence of change there will be no transaction and information costs (cf. Alessi 1987: 27). That is, in the absence of the knowledge problems introduced by a changing economic reality, there will be no costs of discovering contractual partners, drafting and executing contracts, monitoring production, constructing contractual safeguards, judging quality etc. And in the absence of transaction costs, the choice between price-mediated market transactions and firms is indeterminate. As both Hayek (1945) and Mises may be understood to have recognized, in market economies, institutions such as markets and firms perform the function of economizing on dispersed information; that is, they embody constellations of property rights that most efficiently cope with the coordination problems implied by the dispersal of knowledge (Jensen and Meckling 1992).

In a doctrinal perspective, this indicates a link between the Austrian insights in the calculation debate and the Coasian insights in economic organization, though not one that was recognized either by the Austrians or Coase, probably because they had concentrated their attention on different institutions. Where Hayek (1945) praised "the marvel" of the price system, Coase, eight years earlier, had established that the reason firms existed was that the "telecommunications system" of prices did not perform without costs. This may lead to the impression that Hayek and Coase's analyses are strongly opposed. Of course, they are not; it is only in terms of the kind of dynamic economic reality envisaged by Hayek and Mises that Coase's argument acquires its full force.[48]

5. Conclusion

In this chapter, I have argued that Ludwig von Mises should be recognized as an early contributor to the development of the property rights approach. Mises was one of the very first economists to really comprehend the importance of ownership for economic organization and for efficient allocation, grasping, for example, the nature of the agency problem and of the role of capital markets in checking managerial shirking. Furthermore, he pioneered the use of comparative institutionalism.

These findings may hopefully help stimulate a more conciliatory attitude among mainstream economists towards the works of Mises who had a lot more to say than the impression given by his faithful but somewhat narrow modern interpreters among Austro-American economists. Assuredly, Mises pioneered an Austrian process approach, but he was also an important part of the prehistory of property right economics. On the other hand, Mises managed to combine property rights insights and a process perspective. This is something that modern property rights theorists have

[48] This raises, of course, the question of why it was left to Coase to discover an economic rationale for the firm. Why wasn't this task accomplished by the Austrians who had so many of the necessary analytical ingredients? See chapter 8 for further speculations on this and kindred themes.

not done; their theorizing remains largely neoclassical. The single exception is the later work of Douglass North (1990) in which an attempt to bring together property rights and evolutionary economics is made. In the following chapters, I shall pursue further this essentially Misesian theme of the relation between neo-institutionalist economics and process approaches.

6: Market Process Theories and Neo-institutional Economics

1. Introduction

It has often been observed that the term "dynamic" may be more of a rhetorical device than a substantial characterization. For it seems to be primarily applied in economic discourse when economists wish to separate their own contributions favorably from those of other economists. Something similar seems now to be the case with the term "neo-institutional". The literature is in agreement that neo-institutionalism denotes the body of theory that approaches social institutions – their origins, nature and possible change – with economic tools. However, here agreement stops. In a recent contribution, Thráinn Eggertson (1990) wants to reserve the term for neoclassical theories in the Coase-Alchian-Demsetz property rights tradition. In partial opposition to this, Richard Langlois (1986b) seems to apply the criteria whether a given theory 1) says something about institutions, and 2) shows a critical stance towards standard neoclassical economics as the relevant ones. And, we should note, an important part of Langlois' Austrian-influenced evaluation is precisely whether theories are "dynamic". One may infer that trying to grapple with both "dynamics" and "neo-institutionalism" at the same time spells trouble. That is nevertheless my aim in this chapter.

To a limited extent, I shall continue the discussion from the preceding chapters on property rights economics. I shall, however, argue that there are a number of phenomena that this variation on the neo-institutionalist theme cannot satisfactorily address. Most obviously, the property rights approach does not really address processes of change, a characteristic which it shares with some other varieties of neo-institutionalist thought.[49] I shall, however, argue that some of the shortcomings due to this static character may be remedied if neo-institutionalist thought is combined with market process theories, such as evolutionary and Austrian theories. Specifically, through a comparative presentation of "dynamic" theories of the market, I intend to argue that only evolutionary and Austrian theories of the market process ("market process theories", in short) are adequate complementary theories for neo-institutionalist economic thought. In a

[49] Such as agency theory or Williamsonian transaction cost economics.

sense this may be seen as bringing together Austrian and Austrian-influenced theories of the market process with that theory of economic organization to which the Austrians were early contributors. In the context of the preceding chapter, it is an attempt to be a bit more detailed about the Misesian idea of placing economic organization in a dynamic setting.

2. Neo-classical Neo-institutionalism: the Property Rights Approach

2.1. Variety of Neo-institutionalist Approaches

As noted above, one of the problems with the emerging neo-institutional economics is that it exists in a variety of forms, some of them largely neo-classical, others more bent towards a heterodox stance. This is a disciplinary problem, because seemingly neo-institutionalist thought can only be characterized on an overall level by the attempt to make institutions endogenous. And numerous theories satisfy this criterion; however, they are very different in terms of analytical approach (see Langlois (1986a) and Mäki (1987)). Thus, we may see the game theory approach to institutions of Robert Sugden (1986) as neo-institutional economics, as well as Oliver Williamson's (1985) transaction cost economics, agency theory (Pratt & Zeckhauser 1985), the property rights approach (Eggertson 1990), and perhaps even Richard Nelson and Sidney Winter's (1982) evolutionary theory of the firm.

In order to obtain a clear-cut argumentative foil for the following discussion, I propose to discuss briefly one of the oldest and best developed strands of the transaction cost variety of neo-institutionalism, the property rights approach (Alchian 1965; Demsetz 1967; Alessi 1983; Eggertson 1990). I should also like to suggest that some of characteristics of the property rights approach in terms of dynamics – or lack of dynamics – are also present in other strands of neo-institutionalism.

2.2. The Property Rights Approach

To the basic economic concepts and assumptions, such as concavity of utility functions, downward-sloping demand curves, scarcity, decreasing marginal productivity, substitutability in consumption and production, property rights economics adds the concept which it is named after. Property rights are the rights agents possess to the use of resources, as regulated by the laws, norms and mores of society. The system of existing property rights determines how the costs and benefits of actions are allocated among agents (Coase 1960).

In a stationary world there are no transaction and information costs, and solving "the economic problem of society" (Hayek 1945) is at most a matter of computation. Agents know all the relevant "data" confronting them, and the rules of the game as given by the structure of property rights are enforceable at no cost. In the context of the property rights approach, there is a genuine economic problem precisely because agents do not have immediate and full knowledge of changing economic circumstances, and because it is costly to define, enforce and exchange property rights, including searching for contract partners, negotiating contracts and enforcing them. The presence of transaction and information costs introduces new constraints, and produces non-price rationing of resources, and absence of full definition and enforcement of property rights. However, agents' maximizing responses to these constraints produce efficient outcomes, at an individual level as well as at a systemic level (Alessi 1983). Opportunities for gain exist for agents who adopt institutions that economize on the costs of information and transaction. Markets are low-cost institutions for handling the information and transaction costs implied by the division of labor, and firms are special forms of market arrangements, namely contractual coalitions between input owners that arise to minimize the incentive problems associated with team production.

2.3. The Suppression of Process

In its property rights manifestation, neo-institutional economics is a generalization of neoclassical economics, and more so in a substantial than in a methodological sense. Substantially, it is more general since standard neoclassical economics may be argued to be a special case of the property rights approach. For example, the model described in Debreu (1959) obtains in a property rights setting under standard assumptions on convexity etc., *plus* the assumptions that property rights are costlessly defined, enforced and exchanged. Methodologically, however, the property rights approach is distinctly neoclassical in focusing only on efficient outcomes – in terms of individual decisions, contracts, and aggregate outcomes (Alessi 1983). Although the twin pillars of neoclassical economics – maximizing and equilibrium – are generalized, they are *there*. This implies that the property rights approach does not formally investigate

- how agents are able to adopt decision rules that produce maximizing decisions, and how consistency between independently taken decisions arises. That is to say, learning processes are not investigated,
- how property rights (institutions) are defined and changed under the impact of changes. That is to say, institutional change is not directly addressed. Institutional change merely enters in the guise of comparative institutionalism, so that different institutions are compared in terms of efficiency for different parameters,
- how changes arise, and which agents are instrumental in carrying out changes (including institutional innovations). That is to say, the driving forces behind institutional change – such as changing technology and entrepreneurship – are not investigated.

In other words, processes of change at all relevant levels are present in an implicit way at most. Changes are fundamentally taken as given, and the adjustment processes that changes induce are forced into a comparative institutional, functionalist mode of explanation (cf. Demsetz 1967): changes in parameters are directly associated with corresponding (timeless) changes in property rights/institutions, no interest being paid to adjustment processes between these states/institutions. That change is suppressed will typically be defended in this setting by pointing to "the classical defense" (Winter 1987), that is, the use of selection-based reasoning in the service of a defense of maximization and, by implication, equilibrium. The problem with this is not only that this defense is of quite limited generality. It is also that the selection (and variation and hereditary) mechanisms themselves – apparently the real generative mechanisms underlying change – are not themselves theoretically approached, but merely tagged on in an essentially ad hoc manner. This mode of explanation is not only characteristic of the property rights approach; it may also be found in agency theory, and – although somewhat less unambiguously – in Williamson's brand of transaction cost economics.

It cannot be denied that the property rights approach has greatly expanded the domain of application of neoclassical economics (see for example Eggertson 1990). And to suppress change and process may not always be illegitimate, for the simple reason that no theory is designed to explain everything. If the purpose, however, is to investigate institutional and organizational change and the mechanisms that are underneath such changes, we cannot make do with a comparative institutionalism alone; we need a dynamic institutionalism, one that is not casual about the real mechanisms of change. It seems, then, that we need a broader reading of neo-institutionalism. In the following section, I shall present such a reading.

3. A Broader Reading of Neo-institutionalism

I take my starting-point in Richard Langlois' (1986b) very clear and Austrian influenced discussion. Langlois' strategy in this contribution is to identify a number of "common themes", adherence to which is necessary (and perhaps also sufficient) for a theory to qualify as "neo-institutional". The great advantage of his discussion is that it explicitly attacks not only the institutions issue, but also the issues of rationality and process. In fact, the unifying "common themes" are precisely

Rationality: which is not necessarily best understood as conscious and continuous maximization within given and transparent means-ends structures (as in the property rights approach). Under the impact of complexity, ignorance and uncertainty, rationality is also a matter of creativity such as Kirznerian "alertness", Hayekian rule-following, and Simonian "satisficing".

Process: which implies that economic phenomena should not be understood in separation from learning. And this intentional element in human behavior should be combined with genetic explanation on higher levels of analysis – the industry, for example – such that a theory is obtained in which dynamic phenomena on more than one level of analysis may interact.

Institutions: the coordination of economic activities is not only a matter of price-mediated market transactions, but takes place within, and under the impact of, numerous nonmarket institutions that are themselves potential objects for economic explanation.

The identification of these three common themes further allowed Langlois to identify a number of theoretic traditions which he saw as complementary in a larger neo-institutional research program: the radical subjectivism of George Shackle, the Austrian theory of the market process (-Hayek, Mises, Kirzner), Schumpeterian theories of technological evolution (Nelson and Winter, Abernathy and Utterback), evolutionary and institutional game theory (Schotter, Sugden), and organizational economics (Williamson). Undoubtedly, this is a very broad menu of rather different theoretic perspectives, and it is not clear in which ways they are complementary. Obviously, they are characterized by widely diverging levels of analysis, domains of applicability and even units of analysis.

While Langlois was primarily interested in trying to clarify the more explanatory and methodological aspects of fitting these various theories together, I shall be moving on a somewhat more explicitly theoretical level in trying to ascertain how market process theory and neo-institutionalist thought fit together. I shall argue that not all "dynamic" theories of the market are suitable as dynamic underpinnings for neo-institutionalist thought. Quite in line with Langlois (1986a), I argue in the following sections that only market process theories, that is to say, Austrian and evolutionary theories, can serve as adequate dynamic underpinnings.

4. "Dynamic" Theories of the Market

Fritz Machlup (1959) identified 39 different distinctions between "static" and "dynamic" that social scientists since Auguste Comte had put forward. In this section, I shall present a framework (inspired by Ikeda 1990) within which alternative theories of market dynamics can be compared and evaluated.

At the most primitive level, we may associate dynamic analysis with conventional price theory, at least as it is practiced in more elementary or intermediate forms. Here, the restrictions imposed on price theory by the method of comparative statics (see chapter 7) will often not be strictly adhered to. Rather than presenting price-theoretic analysis as merely a comparison of alternative equilibrium values of endogenous variables for a change in a single exogenous variable, an attempt will be made to recount some dynamic, but very loose, story about movements between equilibria. Loose arbitrage arguments are of this type. At a more advanced level, we encounter the analysis of intertemporal models in which time "explicitly" enters through putting "t"-subscripts on selected variables, and where agents maximize over various state variables. At any time of its "dynamic" development, such a system is in equilibrium.

What is common to the mainstream "static" and "dynamic" approaches is that they, in their *formal* manifestations, are solely occupied with analyzing equilibrium states. However, there is also a set of theories, usually thought to "legitimate" equilibrium theories, which address what happens outside equilibrium; for example, will the system move from a disequilibrium situation to one of equilibrium, and how? This is the domain of stability theory. However, like neoclassical economics in general, stability theories assume that agents are equipped with at least probabilistic knowledge of all relevant underlying data. This is not the case in the perspective on the market represented by Austrian and evolutionary approaches. I here call these approaches "theories of the market as a discovery procedure", precisely in order to indicate that data are not given but have to be discovered. This focus on *ignorance* (rather than mere probabilistic risk) implies that agents may in a genuine sense be surprised (cf. Shackle 1972). And equilibrium is not necessarily an aspect of the model.

We are now in such a position that we can present our perspectives in a progression from "static" to "dynamic, a progression that almost corresponds to chronology:

1) Basic conventional price theory
2) Dynamic equilibrium
3) Stability theory
4) Market process theories.

An alternative way in which theories may be classified is to ask which questions they are designed to answer (Machlup 1967). Turning away from Langlois' dynamics theme, and towards his rationality theme, three corresponding questions are relevant:

1) How do agents react, when known data are changed?
2) How do agents react when new data are introduced unexpectedly?
3) Which agents change data and how?

It is intuitively clear that conventional theory, dynamic equilibrium and stability theory are only fully able to address the first question, since there is at most probabilistic risk here. The maximizing framework in these theories only allows the addressing of the first question. As argued later on, questions 2) and 3) are only comprehensively addressed by market process theories. Fundamentally, this is because market process theories are occupied with the analysis of disequilibrium. And as Hey (1981: 201) points out: "...if onc wants to model genuine disequilibrium, then the optimizing model of individual choice must be abandoned". But, as I shall also argue, addressing the two last questions (particularly question number 2) is crucially important to the theory of economic organization. This is how I shall attempt to bring together Langlois' three themes of rationality, process and institutions.

5. Dynamic Theories Briefly Considered

In order to make the distinctions introduced in the above section more concrete, I shall present 5 theories, common to which is that their proponents have argued that they are "dynamic" in one of the above senses. The theories are presented in a progression from less to more "dynamic". As we shall see, in all theories except market process theories, change and process either do not enter or enter only in an ad hoc way.

5.1. The Theory of Contestable Markets

According to Baumol, Panzar and Willig (1982), the theory of contestable markets represents "the building blocks of a new theory of industrial organization", which they think "will transform the field" (p. XIII), and be "no less than a unifying theory as a foundation for the analysis of industrial organization" (Baumol 1982: 15). Such rather high-flown rhetoric should not conceal, however, that the theory of contestable markets in many ways represents an extension and radicalization of traditional industrial economics, particularly theories of limit pricing. In extremely brief summary, a "contestable" market is one in which entry is free and where incumbents believe that potential entrants hold Bertrand-Nash expectations. A firm in a contestable market knows that it will not be able to set prices above average cost without attracting immediate entry. In a fully contestable market, the possibility of immediate hit-and-run entry will keep prices from ever rising above average cost. Of course, contestability requires the absence of sunk cost. A contestable market is furthermore "sustainable" if incumbents are financially viable and there is no possibility of profitably entering under Bertrand-Nash assumptions. Sustainability is a long-run equilibrium condition.

An implication of this analysis is that a market with only two firms can be completely contestable. And that, of course, is why the proponents of the theory argue that it is "a generalization of the perfectly competitive market" (Baumol 1982: 2), since the theory is applicable "the full range of industry structure" (Baumol, Panza, and Willig 1982: 28). Among numerous notable results of the theory are its normative implications: sustainability will always imply a first-best Pareto optimum. It is clear from all this that the theory of contestable markets is truly a generalization of perfect competition theory. And as is the case with this theory, the theory of contestable markets is characterized by very strong assumptions about knowledge and rationality. A contestable market is fundamentally an equilibrium construction in which the efficient industry structure (as determined by the underlying cost structure) "...is essentially a pure matter of calculation" (Baumol 1982: 6). In such a setting, there can no disappointed expectations and no surprises. The efficient structure exists from the beginning, dictated by costs and the perfect foresight of incumbents and entrants alike. The theory of contestable markets is a full-blown neoclassical theory that, in terms of the taxonomy above, belongs in the dynamic equilibrium category. I shall next turn to stability theory.

5.2. Franklin Fisher on Competition and Stability Theory

The case of Franklin Fisher is a very useful one both because he is a prominent contributor to stability theory and because he has applied essentially Schumpeterian (market process theory) arguments in more informal discussions on applied industrial economics. For example, Fisher, McGowan and Greenwood's (1983) economic defense for IBM in an antitrust trial being heard at that time, incorporates discussions of static versus dynamic efficiency, and argues for the social desirability of discounting static deadweight losses of monopoly in favor of the dynamic efficiency of high innovative performance over time. But surely, Fisher, the formal-neoclassical economist knows that all this has a rather meager theoretical foundation in neoclassical economics. This is just one example of how the formal economist often has to twist his concepts or add new, more loose, ones when applying an inherently static theory to a dynamic reality.[50]

It is relevant here to bring in Fisher's (1983) work on stability theory. In his stability theory, Fisher constructs a model of market adjustment in which rational agents drive the economy towards an equilibrium. According to him, stability and fast convergence are standard assumptions among economists. However, a well-developed stability theory is a "...necessary foundation for the equilibrium analysis of economic theory. If stability theory is unsatisfactory, then that foundation is lacking" (1983: 2). A sound "foundation" has to be laid or economic theory must be "be drastically altered". This will be the case if the world is "not close to equilibrium at all ..[then]... the study of disequilibrium...becomes the main business of economists" (ibid.: 5). However, Fisher chooses the first alternative.

The innovative aspect of his discussion is the introduction of what he calls "favorable surprises", that is to say, new unanticipated possibilities

[50] Cf. Nelson and Winter (1982) on "formal" and "appreciative" theory.

for trade. In other words, Fisher's stability theory can, in principle, handle question 2) above: how do agents react when new data are introduced unexpectedly? Fisher shows that within his specific model, convergence is guaranteed in the absence of "a stream of perceived new opportunities, real or imagined" (ibid.: 89). "New unforeseen opportunities" become a necessary condition for "instability – for continued change" (ibid.: 88). What these unanticipated changes are, *who* introduces them, *which* economic mechanisms underlie their emergence etc., are, however, questions left unaddressed by Fisher. For tentative answers to them, we have to proceed to market process theories.

5.3. Market Process Theories

Market process theories encompass evolutionary (Nelson and Winter 1982) and Austrian (Hayek 1937; Mises 1949; Kirzner 1973; Lachmann 1986) theories of the market process. What unites these two approaches is, at an overall level, that they both highlight processes of change and, at a more specific level, that they both conceptualize competition as a discovery procedure (to borrow Hayek's (1978) expression); that is to say, as a mechanism for social experimentation broadly conceived. I shall discuss evolutionary theory first.

One of the main motives for the work of Nelson and Winter (1982) – my first example of a theory of a market process theory – is to formalize the kind of evolutionary reasoning that they argue has always been at the back of the economist's mind when he engages in informal discussion with colleagues or explains things to the outsider. Such "appreciative" theory has traditionally been particularly prevalent in connection with innovation-related problems, as exemplified by Fisher's use of Schumpeterian arguments. However, in contrast to Fisher, Nelson and Winter do want economic theory to be "drastically altered" and the study of disequilibrium made "the main business of economists" (Fisher 1983: 5). This is completely in line with the call in such Austrian treatises as Kirzner (1973) or Lachmann (1986) for a process approach to market activity.

Many economists will probably in their more informal moments admit that in some sense the economy may be said to be in disequilibrium most of the time. But in their formal moments, economists – at least neoclassical economists – argue that 1) excess demands cannot be identified, that is, have no observational equivalents (a new classical response), or 2) that the economy is fundamentally stable and constantly in the neighborhood of an equilibrium, and/or 3) that natural selection processes in the market work so efficiently that only maximizing behavior forms "survive", and steady states for adaptive process are by implication quickly reached (more on this in chapter 7).

A part of the background for Nelson and Winter's work is precisely this natural selection defense most forcefully put forward by Milton Friedman. Sidney Winter in particular was able to isolate the strong assumptions that had to be made for Friedman's conclusions to be valid (e.g. Winter 1975). Furthermore, if Friedman essentially defended profit maximization on the basis of disequilibrium selection processes on the supply side of the market, why should these processes not be the really interesting object of investigation? On the basis of an underlying realistic conception of science (in contrast to Friedman's instrumentalism), according to which it is in fact possible to identify and theorize about the underlying mechanisms, Nelson and Winter view the investigation of dynamic disequilibrium market processes as the real task of economists.

Their theory clearly has, then, a background in methodological debates. But there is also a more substantial theoretical background which may derive more from Richard Nelson's lifelong attempt to obtain a theoretical understanding of the process of technological competition than from Winter's critique of Friedman. Technological innovation introduces a theme that has traditionally been problematic for neoclassical economics, and has, accordingly, traditionally been suppressed. It indicates the essential open-endedness of the economy, that is, the fact that novelties emerge. There is a standard philosophical argument that, logically, new knowledge cannot be anticipated, for if it could, it would not be new in any meaningful sense. And innovation is usually defined as the production of new knowledge, that is, as novelty.

The traditional strategy in economic research for handling this problem has been to flatly ignore it. In modern "patent race" models, for example, all market participants have full and precise knowledge about the innovation; what is uncertain is who may commercialize it first. The problems for neoclassical economics derive from the circumstance that neoclassical economics is basically ill-suited to handle the unexpected. The theory does not theorize about how agents react to unexpected changes (question 2 above), or how and why some agents – innovative entrepreneurs – may introduce novelties. The reason is not difficult to discover: it is difficult to give (intertemporal) equilibrium meaning if the goods space is unexpectedly expanded through product innovation. And maximization necessitates a finite list of possible states. This is the reason why Richard Nelson say that, "We [Nelson and Winter] believe that the profession will ultimately be driven to adopt our approach...*if it attaches high priority to characterizing and explaining significant unforeseen economic change*" (1986: 450; my emphasis.).

For there is a fundamentally evolutionary approach that can handle (at least some of) the problematic aspects of the process of technological change. In an evolutionary conceptualization of market activity, for example with biological natural selection as an analogy, there is 1) no presumption that equilibrium is a necessary aspect of the model, and 2) no presumption that agents continually maximize. And if optimality is relevant at all in an evolutionary setting, it is just as much – and probably more – a matter of systemic rationality than of individual rationality (Alchian 1950). Economic change through the novelty creating mechanism of innovative activity is a quite natural part of such a conceptualization – it is the analogy to mutations, and what ultimately underlies variation. This does not imply that we have opened up the way to analytical chaos. For selection in the market, operating over a population of firms with differential revealed performances, guarantees that the outcomes of evolutionary processes are not wholly random and unpredictable. For example, it may be possible to formulate criteria for survival; an obvious, though trivial, one is simply positive realized profit over some span of time.

Firms are portrayed by Nelson and Winter as profit-motivated, though not maximizing. Furthermore, Firms follow "routines", which in their theory constitute the analogy to genes and biological heredity. Routines are hierarchically arranged, with upper-level routines directing the search for more efficient lower-level routines (i.e., process innovation). Taken together with selection effects in the market, such innovative search determines profitability and, therefore, changes in the real capital of firms. In a complex world, firms do not have automatic and costless access to best productive techniques. Such techniques have to be discovered, and discovered anew, as the Austrians emphasize.

Furthermore, firms are strongly constrained in what they can do by where they have been, so that their innovative performance and technology development are strongly path-dependent. That is one reason why different firms react in different ways to the "same" changes. Different reactions, however, mean different profitability and different growth so that "...over time, the economic analogue of natural selection operates as the market determines which firms are profitable and which are unprofitable" (1982: 4). In the absence of any reliable ex ante knowledge about which processes of production are the most efficient, which products are most profitable etc., the market thus acts as a discovery procedure: "...the market system is (in part) a device for conducting and evaluating experiments in economic behavior and organization" (Nelson and Winter 1982: 277) (compare Hayek 1978).

Much of the work of Nelson and Winter converges with the Austrian theory of the market process. Inspired by the work of Ludwig von Mises and Friedrich von Hayek, Israel Kirzner (1973) in particular has constructed a closely reasoned argument that incorporates the notion of the market process as a process of the entrepreneurial discovery of new possibilities for trade. Central to Kirzner's argument is the point that, what he calls "Robbinsian maximizing" (after Lionel Robbins), is inadequate to form the individualistic basis for a theory of the market as a dynamic process. This is because in the conventional conceptualization of the problem confronting the individual decision-maker, the whole decision structure is *given*. What should be included in the behavioral make-up of agents is what Kirzner calls "alertness", that is, the ability to recognize and act on new possibilities for trade.

The conclusion of this section's survey of dynamic theories of the market is that, although they all incorporate some notion of "dynamics", it is only theories of the market as a discovery procedure and Fisher's stability theory that can handle our question 2) above, that is, address how agents react when they are initially ignorant about some changes. However, Fisher's and also Kirzner's theories are not really theories about how agents create new data; they are theories about how agents react to new data, and they are designed in order to examine convergence to equilibrium. In principle, although it is not well described in their work, Nelson and Winter's (1982) agents can initiate changes, so that their theory can (partially) address question 3 above. What now remains is to show that market process theories are the natural complements to neo-institutionalist economic thought. That means, having addressed Langlois' process and rationality themes, I shall now turn towards the institutions theme, showing how the other two themes have a bearing on this.

6. Why Neo-institutionalism Needs Markets Process Theories

6.1. Important Explananda

Among the reasons for bringing together hitherto separately existing theories is that they may somehow complement each other. That may not be a very compelling reason, however, since it could still be maintained that of two theories, each has its own domain of application, and that we can shift from theory to theory when approaching different domains. Something more is needed for a convincing argument of why we should combine theories. That may well be that objects needing explanation exist that cannot be fully approached by any two (or more) theories in isolation, but need a combined theory. Consequently, the unified theory should possess greater problem-solving power than any two theories in isolation.

In the context under consideration here, the relevant objects for explanation could be, in arbitrary order, the influence of path dependence on economic organization, the influence of changing industry structure on economic organization, entrepreneurship and economic organization, the organization of technological changes etc. Intuitively, such objects cannot be fully comprehended by either neo-institutionalist thought or by market process theories of the Austrian or evolutionary variety alone; a satisfactory explanation of such objects needs insights from *both* theories.

6.2. History and Explanation

A second reason makes use of a general social-scientific point: normally, a social phenomenon can only be fully comprehended if its history of emergence is factored in the explanation. Otherwise, the "explanation" will easily degenerate into mere description of the thing to be explained (the explanandum). Merely listing a set of equilibrium prices and quantities is no *explanation* of that equilibrium, since the explanans, the "historical" process through which the equilibrium emerged, is not taken into consideration. This is the explanatory dimension to Hayek's (1937) early critique of equilibrium theory, and his call for more attention being paid to processes of knowledge acquisition. To use another example, we shall only be fully able to understand why a particular firm has diversified in the way it in fact has by incorporating its prior development of competencies into the explanatory apparatus (Penrose 1959). Another closely related interpretation of the "history and explanation" theme is that "history matters" in the well-known sense of small historical events that lock-in a course of development along a certain path. In fact, arguments such as Penrose's may be given precisely this interpretation (Dosi, Winter, Teece, and Rumelt 1993).

Much neo-institutionalism of the transaction cost variety suppresses historical processes in its explanation of institutions. By analogy to comparative static explanations in standard neoclassical economics, attention is metaphorically devoted only to a "snap-shot" portrayal of economic organization; not to the "film" in which each picture emerges from the preceding one. Intuitively, the explicitly causal character of market process theories may remedy what I have argued to be an explanatory shortcoming of transaction cost economics.

6.3. Functionalism

The third reason is closely related to the preceding reason, and may in fact be seen as focusing it in a more specific direction. It relates to the functionalist mode of explanation that has traditionally been applied in neo-institutionalist work of the transaction cost species (Dow 1987; Williamson 1987). That is to say, when explaining the existence of an institution or organization, the theorist points to its beneficial consequences for the participating agents. But at the same time, for the explanation to be truly functionalist, these consequences must be unanticipated for the relevant agents.

As an extensive literature on the legitimacy of functionalist explanation in the social sciences has shown, this kind of explanation is legitimate only to the extent that a causal feedback mechanism/process can be specified, one that shows how agents can maintain an institution/organization over time when the beneficial consequences are unanticipated (Elster 1983). One such mechanism is natural selection (ibid.), so this variation on the explanation/process theme, too, suggests the necessity of integrating market process theories (particularly of the evolutionary variety) with neo-institutionalist thought.

6.4. What Can (Legitimately) Be Taken as Given?

This reason has to with what should be taken as *data* in economic analysis (Hayek 1937). In the analysis of the competitive firm of conventional price theory, inputs, outputs and technology are taken as given, and the economic problem has to with combining them in a profit-maximizing manner given prices. The economic problem of the firm of transaction cost economics is not *substantially* different from this; here the economic problem has to do with combining inputs, outputs etc., in a transaction cost minimizing way, given contractual hazards. Implicit in this is that outputs, inputs and technology are *given* through some process that is logically and historically prior to the issue of the organization of economic activities. This is what Williamson (1985: 84) means when he says that the presumption that "in the beginning there were markets" informs the transaction cost perspective.

To abstract from this process may be legitimate to the extent that the phenomenon under consideration is the economic organization of *existing* resources that are present on more or less well-working markets. This is, of course, how the economic problem is conventionally understood in neoclassical economics. However, it is grossly inadequate if technological changes – changes in the menu of inputs, outputs, and technology – significantly influence economic organization, for example, because they influence transaction and information costs (cf. North 1990; Langlois 1991). Understanding variations in economic organization would then presuppose an understanding of variations in technology etc. Furthermore, the whole procedure of examining only existing resources that are traded on more or less well-functioning markets, sidesteps the issue of market creation; an issue that was central to the work of such seemingly different marginalist pioneers like Carl Menger (1871) and Alfred Marshall (1925), and was later emphasized by Schumpeter.

It is of course not methodologically legitimate to criticize a theory for not addressing a phenomenon which it was never the designed to address. And theories of economic organization are not normally designed to address the process of technological change. But technological changes are fundamentally injected into the economic system in the form of transactions. This implies that the organization of technological changes is not, in principle, out of reach of theories of economic organization.[51] But that would seem to necessitate some account of the emergence of technological changes as part of the explanatory task. That story is supplied by market process theories, particularly of the evolutionary variety (Nelson & Winter 1982).

Furthermore, the activity creating markets have surely implications for economic organization, as empirically illustrated in Chandler's (1977) work on American business history.[52] We should not forget that markets are goods with strong public goods characteristics. Since set-up costs of markets may be quite high compared with their recurrent costs, it seems sensible to associate this capital commitment with the creation of the longer-lived entities known as firms. Only by a longer-lived interaction with

[51] In fact, David Teece (1986) tries to tell a transaction cost oriented story about the organization of technological changes. Teece primarily focuses on the commercialization aspects of the innovative process. Characteristic of transaction cost oriented analysis, this implies that the innovation itself is given. What may vary is how it is commercialized.

[52] This is in fact the fundamental reason why Chandler (1992) has grown increasingly skeptical towards transaction cost economics.

customers can the initial commitment be recouped (Casson 1982). The creation of markets, and hence, new firms, is not a theme normally associated with neoclassical economics. It is a theme that is primarily associated with research in entrepreneurship, and therefore, inter alia, with market process theories.

6.5. Change is Necessary for Understanding Economic Organization

Although the transaction cost wing of neo-institutionalism may present a largely static picture, change does in fact enter in some dimensions. In, for example, Williamson's (1985) theory of economic organization, concepts such as complexity, uncertainty, asymmetric information, opportunism, incomplete contracts, and frequency are crucial. Other theories of economic organization – such as the nexus of contracts approach associated with, for example, Alchian and Demsetz (1972) – operate with a more narrow menu of determinants of economic organization including moral hazard and team production. But all transaction cost theories of economic organization, whatever their differences may be, utilize concepts – such as uncertainty, incomplete contracts, asymmetric information – the meaning of which is only fully comprehensible against the background of an economic reality characterized by change. In other words, change is implicitly necessary to make sense out of these theories and it is necessary for meaningfully discriminating between alternative forms of economic organization. The theories that explain – make endogenous – economic and technological change are market process theories. But which kind of change is relevant?

6.6. Which Kind of Change?

That is a complicated question, for not all kinds of change may be relevant for economic organization. An important distinction to draw relates to whether change is anticipated or not. If the relative price of some good changes at a future date and this is known by everybody, the change will of course have economic consequences, since it will induce the usual substitution effects in consumption and production. But such an anticipated change will not influence economic organization since no transaction or information cost will change. To underscore this point and isolate which kind of change matters to economic organization, let us take a brief look at some themes from the history of economic ideas.

That change and economic organization are somehow related is a theme that does not seem to emerge until the socialist calculation debate of the 1930s between Hayek and Mises on the one side, Lange, Lerner et al., on the other (cf. chapter 4). A reconstruction of the Austrian position might be the following. It is only when change enters into consideration that economic organization makes a difference in terms of allocation and optimality. In a stationary state, economic organization is indeterminate, which implies that, for example, the choice between central planning or private property market organization is economically insubstantial (Mises 1936). Basing their socialist schemes on the economics of the stationary state allowed the market socialists to suppress all relevant questions of economic organization, and portray market socialism in a much too positive light.

This Austrian position is an expression of the point presented above: fully anticipated economic change – as in the stationary state – bears no implications for economic organization. But conclusions on economic organization derived from the economics of the stationary state are of no relevance for real-world economic organization. The other side of the coin is, of course, that nontrivial problems of economic organization derive from economies not being stationary. This is precisely what Hayek meant by saying that "It is...worth stressing that economic problems arise always and only in consequence of change" (1945: 82). Updating Mises and Hayek's insights, we might say that in the absence of change there would be no costs of searching for contract partners, drafting contracts, monitoring production, inspecting quality, credible commitment etc., in short, no transaction and information costs. In the tranquil state of stationarity, the existential question related to economic organization would not arise.

Hayek's solution to the problem of what guarantees a tolerable degree of consistency of plans in a changing economy was to point to "the telecommunications system of prices". This meant that he conceptualized institutions in informational terms: the institution of the price system economizes on information and bounded rationality and allows effective adjustments to unanticipated change. At approximately the time at which Hayek reached these insights, Ronald Coase (1937) presented an insight that, on the face of it, ran totally counter to Hayek's. The existence of the firm had to be rationalized in terms of failures of Hayek's telecommunications system. And Coase furthermore suggested that for some activities, the firm was superior to the price system in terms of handling unanticipated change.

However, these two arguments are not at all contradictory; it is precisely in the Hayekian picture of the changing economy that the existence of Coase's "costs of using the price system" may be rationalized. As Coase (1937: 393) observed, it is "...improbable that a firm would emerge without the existence of uncertainty", and it is clear from the context that what he has in mind is Knightian uncertainty. What neither Hayek nor Coase supplied, however, was a principle that could satisfactorily discriminate between the firm and the market in terms of which institution best secured adaptation to unanticipated change. To supply this principle – centered around the concept of asset specificity – is the way that Oliver Williamson now interprets his own work (cf. Williamson 1991b).

Both Hayek and Coase may be seen as identifying the kind of economic change that is crucial in the present context, that is, the kind of change that makes a difference to economic organization. Hayek is clear that the institution he focuses on derives its primary efficiency properties from its ability to handle unanticipated change, and Coase makes essentially the same point about the institution that concerns him. For one aspect of the efficiency of the firm has to do with its *flexibility* in adjusting to certain kinds of unanticipated change. As Coase observed, interesting contracts were not only long in duration but also open-ended because it is usually too costly or epistemically impossible to specify all future contingencies.

This is a theme that has been comprehensively addressed by Oliver Williamson and incomplete contract theorists such as David Kreps (1992), Sanford Grossman and Oliver Hart (1986). As these writers make clear, some notion of unanticipated change, as embodied in the notion of an incomplete contract, is necessary to make economic sense out of the institution known as the firm. In the formal manifestations of this idea, agents are, however, typically portrayed as so clever that they are able to design ex ante contracts that can efficiently handle unanticipated future change, so that later revisions of contracts are not necessary. Characteristically, Kreps' (1992) title to his formal modelling of this is "Static Choice in the Presence of Unforeseen Contingencies" (my emphasis). Dow (1987) argues that it is logically problematic to claim that agents can rationally ex ante design *efficient* responses to future unanticipated change, since one can only adjust efficiently to something that is foreseen.

Obviously, the crux of the matter here is the precise interpretation of the term "unanticipated". This may be given an interpretation ranging from the moderate interpretation of an event that is perceived in broad outlines to the more radical (Shacklian, perhaps) interpretation of the completely novel event. All interpretations on this spectrum may be relevant to economic organization; however, it is only the moderate interpretation that suits the ex ante efficient design perspective of the incomplete contract theorists (cf. Kreps 1992). That does not mean that an interpretation that also incorporates the more radical side of the spectrum is impossible; it just cannot be given an efficient ex ante design interpretation. It may, however, be given an ex post interpretation so that firms that – accidentally – choose a right response to a novel situation prosper at the expense of less lucky firms. "A right response" would here mean adopting a governance structure that made possible efficient – transaction cost minimizing – adaptation to the unforeseen change. In such a reading, transaction cost economics supplies some of the survival criteria of a broader evolutionary story (much in the way outlined by Alchian 1950).

6. Towards a Processual Neo-institutionalism

As argued above, changes in the sense of unanticipated changes have traditionally been a cumbersome theme in economic analysis, and have proved particularly troublesome for neoclassical economics. However, an implication of the analysis is that, in order to make economic organization determinate, we have to introduce at least some measure of the unexpected; not necessarily in the sense that the future is impossible to anticipate in any sense, but perhaps more realistically in the sense that only the contours of the unexpected may be glimpsed. For example, entrepreneurs may rationally expect some new technological innovation that will render their products obsolete but not be able to tell its precise characteristics (if they could, they could make the innovation themselves). Or self-interested agents may have reasons to adopt institutions (constitutions, governance structures) which they believe will best guard them against the problems caused by the emergence of the unexpected. I shall leave the troublesome epistemics of the unexpected here but I shall have more to say on its institutional consequences later on.

What can be noted, however, is that it is fundamentally in the importance of economic change for neo-institutionalist economic thought that it makes contact with evolutionary and Austrian theory. Theories of the market process make explicit the variation and change which is necessary to understand the existence of institutions, and by implication institutional change. In this sense, these theories and neo-institutionalist economic thought are complementary. Mises (1936) was, in the context of the socialist calculation debate, the first to point out that the process theme and the institutions theme in this sense belong together. In order to drive this point further home, let us again focus on the theory of the firm.

Why do firms exist? The answer given by neo-institutionalist thought involves a mix of scale advantages, specialization (asset specificity), and opportunism/moral hazard. What is vital, however, is that firms derive their comparative advantage in handling some type of productive activities relative to the market only in the presence of two central behavioral assumptions:

> "But for the *simultaneous* existence of *bounded rationality and opportunism*, all economic contracting problems are trivial and the study of economic institutions is unimportant" (Williamson 1981: 1545).

As Hayek (1945) argued, bounded rationality causes problems for the centrally planned economy, particularly in the presence of unexpected change. The "telecommunications system" of prices was, in this perspective, a low-cost arrangement for economizing on bounded rationality. However, as we saw, Coase argued at almost the same time that Hayek's telecommunications system does not always work effortlessly; in fact, that is why firms exist.

These insights are, of course, the central ones in modern organizational economics; much of the field can indeed be said to be primarily preoccupied with clarifying the precise circumstances under which alternative forms of economic organization are most efficient. But as we shall see in chapter 8, the field is not homogenous. There is, for example, a distinction to be made between "the nexus of contracts approach" and "the asset specificity approach" as the two dominant approaches to economic organization.

The nexus of contracts approach, which is an outcome of property rights theory and also includes agency theory, is primarily occupied with the efficient ex ante design of contracts, that is, the search for incentive compatibility. When the incentives are in place, the contract partners essentially react predictably.

Williamson's focus is much wider, since he tries to give a real time account for contract evolution. It is precisely here that "the economics of time and ignorance" (O'Driscoll and Rizzo 1985), enters since the assumption of opportunism introduces "surprise", that is, the emergence of novelty (Williamson 1985: 56-59). In other words, the behavioral quality of opportunism is broader than the shirking assumption that plays a similar role in the incentive branch of modern organizational economics. This is because opportunism as Williamson portrays it is basically about taking advantage of contracting partners in a way that is unexpected to them. If contract partners could have anticipated the opportunism, either they would not have entered into the relationship or the future opportunism would have been reflected in contract terms. Various governance mechanism can to some extent handle these problems – the broad contours of future potential opportunism may be anticipated – but external unexpected events may further complicate the picture. It is with good reason, then, that the essential incompleteness of most interesting contracts is so emphatically emphasized in the Williamsonian approach to organizational economics.

Within this scheme of thought, the function of institutions – including contracts – can be interpreted as responses to situations where the parties "expect the unexpected". In other words, the embodiment of property rights in institutions to some extent reflects how and by whom uncertainty should be handled – who, for instance, should have the right to control the firm's physical assets in unexpected situations (cf. Grossman & Hart 1986).

However, the emergence of various institutional arrangements do not have to be a result of conscious calculation in which the parties react efficiently to a rational expectation that something unforeseen will happen (as in Grossman & Hart 1986). As the Austrian school since Menger has emphasized, the rational design perspective is too narrow and often misleading since many institutions have in fact spontaneously emerged. In such an interpretation, the emergence of "the economic institutions of capitalism" (Williamson 1985) may be seen as the result of various kinds of social experiments with different kinds of behavioral rules, the surviving results of such trial and error learning being spread through the mechanism of imitation since they were able to cope most efficiently with the problems introduced by bounded rationality and opportunism. In other words, such a reading – inspired by market process theory – of organizational economics allows us to address question 2) above, how agents react to unanticipated changes. The answer suggested is that they imitate behavioral rules that have a successful historical track record.

One could argue that the role reserved for the unexpected in, for example, Williamson's theory is rather limited: it only surfaces when one party in a contractual relationship involving highly specific assets opportunistically "holds up" the other party. This limitation is dictated, I think, by the fact that Williamson's primary interest lies in understanding "nontrivial" economic organization. And he does not really present an overarching perspective on the market economy, despite the ambitious title of his 1985 book, "The Economic Institutions of Capitalism". The economic problem in Williamson's writing involves combining existing inputs (allowance being made for "the fundamental transformation") and outputs in a transaction cost-minimizing way. Innovation, firm and market creation, and entrepreneurship are not explicitly factored in. However, a consistent perspective on economic activities informed by market process theories surely cannot neglect the more general presence of the unexpected. It cannot, as Williamson for heuristic reasons does, neglect the expansion of the goods space that takes place through product innovation, and it cannot neglect the formation of new firms and markets.

However, it is definitely one our discipline's oldest empirical truths that the menu of inputs and outputs and the corresponding markets have continuously expanded, through the growing "extent of the market", through the division of labor, and the process and product innovations this dynamic process brings with it. As Mises (1936) understood, the economic problem of society – or any economic organization – does not relate to combining given inputs and outputs in an efficient way *per se*; rather, it relates to the problem of which institutions will most efficiently cope with the calculation, incentive and coordination problems introduced by economic change.

Basically, Adam Smith and Mises give us the same overall answer here, that the market society is best equipped to deal with these problems. However, none of them allows us to go further and examine which of "the economic institutions of capitalism" will best handle the problems introduced by economic change. It is here that we may get help from Williamson since he has at least made an attempt to lay bare the conditions under which alternative institutions most efficiently handle the unexpected, although the domain of the unexpected that he focuses on is quite limited. In other words, for a processual neo-institutionalism – in the sense of a theory that can say something about economic organization under the impact of changes in the division of labor and innovation – we need both Adam Smith, Ludwig von Mises and Oliver Williamson.

What would a research program for such a dynamic neo-institutionalism look like? One tentative answer is that it would involve isolating the determinants of transaction costs, and theorizing about how transaction costs changed over time. Transaction costs, we have seen, exist in the end because of economic change and the information problems caused by economic change. And such information problems are not only related to opportunistic behavior in a bilateral monopoly with highly specific assets etc. The sources of information problems, and therefore information and transaction costs, are many and varied. They may relate to establishing behavioral and technical standards; to the problems of appropriating rent from, for example, technological innovation; to the problems of coordinating throughput in the vertical chain of production; to educating suppliers; and much else beside.

It seems to me that an excessive preoccupation with the contracting problems caused by morally hazardous or opportunistic behavior has blinded theorists of economic organization to the existence of a much broader menu of determinants of information and transaction costs, many of which relate to the process of the division of labor and technological change. Technological change involves, almost by definition, the unexpected. And it has for some time now been the favorite explanandum of evolutionary theories (Abernathy and Utterback 1978; Nelson and Winter 1982; Dosi et al 1988), indicating again the complementarity of theories of economic organization and market process theories. Evolutionary theories often incorporate numerous stylized facts on how technology changes over time (see for example Abernathy and Utterback 1978). This may form a possible basis for theorizing about the information and transaction costs that are caused by the evolution of technology changes, which means that it may become possible to say something determinate and empirically relevant about how economic organization changes. For example, whether a technology is in its "fluid" or "mature" (ibid.) phase surely influences information and transaction costs and therefore also economic organization.

7. Conclusion

This chapter has made an attempt to bring together market process theories, including the Austrian theory of the market process, with theories of economic organization, particularly Williamson's theory. In a sense, this involves bringing together again two strands of thought that were both embryonically present in the Austrian school, particularly in Mises and Hayek's work. I have argued that due to the presence of unexpected change in market process theories, these are the prime candidates for forming a dynamic underpinning for theories of economic organization. However, as argued elsewhere (chapter 8 and Foss 1993b), the modern theory of economic organization seems to be branching in a more neoclassical and a more heterodox direction, respectively. The more heterodox direction includes, among others, Oliver Williamson. Presumably, it will be here that the possibilities of successfully merging market process theories with theories of economic organization will be the most favorable.

7: Varieties of Price Theory: Orthodox, Austrian and Evolutionary

1. Introduction

In this chapter, I aim to focus on how price theory – or the theory of markets – is covered in three competing approaches. I shall also bring *modern* (post Mises and Hayek) Austrian economics into the picture much more explicitly than I have done hitherto. I shall take a look at how orthodox economists, (modern) Austrian economists and evolutionary economists conceive of price theory and how these conceptualizations differ. I shall argue that while there may not be qualitative differences between the price theoretical results of orthodoxy, Austrian economics and evolutionary economics, the two latter approaches are (given the standards of assessment I have chosen here) superior to the orthodox approach in an explanatory and methodological sense. Briefly, this has to do with the preoccupation with process in Austrian and evolutionary economics and the neglect of the same phenomenon in orthodoxy. I shall further argue that Austrian and evolutionary price theory may be seen as complementary to one another.

2. Machlup, Price Theory and Comparative Statics

Let us start with a seemingly simple question: for what purposes do we apply price theory? The late Fritz Machlup brought a number of pertinent ideas to bear on this question in his 1967 presidential address to the American Economic Association, "Theories of the Firm: Marginalist, Behavioral, Managerial". Specifically, he asks us to

> "...pose four typical questions and see which of them we might expect to answer with the aid of price theory. 1) What will be the price of cotton textiles? 2) What prices will the X corporation charge? 3) How will the prices of cotton textiles be affected by an increase in wage rates? 4) How will the X Corporation change its prices when wage rates are increased?" (p.8).

As Machlup argues later on in the paper, conventional price theory is only able to say something determinate on question 3, and give some indications on how question 4 should be answered. But questions 1 and 2 are "out of reach".

Machlup's conception of price theory is decidedly not unproblematic (and in this assessment, I also include Machlup 1959, 1963b).[53] For one thing, it is inconsistent with modern notions of the method of comparative statics, that is, the standard way in which price theory is focused. As William Baumol explains, it is

> "...easy but incorrect to say that the analysis shows that the imposition of an excise tax will lead price to rise from its previous level, but by less than the amount of the tax...But...comparative-static analysis makes no such intertemporal assertions" (Baumol 1977: 322).

Substitute Baumol's "imposition of an excise tax" by Machlup's "increase in wage rates", and the above passage implies a perfect negation of Machlup's conception. Price theory as a formal technique has *nothing* directly to say about how the price of "cotton textiles" will be influenced by "an increase in wage rates". The comparative static method consists in the comparison of equilibrium values of endogenous variables for selected values of the parameters. And different values of the parameters do not imply anything temporal.

3. Explanatory Aspects

Baumol's conception would seem to imply that price theory has lost all direct contact with economic reality. But that implication is in fact a false one, as strongly argued by Paul Samuelson (1947). Samuelson's principle of correspondence is precisely an attempt to provide this realistic connection, thereby establishing what Samuelson called "operationally meaningful theorems". More specifically, Samuelson tried to establish a realistic "correspondence" between price theory and economic reality by associat-

[53] Loasby (1976: 45) thinks that Machlup's analysis is completely wrong, since price theory can only give answers to *the first two* questions. This is because "...the solution of all equilibrium models rests on given data; there is provision for alternative solutions for different data; but no provision within the model for a response to any data which is not included in the original specification". If by "price theory" is meant general equilibrium theory, Loasby is undoubtedly correct in his critique of Machlup.

ing the "initial" and the "resulting" (we have to put these words in quotes in order to avoid any direct reference to causality) with real states, and by identifying differences in the values of parameters with real identifiable changes in data. And this is where the principle of correspondence becomes important, for this identification procedure is only warranted if the relevant equilibria are stable. But the principle of correspondence cannot be associated with causal developments between equilibria. It is simply a check on the applicability of comparative static analysis. Comparative statics is for Samuelson, as it is for Baumol, the comparison of alternative equilibria "...without regard to the transitional process involved in the adjustment" (1947: 8).

In the last analysis, Samuelson and Baumol's conception of price theory and the role and nature of comparative statics are identical. And it is for both of them a necessary condition for price theory to be practically applicable that the relevant equilibria approximate to real states. But how can this assumption be justified? The only direct, "operational", contact that neoclassical price theory makes with reality hinges on observed prices and quantities, but what justification is there for associating observed time series of prices and quantities with a string of equilibria?

Different answers to this have been put forward. One answer is that economic theory by definition is only concerned with the study of steady states for adaptive processes (Lucas 1987b), that is, equilibria, static/stationary or dynamic/time-dimensioned. This may be argued – and Austrian and evolutionary theorists would certainly argue so – to be excessively restrictive: there are a number of interesting disequilibrium phenomena which cannot meaningfully be classified as "noise", and about which economists are certainly able to say something meaningful (Winter 1987). This has recently been echoed by the orthodox economist, Frank Hahn, when he says that "Economic theory thus narrowly constructed makes many important discussions impossible" (1984: 4). At least, "If disequilibrium effects are in fact unimportant we need to prove that they are" (Fisher 1983: 217). According to the critics, that proof has not been forthcoming.

On a more methodological level, it may furthermore be argued that the history of the emergence of a social phenomenon – how it came into being – is an extremely important part of its explanation (Ullman-Margalitt 1978). As the prominent contributor to stability theory, Franklin Fisher has explained, it is finally, and perhaps even more fundamentally, a condition for the applicability and explanatory power of price theory that "...the equilibria of economic models are not only stable but that convergence to a neighborhood of equilibrium is achieved relatively quickly" (1983: 2). This "necessary foundation" is, according to Fisher, not yet existent since stability theory is theoretically undeveloped.[54] As Fisher explains, approaches – such as that of Robert Lucas (1987b) – that only focus on steady states for the adaptive process, fundamentally sidestep the important problem of contributing to the provision of a sound stability-theoretic "foundation"; they do not solve the problem. Friedrich Hayek, as we saw in chapter 3, said essentially the same thing in 1937.

Historically, economists have not in fact remained content with focusing their analyses in terms of only steady states for adaptive processes. In their discussions of the explanatory and realistic content of economics, most economists have fully recognized that equilibria, maximizing behavior etc., are the results of previous dynamic adjustment processes on the market and, in the last analysis, in the market behavior of individual agents.

But to admit that is, of course, not the same thing as saying that adjustment processes should be theoretically approached. One of the most famous illustrations of the character of the processes – and ironically at the same an argument for their ultimate theoretical irrelevancy – is Milton Friedman's (1953) famous application of evolutionary biology to the theory of the firm:

> "Let the apparent immediate determinant of business behavior be anything at all – habitual reaction, random chance or whatnot. Whenever this determinant happens to lead to behavior consistent with rational and informed maximization of returns, the business will prosper and acquire resources with which to expand; whenever it does not, the business will tend to lose resources...The process of natural selection thus helps to validate the hypothesis – or, rather, given natural selection, acceptance of the hypothesis can be based largely on the judgment that it summarizes appropriately the conditions for survival" (1953: 3).

In other words: the processes that underlie the supply side of the market are selection processes. But since profit maximization is the relevant criterion of survival, and since behavior based on profit maximization over time will dominate through the mechanism of differential survival, econo-

[54] Fisher wrote in 1983; a decade after, his assessment still holds true.

mists are best served by focusing their interest on profit-maximizing behavior – and by implication: equilibria – only.[55]

Largely due to the work of Sidney Winter (1964; see also Schaffer 1989), we know today that there are a number of problems with Friedman's argument: strong assumptions on the height of entry barriers, the intensity of competition (i.e., the selection pressure), how much of the realized profit firms plow back into investments in real capital etc., have to be made in order to produce Friedman's conclusions. A perhaps deeper problem in Friedman's case is that his making use of an argument based on disequilibrium behavior, with agents that vary strongly in terms of motivation, knowledge and rationality etc., in itself is inconsistent with the formal core of neoclassical economics, maximization and equilibrium. This obvious inconsistency does not hinder many formal economists in making much use of selection-based reasoning in their more informal discussions. To take one example, Stiglitz (1975) in a formal discussion of the economic theory of contracts, defended the conclusions of his analysis with the remark that "...it might be argued that there is an evolutionary tendency of the economy to gravitate to the contractual arrangements analyzed here" (p.556).

What is interesting in this context is that informal, dynamic, selection-based, arguments that incorporate the diversity of agents in terms of behavior, knowledge and rationality are implicitly an important part of the way the applied economist often approaches his subject.[56] The applied economist makes little use of formal general equilibrium theory; his toolbox is one that has basic Marshallian price theory in it, supplemented with loose, dynamic reasoning such as Friedman's selection arguments. It seems, then, that the practice of the applied economist is much closer to older price theory tradition than it is to the modern formal conception. The applied economist will to a large extent be interested in dynamic developments; for example, in which precise path the price of cotton textiles follows when it is disturbed by an increase in wage rates, to borrow Machlup's example. He will, in other words, be an analyst of the "market process", as Austrian economists would say (Kirzner 1973).

[55] This argument is also related to Friedman's advocacy of methodological instrumentalism, which implies that he is an adherent to the so-called "underdetermination thesis", viz. the proposition that given "facts" may be explained by an infinite number of incompatible theories. For example, profit maximization may be explained both by conscious decision making and by the evolutionary argument. As a conventionalist, Friedman reacts in the present context by choosing the simplest and most elegant explanation, that firms act "as if" they consciously maximize profits.

[56] See Nelson and Winter (1982) on the difference between "formal" and "appreciative theory", and Benjamin Ward (1972) on "story-telling".

4. Back to Machlup

Which bring us back to Fritz Machlup. For Machlup presented as an integral part of his conception of price theory a procedure for actually applying price theory to questions such as, "How will the prices of cotton textiles be affected by an increase in wage rates?". This is the procedure that seems to be applied by the nonformal economist when he approaches an empirical problem with his price theoretic tool-box. And it is a procedure that is wholly inconsistent with the methodological stipulations of Baumol and Samuelson. On the other hand, it is – as I shall argue later on – consistent with the approach to economic analysis represented by evolutionary and Austrian theorists. Machlup's approach is contained in the following four-step procedure:

> *1. step*. Initial position: equilibrium, "i.e. 'Everything could go on as it is'".
>
> *2. step*. Disequilibrating change, "i.e. 'Something Happens'". The analyst introduces a change in "data".
>
> *3. step*. Adjustment, "i.e. 'Things must adjust themselves'". The analyst traces the effects of the change.
>
> *4. step*. Final position: a new equilibrium, "i.e. 'The situation calls for no further adjustments'" (Machlup 1963b: 47).

In this procedure, the role of equilibrium is primarily to ensure that all ceteri are kept *pariba*: the initial equilibrium position allows us to postulate that the disequilibrating change introduced under the second step is the *only* relevant change, the only cause of the effects traced under step 3. And the final equilibrium position allows us to postulate that all the effects that were caused by the change have been accounted for. Clearly, this explicitly causal analysis is inconsistent with the Samuelson/Baumol procedure. For Machlup it is a part of the application of price theory to tell a dynamic story about what happens between equilibria. How this differs in an explanatory and methodological sense from the standard procedure will be examined in the following section. I shall focus the discussion in terms of the explanatory approach known as "invisible hand explanations" (Ullman-Margalitt 1978).

5. Invisible Hand Explanations and Price Theory

The term "invisible hand explanation" finds its origin, of course, in that famous passage in "The Wealth of Nations" in which Adam Smith explains that: "Every individual intends only his own gain, and he is in this, as in so many other cases, led by an invisible hand to promote an end which was no part of his intention". Cleansed of metaphysical and ideological connotations, invisible hand explanations may be seen as an expression of the fundamental insight that there will often be a qualitative difference between aggregate social outcomes and individual actions. To commit a fallacy of composition in a social scientific context will usually be a result of lack of understanding of this basic principle. In somewhat more precise terms, providing an invisible hand explanation means explaining selected social phenomena as the unintended result of the interaction between many individuals acting intentionally (so that invisible hand explanations are inapplicable to both nature and Robinson Crusoe). In these broad terms, it is intuitively clear that most of the important objects of explanation in economics are phenomena that are given to such explanation: the study of relative prices and allocative efficiency is precisely the study of phenomena that are not intended per se by any single agent, but emerge as the unintended results of the interaction of rational agents.

However, If we broaden our view to incorporate the methodological restrictions placed on invisible hand explanations, it becomes a good deal more doubtful whether (orthodox) economic theory can be said to consistently adhere to invisible hand explanation. In a classic contribution, the philosopher Edna Ullman-Margalitt (1978) provided the following restrictions that should be adhered to in any good invisible hand explanation:

> 1. *The domain of the explanation*: social phenomena.
>
> 2. *The explained phenomenon (explanandum)*: the social phenomena that are susceptible to invisible hand explanation are "well-structured...patterns", that are the unintended and unforeseen result of the interdependent actions of many interacting agents.
>
> 3. *The nature of the explanation*: an invisible hand explanation is a "genetic" explanation, that is, it explains a process in

time, when it accounts for the emergence of the explanandum.

> 4. *The mechanism of the explanation*: the explanation implies providing a plausible mechanism or principle of composition that aggregates individual choice acts to the relevant explanandum.

Given these stipulations we are now in a position to examine how economic theory conforms to an adequate invisible hand explanation, starting with Samuelson and Baumol's conception of price theory and then comparing that with Machlup's. A relevant price theoretic example that can serve as "testing ground" could then be tracing the effects of the discovery of some new natural resource. In this example, the invisible hand explanandum is the new equilibrium in which all adjustments have played themselves out. Samuelson and Baumol's approach would be to specify a set of equations describing the equilibrium at the point when the new resources had not yet been discovered. Having done that, the next thing to do is to specify a new set of equations in which the new "data" are incorporated. The relevant equilibrium constellations of prices and quantities can then be compared (provided the equilibria are stable).

Clearly, this procedure is not in conformity with the restrictions with which an adequate invisible hand explanation must comply: there are no "genetic" elements in it (point 3 above), and there is no attempt to detail the mechanism through which the explanandum (the new equilibrium) emerges over time as the result of the interaction of many interdependent and rational agents. What this kind of approach to price theory does is to describe the explanandum; it does not explain it. That is the methodological side of the traditional complaint that neoclassical price theory makes some fictitious person, the auctioneer, coordinate everything. It could be argued, of course, that I have "cheated" by focusing so much on comparative statics since that method explicitly specifies that adjustment processes between equilibria be paid no attention. However, as Frank Hahn indicates in the following metaphorical terms, the problem is there and it is a general problem for neoclassical economics:

> "Suppose, for instance, it is possible for an egg to stay standing on its tip until it is disturbed. We should not attach great practical significance to this equilibrium of the egg until we are told some causal story of how it comes to be in that state.

> In exactly the same way, the proposition that, in certain circumstances, there is a set of prices which ensures equality between demand and supply in all markets tells us nothing of whether these prices will indeed be established by a market economy" (Hahn 1982: 13).

The problem that Hahn identifies links up with Fisher's (1983) point about the lack of a sound stability theoretic foundation for equilibrium theory. And translated into our terminology, we can interpret Hahn as calling for formal economic attempts to adhere to restrictions number 3) and 4) above which any adequate invisible hand explanation should adhere to. In other words, he calls for formal models that offer mechanisms (point 4), describing how economic agents over time (point 3) may home in on a coordinated state, that is, equilibrium ((point 2); explanandum), even when they initially have little or no knowledge about possibilities for trade.

In marked contrast to the Samuelson/Baumols conception of price theory, it is clear that the structure of *Machlup's* adjustment model is much closer to the restrictions described in the above: his adjustment model is explicitly designed to tell a dynamic, causal story about what happens between equilibria (point 3). However, he does not have very much to say about the precise nature of the mechanism that brings us over time from the initial to the final equilibrium. And in fact, that is a serious problem. In the next section, I shall interpret the modern Austrian theory of the market process and Richard Nelson and Sidney Winter's evolutionary theory as attempts to provide detailed views of the invisible hand mechanism that aggregate individual choice acts to a consistent outcome. I shall also argue that although these two theories approach the invisible hand mechanism differently, they may nevertheless be argued to be complementary.

6. Austrian and Evolutionary Theories of the Market Process

6.1. Modern Austrian Theory

In a sense, the central Austrians of the later generations – particularly Mises, Hayek and Kirzner – may be argued to have always placed at center stage the attempt to provide a price theory that conforms to the dictates of invisible hand explanations. Hans Mayer's (1932) early distinction between "functional" (general equilibrium theory) and "causal-genetic" (Austrian theory) theories of price is the first Austrian expression of something like this. And when Hayek (1937) criticized the economics of his time as being unduly occupied with examining "the pure logic of choice" to the neglect of out-of-equilibrium learning processes, what he meant was that economics did not identify the generative mechanisms that over time produced the explananda of economics, such as market equilibria.

I have argued elsewhere that it was the recognition of this problem that led Hayek to focus on institutions that bear a number of similarities to the concerns of modern neo-institutionalists (chapter 3). The existence of behavior-coordinating institutions supports the existence of a tendency towards coordinated states, that is, "spontaneous orders". But in some sense this is evading the issue, for the tendency is predicated on the existence of institutions; it is not fundamentally investigated. Consider, for example, Hayek's (1945) famous conceptualization of the price system as a "telecommunications system". The way this has been usually interpreted in mainstream economics is simply that the market economy operates efficiently with a minimum of information, since *equilibrium* prices supply all the correct incentives. Local producers and consumers do not have to bother with, for example, strategic interaction. In other words, Hayek merely describes the explanandum – equilibrium prices – and does not provide a causal explanation.

This is one interpretation of Hayek's article, which certainly cannot be rejected per se. On the other hand, Hayek *also* says that the "limited individual fields of vision" of market participants "...sufficiently overlap so that through many intermediaries the relevant information is communicated to all" (1945: 86). Now, under perfect competition, "individual fields of vision" do not overlap; and there are no "intermediaries". I submit that what Hayek indicated, but did not elaborate, in such passages was the existence of entrepreneurs who drove the market process towards equilibrium.

It has been left primarily to Israel Kirzner (1973, 1979, 1984) to provide a detailed view of this adjustment process. His is a self-consciously Hayekian starting point. As he says:

> "...to make the assumption that markets are close to equilibrium is essentially...to *beg* (rather than to overcome) the Hayekian problem of dispersed knowledge...One does not "solve" the problem of dispersed knowledge by *postulating*

> prices that will smoothly generate dovetailing decisions" (Kirzner 1984: 415).

In order to "overcome" this problem, Kirzner introduces a function that perhaps owes more to Mises than to Hayek, namely the entrepreneur. Central to his argument is the distinction between "Robbinsian maximizing" – the mechanistic activities of the neoclassical agent – and "alertness", the active entrepreneurial quality which allows agents to perceive and act on hitherto undiscovered possibilities for trade. And

> "Robbinsian theory only applies after a person is confronted with opportunities; for it does not explain how that person learns about opportunities in the first place" (Kirzner 1973: 6-7).

The entrepreneurial exercise of alertness closes pockets of ignorance in the market and thereby moves the economic system towards a coordinated state (for an attempt at formalization, see Littlechild 1979).

However, as many of Kirzner's critics (particularly among the so-called "radical subjectivists") have argued, there is no theoretical guarantee for such a tendency. The actions of the entrepreneur may just as well act to destabilize the system in a more or less Schumpeterian manner (Lachmann 1976, 1986: chapter 7). And the possibility of coordination failures cannot be overlooked. But to downplay Schumpeterian entrepreneurship and neglect coordination failures is precisely what Kirzner wants to do. There is currently a heated debate within the modern Austrian school on these issues (see Vaughn (1992) for a summary). Much of the debate seems, however, to be a matter of terminological differences. For example, when Kirzner talks about "equilibration", the case of producers/entrepreneurs alerting consumers to new products would seem to fall under this category. Whereas for some of Kirzner's opponents, product innovation would constitute a clearly disequilibrating force.

It seems fair to say in summary that the dominant Austrian attempt to provide a genetic approach to price theory – one that can be understood as conforming to the dictates of invisible hand explanations – is one in which the conception of rationality is broadened to include the propensity to discover those opportunities for trade, the presence of which is tantamount to the existence of disequilibrium. Very little is, however, said about the institutional context in which the entrepreneur operates; but as Hayek argues, the tendency towards coordinated states is not invariant relative to the institutions of society. Furthermore, there is very little mention of the firm; in fact, the pure Kirznerian entrepreneur is wholly distinct from the manager/producer. Finally, in the Austrian theory of the market process there is actually very little discussion of the psychological mechanisms that motivate people to discover opportunities, limit who discovers them etc. All that is asserted (presumably as a matter of apodictic knowledge) is that there is *some* inherent propensity in human beings to exercise entrepreneurial alertness.

In contrast, the next theories to be considered explicitly incorporate the firm, partially build on psychological foundations (through the concept of bounded rationality), build (implicitly) on a Hayekian theory of evolved rules (in firms), but have a rather different view of rationality. As a result, their genetic accounts about out-of-equilibrium behavior are very different. Instead of alertness, evolutionary theories tend to emphasize resistance to change, path dependence, and bounded rationality. To be sure, these themes have not been neglected in the wider corpus of Austrian theory. For example, as argued in the preceding chapter, Mises had a rather clear evolutionary understanding of the market process as a process of differential firm growth (Mises 1936). And evolutionary arguments figure prominently in Hayek's later work (for example, Hayek 1973). Unfortunately, these insights have not been elaborated with reference to the market process by the modern Austrians, but by a group of modern evolutionary theorists. This does not mean that modern Austrians neglect evolutionary insights per se; merely that while these insights may be applied to the evolution of *institutions*, they are not applied to the market process as a process of purposive entrepreneurial process of discovery.[57] So while institutions – the rules of the game -may change in an evolutionary way, the game itself is not best analyzed in an evolutionary manner.[58]

6.2. Evolutionary Theory

Although Alfred Marshall has often been invoked as an early reference (e.g. Foss 1991), the first systematic application of social scientific analogies to biological natural selection seems to have been Armen Alchian's famous 1950 article, "Uncertainty, Evolution and Economic Theory". The

[57] For some pertinent remarks, see Kirzner (1992) and Koppl (1992).

[58] For a different and somewhat broader reading of the evolutionary/Austrian economics connection, see Witt (1993).

three fundamental concepts in the biological theory of evolution through natural selection are 1) the principle of variation – that members of a population vary in terms of at least one trait of selective significance; 2) the principle of heredity – that copy mechanisms that ensure intertemporal stability in the forms of species exist; and 3) the principle of selection, that some forms are better adapted to the pressure of the environment and therefore increase in weight in the population through differential reproduction. The lack of legitimacy of uncritically applying these concepts to the social domain is well-recognized among economists who have usually surrounded their applications with strong reservations. However, the analogies that have actually been put forward are innovation (variation, mutation), imitation of rules and/or institutions as knowledge bearers (heredity), and firm growth and decline in the market process (selection).

That such analogies could be extremely useful in economic analysis, because they allowed simultaneously addressing stability and change (something that neoclassical economics is not satisfactorily capable of), was first argued by Alchian. His starting point was that profit maximization is, in general, ill-defined under uncertainty. Although Alchian's specific reasoning is a bit shaky on the exact decision-theoretic aspects – his article was written before expected utility theory became standard fare – his point is that firms, confronted with exogenous changes, will react in a number of different ways, many of which are not predictable by an outside observer. Nonetheless, Alchian explains, the effects of changes can be predicted on an aggregate level, provided the market mechanism is conceptualized as a selection mechanism, selecting over different behavioral forms, realized profit fueling the process. The behavior of individual firms may be wholly myopic, irrational or whatever, yet predictions will still be possible on an aggregate (industry) level.

Using the following analogy, Alchian provides an illustrative example of the nature of his reasoning:

> "Assume that thousands of travellers set out from Chicago, selecting their roads completely at random and without foresight. Only our "economist" knows that on but one road are there any gasoline stations. He can state categorically that travellers will *continue* to travel only on that road; those on other roads will soon run out of gas...The correct direction of travel will be established. As circumstances (economic environment) change, the analyst (economist) can select the type of participants (firms) that will now become successful;

> he may also be able to diagnose the conditions most conducive to a greater probability of survival" (1950: 22).

Completely independent of the motivation and rationality of firms, there exist survival criteria such as positive realized profit: "As in a race, the award goes to the relatively fastest, even if all the competitors loaf. Even in a world of stupid men there would still be profits" (Alchian 1950: 20). The economist knows about the criteria as they are dictated by the economic system, and it is his knowledge of them that allows him to make predictions, although only of a qualitative kind.

The following variation of an example given by Alchian can usefully illustrate his evolutionary reasoning: in a society – let us call it "Ceteris Paribus" – there are a number of firms that produce products that are near substitutes. All the firms use oil in their production processes. The economy is stationary until it is hit by a sudden increase in the price of oil. A questionnaire conducted among firms in Ceteris Paribus reveals, however, that no firm intends to changes its production process (so Ceteris Paribus does not lie on the neoclassical continent). It is now that Alchian's reasoning shows its force. For even if no firm consciously changes its production process, an evolutionary pressure will nevertheless operate on the population of firms in such a way that the observed qualitative results conform to the results of a formal comparative static analysis. The precondition for evolutionary reasoning being applicable in this case is that there is variation in terms of how much oil firms use. Those firms that use comparatively little oil will over time increase in weight in the population of firms, and as a result the average use of oil per unit of output in the population will fall – which is precisely the result one would expect using a formal comparative static approach.

Notice that this story implies no, or almost no, appeal to rationality and conscious decision-making – at least on the supply side of the market; implicitly, the story presupposes some rationality on the part of the demand side, since it has to be assumed that consumers prefer and search out the less expensive goods (cf. Kirzner 1962). However, later in his discussion Alchian relaxes the assumption of wholly myopic or stochastic behavior and introduces assumptions of bounded rationality and conscious imitation of successful rules of behavior. So where changes in the weight of individual firms/rules of behavior in the overall population, in the scenario with little intentionality, are primarily a matter of pure selection effects and life and death, the more Lamarckian mechanism of imitation is present in the scenario with more intentionality. Alchian's use of biological analogies is, in other words, not dependent on an assumption of total lack of intentionality, rationality etc.

Alchian's approach is the starting point for Nelson and Winter's many contributions from the beginning of the 1970s, culminating in their joint 1982 book, "An Evolutionary Theory of Economic Change". In terms of intellectual influence, Alchian is to Nelson and Winter what Ronald Coase is to Oliver Williamson. Like Alchian, Nelson and Winter conceptualize the market mechanism as a selection mechanism operating on a population of firms with different revealed performance. And even more explicitly than Alchian, Nelson and Winter identify firms by their decision rules, or "routines", which embody their productive and organizational knowledge, much of which is tacit. To stay with the biological analogy, routines are the analogy to genotypes; they constitute the hereditary system of the firm. Furthermore, the notion of routines supplies that rigidity which is necessary for selection arguments to be meaningfully applicable. In Nelson and Winter's "organizational genetics", routines are portrayed as hierarchically arranged, higher-level routines (R&D routines, for example) manipulating lower-level routines. Routines for process innovation, for example, are "search routines" which, triggered by the pressure of the market, select from among lower-level routines. However, there is no guarantee that the firm will in fact choose an efficient routine; this can only be fully determined through tests in the discovery procedure of the market.

Although the primary interest of Nelson and Winter lies in obtaining a realistic understanding of the process of technological change and Schumpeterian competition through innovative activities, their evolutionary reasoning is, however, also applicable in price theoretic problems – such as the analysis of Machlup's question number 3, "How will the prices of cotton textiles be affected by an increase in wage rates?". And the way evolutionary reasoning is applied in such price theory is remarkably similar to Machlup's stipulations of the method of price theoretic problems. That is, Nelson and Winter attempt to provide a dynamic analysis of the genetic process between industry equilibria (really, absorbing states for Markov processes), identifying the mechanisms that are operative during this process. In other words, they try to identify the generative mechanisms that produce the explanandum (for example, a new equilibrium with changed prices for cotton textiles), rather than merely describing the explanandum. This indicates a further reason behind the development of the Nelson and Winter approach: the wish to develop a framework within which conventional price theoretic analysis may be treated as a special case.

As we have seen, it is fundamental for Nelson and Winter to understand the firm as fundamentally a bundle of routines and decision rules that decide input requirement and output for given market conditions. In their portrayal of market dynamics – and this, rather than the firm, is what occupies their interest – there is a clearly intentional element, since firms intentionally apply decision rules when market decisions change ("along-the-rule effects"). At the same time, it is the rigidity of these rules – which implies the general impossibility of immediate adaptation to changing market conditions – that makes selection effects relevant: some rules are simply more efficient in terms of realized profit for given market conditions. The relatively more efficient rules and routines will therefore increase in weight in the population through the expansion of the firms that embody them. However, although they are quite rigid, lower level routines may be modified through the operation of higher-level search routines. There is, then, also an element of "mutation" in Nelson and Winter's evolutionary conception. The following version of Nelson and Winter's basic model (1982: chapter 7; Nelson 1987: 24-30) may more clearly illustrate the nature of their approach.

Assume that at time t firm i's decision rule on how to utilize a given input has the following form:

$$(x_i/k_i) = D(P,d_i) \qquad (1)$$

The left-hand side of 1) is the amount of variable input (x) per unit of capital (k) employed in firm i; P is a vector of input and output prices; and d is a vector of parameters of decision rules which determine (x/k) given P. All techniques are assumed to have the same capital/output ratio, but different input/output ratios.

If $X = \Sigma\, x_i$, and $K = \Sigma\, k_i$, then for the industry the following must obtain:

$$(X/K) = \Sigma\, D(P,d_i)\ (k_i/K) \qquad (2)$$

Now, what happens to (X/K) *over time* when factor prices change? And is (X/K) able to change for constant market conditions? The first question is interesting because it may be seen as a classical question of comparative static price theory, answered here by means of an evolutionary approach. The second question is interesting because, in an orthodox context, the answer would be "no" – but possibly not in an evolutionary context.

Answering these two questions may involve setting up two different scenarios. In *scenario 0*, prices are always P_0. In *scenario 1*, prices are P_0 until time *t*, and P_1 after *t*. For a given point of time, *T* (larger than *t*), (X/K) at time *T* in *scenario 0* can be expressed thus:

$$(X/K)^T{}_0 = \Sigma\, D(P_0, d^t)\, (k_i/K)^t + \Sigma\, [D(P_0, d^T{}_{i0}) - D(P_0, d^t{}_i)]\, (k_i/K)^t$$

$$+ \Sigma\, D(P_0, dT_{i0})\, [(k_i/K)^T{}_0 - (k_i/K)^t]. \qquad (3)$$

In 3) upper signs *T* and *t* identify the points of time at which the relevant variables are measured. The lower sign 0 identifies the variables that can be different at *t* and *T* in scenario 0 and 1 respectively. The first summation is then $(X/K)t$. The second summation expresses the effects of the evolution of routines/decision rules in between *t* and *T* (through innovation). And the third summation expresses selection effects, which change the weights of firms' routines in the overall population of firms.

A similar expression shows what (X/K) is at *T* in *scenario 1*:

$$(X/K)^T{}_1 = \Sigma\, D(P_1, d^t{}_i)\, (k_i/K)^t + \Sigma\, [D(P_1, d^T{}_{i1}) - D(P_1, d^t{}_i)]$$

$$(k_i/K)^t + \Sigma\, D(P_1, d^T{}_{i1})\, [(k_i/K)^T{}_i - (k_i/K)^t]. \qquad (4)$$

Subtracting (3) from (4) expresses the difference in (X/K) under the two scenarios:

$$(X/K)^T{}_1 - (X/K)^T{}_0 = \Sigma\, [D(P_1, d^t{}_i) - D(P_0, d^t{}_i)]\, (k_i/K)^t +$$

$$\Sigma\, [D(P_1, d^T{}_{i1}) - D(P_1, d^t{}_i) - D(P_0, d^T{}_{i0}) + D(P_0, d^t{}_i)\, (k_i/K)^t +$$

$$\Sigma\, [D(P_1, d^T{}_{i1})\, [(k_i/K)^T{}_1 - (k_i/K)^t] - D(P_0, d^T{}_{i0})\, [(k_i/K)^T{}_0$$

$$- (k^i/K)^t]] \qquad (5)$$

5) offers one way in which "the canonical question of comparative statics; what is the effect of a change in price" (Nelson 1987: 27) can be analyzed in a dynamic context. The first summation can be seen as expressing the effects of firms moving along their routines/decision rules when prices change from P_0 to P_1. The second summation expresses that routines/decision rules may develop differently under the two scenarios. In other

words, these two summations stand for the more intentional elements in the Nelson and Winter set-up, since they incorporate the direct reaction to a factor-price shock and the attempts to change routines/decision rules. The second summation could perhaps also be argued to capture the effects of what the Austrians call entrepreneurial "alertness" (Kirzner 1973); in this context the *discovery* of new, more profitable routines. The last summation expresses the *difference* in selection effects in the two scenarios. Summing up, 5) expresses three fundamental mechanisms in an evolutionary conception of price theoretic questions: 1) response when prices change, applying existing routines/decision rules; 2) change of routines/decision rules (innovation); and 3) competitive market selection.

Does such reasoning produce the same qualitative results/predictions as orthodox price theory? Formal price theory obtains its results/predictions under the assumption that firms know all relevant alternatives and maximize profits. That is, mechanism no. 1. However, the two other mechanisms (innovation and selection) are not present in orthodox price theory. This is the reason why (X/K) cannot change for given market conditions. In spite of such differences, it is easy to argue that the (qualitative) results/predictions of orthodox price theory correspond fairly close to the results/predictions of evolutionary price theory, since the assumption of profit-seeking is all that is required to ensure that the summations generally will have "orthodox" signs.

7. Concluding Comments

7.1. More Generality

What may now be said in favor of conducting price theory within the confines of an Austrian or evolutionary approach as distinct from within an orthodox approach? To start with the relatively obvious, the evolutionary process approach to price theory, here exemplified by a basic Nelson and Winter model, is in an important sense more general than the orthodox approach: the economic consequences of variation in many dimensions can conceptually be handled by an evolutionary model, whereas variety, at least in terms of behavior, is ruled out by a neoclassical approach. In other words, evolutionary economics is compatible with a larger menu of behavioral assumptions. Austrian economics is not limited to maximization either since it also includes the category of entrepreneurial alertness. However, with the exception of the later work of Hayek (such as Hayek 1973),

Austrian economists have not shown an interest in conceptualizing rule-following or routinized behavior, not to mention Simonian satisficing or other notions that smack of psychologism. Given this, it may not be surprising to find Israel Kirzner (1973) tending to see the relation between Austrian economics and orthodox economics as Austrian economics supplying a basically sound orthodoxy with the category of alertness. In such a reading, Austrian economics may be seen as closer to orthodoxy than to evolutionary economics. However, we may also see Austrian economics as supplying evolutionary economics with the behavioral category of "alertness" to hitherto undiscovered profit opportunities (Kirzner 1973), so that it is really these two approaches that are complementary.

7.2. The Relation between Evolutionary and Modern Austrian Economics

In Nelson and Winter's evolutionary models, the product market is assumed to clear on every single market day, although expectational equilibrium does not obtain.[59] Thus, firms confront an equilibrium price. However, how precisely that price is established is not investigated by Nelson and Winter. Just as much as in standard orthodox analysis, the invisible hand process that produces an equilibrium price is suppressed. This is where Kirzner's analysis of the alert entrepreneur complements their analysis, since that analysis is essentially designed to examine the dynamics of price.[60] So, although they are complementary, Kirzner's analysis is, in a sense, logically prior to Nelson and Winter's: it is when Kirznerian entrepreneurs have moved the market towards an equilibrium that Nelson and Winter's firms enter the scene. To an extent then, Kirzner's analysis may bear the same relation of logical priority to evolutionary economics as it does to orthodoxy. Like orthodox agents, the agents of evolutionary economics are not alert in Kirzner's sense; the discovery factor is not systematically brought into the picture. Of course, firms may innovate, but this is conceptualized in the stylized way as a matter of drawing from a probability distribution of innovations. In this sense, the innovations are already there; they do not have to be discovered in Kirzner's sense.

[59] In this sense, their theorizing is more Marshallian than Walrasian.

[60] Kirzner (1983: 1502) noted the existence of possible complementarities. Talking about the increasing dissatisfaction with Walrasian models, he noted that there "...appears, in fact, in the work of Nelson and Winter and others, a significant beginning towards...a shift in emphasis...It is not at all unthinkable...for a revival of Schumpeterian economics to develop as a linkage with the ideas, more consistently pursued in the narrower Austrian tradition by Schumpeter's less flamboyant but equally self-assured and brilliant Austrian contemporary, Ludwig von Mises, currently being developed by the followers of the latter (and of Friedrich Hayek) in the form of a modest revival of the older Austrian tradition".

As this indicates, entrepreneurial creativity is not yet incorporated in a comprehensive way in standard evolutionary economics (Witt 1987a), in spite of the emphasis put on innovation and technological change. This circumstance may partially derive from the fact that routinized behavior is necessary in any evolutionary model since it supplies the rigidity that is necessary for the meaningful application of selection-based reasoning. Furthermore, the evolutionary approach – at least as represented by Nelson and Winter (1982) – is not really a theory about the firm or the individual decision-maker per se. Like its distant neoclassical cousin, it is a theory of what happens at the industry level. However, an evolutionary theory should be able to more fully address the economic consequences of creativity and its embodiment in novelty – which is where Austrian insights may assist.

7.3. Mechanisms, Realism and "Appreciative" Theory

On an explanatory level, the evolutionary and Austrian approach have the characteristic that they explicitly attempt to identify the economic mechanisms that underlie economic activity outside equilibrium. In other words, these two approaches conform much more closely to the methodological dictates of invisible hand explanation. And they conform more closely to the dictates of a realist meta-theory, according to which the aim of science is precisely the identification and theorizing of "generative mechanisms" (Bhaskar 1978), rather than prediction.[61] As Ludwig Lachmann (1982: 635) summarizes this: "Causal genetic explanation comes into its own when we turn from the construction of models to an endeavor to understand the course of real events". And in Lachmann's opinion, there should be more feedback from "real events" to "the construction of models"; any evolutionary economist would, I believe, concur.

Closely related to the above is the argument that Austrian and evolutionary approaches should be preferred simply because their "...richer formulation...corresponds much better to what economists' really believe, their "appreciative" theory about what happens, than the neoclassical formulation" does (Nelson 1987: 29). That is, they are more consistent with the kind of analysis that takes place at the mundane, street level, in the building of economic theory, than they are with theorizing conducted at or near the penthouse level. For the formal economist – the proponent of rig-

[61] On realism and evolutionary economics, see Foss (1994), and on realism and Austrian economics, see Mäki (1993)

or and simplicity – such an argument borders on open confession of ignorance. Surely, he will say, the work being done on the upper floors should direct what is going on at the lower floors. To this we may retort with the argument that a sound development of a theory cannot be relied upon to proceed in this way, since it may insulate theorizing from reality. Rather, theoretical development in any well-working scientific discipline consists in a sound dialectic between formal and "appreciative" theory (cf. Nelson and Winter 1982; see also chapter 9), that is in a conversation between the upper and the lower floors.

7.4. An Improving Orthodoxy?

In this connection, we may note that the conventional complaint that has been levelled at evolutionary and Austrian economics from orthodox perspectives is that these approaches generally lack a formal analytical structure. This complaint can relatively be dealt with easily since numerous formal evolutionary models have been forthcoming in the last decade following Nelson and Winter's pioneering formalizations (such as, for instance, Schaffer 1989). However, in the accusation of a lack of analytical structure, more seems to be involved than the (fallacious) complaint that evolutionary economics is unformalized. Fundamentally, the complaint seem to center around the ad hockery of evolutionary economics: evolutionary models are not in general derived from a rigorous choice-theoretical foundation. And the behavioral assumptions employed (such as "bounded rationality", "satisficing" etc.) do not imply determinate implications of behavior (Winter 1986). Rather than conducting informal and ad hoc evolutionary theorizing, the economist is, therefore, much better advised "...to stick with the standard model of maximizing behavior, complicating the environment" (Kreps 1990: 738-739).

Recent significant results from game-theoretic research (such as Binmore 1989) seem to imply, however, that this is not an approach that can be generally recommended. Intuitively, these results indicate that perfectly rational agents will run into infinite regresses in their decision making which make them unable to act. Such problems have in fact been handled, but only through invoking assumptions that are themselves completely ad hoc (such as Reinhart Selten's concept of "trembling hands"). Such results and problems have caused increasing interest among formal economists in broadening the behavioral foundation of neoclassical economics, recommending that, for example, bounded rationality should be modelled (see Kreps ibid.). Furthermore, the constant problems with providing a sound stability theoretic foundation for economics have, at least among some formal economists, indicated the need for a broadened behavioral foundation. For example, in order to examine stability, Fisher (1983) equips the agents of his model with the ability to react to unanticipated changes. Furthermore, recent work in organizational economics seems to indicate the necessity of such a broadening, since, for example, a sound understanding of the nature of the firm seems to necessitate that unanticipated changes be incorporated in the analysis (cf. chapter 6).

Nonmaximizing modes of behavior and unanticipated changes are precisely among the hallmarks of evolutionary economics (Nelson and Winter 1982; Winter 1986; Nelson 1987; Witt 1987a). To the extent that these notions are beginning to be taken seriously in the mainstream of orthodoxy, it is the nature of orthodoxy that is changing, and changing towards something like the metaphysics that underlie Austrian and evolutionary economics. This metaphysics is one that sees the economic world as fundamentally open-ended, and the future as emerging more or less unpredictably out of the creative choices of men. It is on this basis that evolutionary, Austrian and post-Keynesian economists for a long time have complained that neoclassical economics is fundamentally static: it operates within a deterministic world in which everything is settled from the beginning.

This complaint may have lost some of its force in the face of the increasing attempts to incorporate path dependence under the umbrella of formal neoclassical economics (for an informal discussion, see Hahn 1987), the recent work on sunspot equilibria, on strategic complementarity, the application of the mathematical theory of chaos to economics, etc. If, however, the complaint should be interpreted as meaning that orthodoxy continues to be equilibrium oriented, then in this sense orthodoxy is surely "static". That critique of orthodoxy should be carefully guarded, but that it is surely a possible endeavor, is argued by Nelson and Winter (1982: 8) when they observe that

> "...although it is not literally appropriate to stigmatize orthodoxy as concerned only with hypothetical situations of perfect information and static equilibrium, the prevalence of analogous restrictions in advanced work lends a metaphorical validity to the complaint".

The issue of "analogous restrictions" may or may not be thought to be the fundamental division. However, the general expansion of the interest of mainstream economists in incorporating notions such as path dependence and broadening orthodoxy's behavioral foundation, combined with the growing possibilities of formalizing evolutionary and Austrian insights may indicate the possibility of a real convergence between these hitherto separately developed perspectives. This is all to the good, since it will in a fundamental sense make economic theory much more realistic, reducing the distance between the formal upper floors in the economics building and those at the more practical street level. And it will also make more credible the saying ascribed to Milton Friedman that "There is no Austrian [or evolutionary or orthodox] economics, only good and bad economics".

8: Austrian Economics and Neo-institutionalism: the Case of the Theory of the Firm

1. Introduction

In this chapter, I shall take a look at the Austrians as precursors of neo-institutionalism with reference to a relatively narrow subject, namely the theory of the firm. Although focusing on the theory of the firm allows me to survey a number of pertinent subthemes, it may seem an awkward place to begin. For as more than one commentator has observed, a distinct theory of the firm is conspicuously missing from the body of Austrian thought (for example, Minkler 1991: 8). As two Austrian economists observed some years ago: "...there is no...Austrian theory of the firm" (O'Driscoll & Rizzo 1985: 123). That is still the situation. By the term "theory of the firm", I understand a theory that has something to say about the existence, the boundaries and the internal organization of the firm (Holmstrom & Tirole 1989). And by the term "firm", I mean an organization that is planned with the purpose of earning profit. In Hayekian terms (Hayek 1973), the firm is a "planned order", an element of "taxis". It exists in the interstices of the unplanned market order, that is, "kosmos".

That social institutions have always occupied center stage in Austrian economics is a proposition that commands rather widespread assent today (Hodgson 1988; Langlois 1986b, 1991). The Austrians are no longer thought of as aloof apriorists, only concerned with spinning out the logical implications of a few incontestable axioms. For many economists recognize the distinctiveness of the Mengerian theory of the origin of a medium of exchange (Menger 1871: chapter 8), and probably even more economists are familiar with the Hayekian account of the information providing function of the price system (Hayek 1945). Many economists also know that Hayek's insight stemmed from his involvement in the socialist calculation debate, which was first and foremost a debate about the *organization* of economic activities. Indeed, Hayek's "The Use of Knowledge in Society" has become a standard reference in the literature on economic organization.[62] More generally, many writers (e.g. Langlois 1986b) have pointed out the affinities to Austrian economics of much of neo-institutional-

[62]1. For example, Ricketts (1987: 59), Milgrom and Roberts (1992: 56), Douma and Schreuder (1991: 9), and Williamson (1985: 8, 1991: 160).

ism, that is the modern analysis of social institutions with the aid of economic analysis.[63]

So the Austrians, right from the beginning of their school with Menger's "Grundsätze" in 1871, have approached institutions and theorized about the organization of economic activities. This has not only been a matter of giving efficiency rationales for existing institutions, such as in Menger's account of the evolution of money. It has also been a matter of *comparing* existing institutions in terms of their efficiency properties. That is to say, the Austrian approach to institutionalism has not only been a matter of tracing the emergence of institutions in a causal-genetic way, it has also been a matter of comparative institutionalism. Of course, these two tasks are complementary, although there is a tendency in modern neo-institutionalism to downplay the first task.[64] But the institutions that have traditionally been confronted in Austrian economics are mainly central planning – either in its comprehensive or its market socialism manifestation – and private property rights based market organization, that is, "capitalism". This means that the hierarchical direction that takes place within a market economy has been comparatively neglected,[65] although Austrians have never denied the fact of planned order existing within spontaneous order. Along with many other economists, the Austrians could be seen as assimilating the message of Machlup (1967) that, for the purposes of market analysis, we can make do with a very stylized (anonymous) conceptualization of the firm. And economics per se has no business breaking up the black box of the firm; that may be left to organization theory or social psychology. In fact, Austrian analysis of market phenomena has even manifested a tendency to dispose of the concept of the firm, resting content with analyzing the extra-Robbinsian – as Israel Kirzner puts it – activities of the entrepreneur.[66]

However, as we shall see, it is something of a doctrinal puzzle that the Austrians never took steps toward formulating a theory of the firm. It is surprising because many of the analytical components that are necessary

[63] It should be noted that the term "neoinstitutional" is often applied generalized neoclassical economics (property rights theory) (e.g. Eggertson 1990) as well as more processual and heterodox influences (e.g. Langlois 1986a). As I have argued elsewhere in this book, the Austrians can be seen as precursors of both the property rights strand (chapter 5) and the more processual strand (chapter 6) of neoinstitutionalism.

[64] Property rights economics is arguably the best example of this tendency, but it may also be found in agency theory and transaction cost economics.

[65] Among the few Austrian contributions that deal explicitly with the theory of the firm are O'Driscoll and Rizzo (1985: 122-125), Littlechild (1986: 35), Boudreaux and Holcombe (1989), Thomsen (1989, chapter 4), and Ikeda (1990). Contributions explicitly influenced by Austrian economics are Malmgren (1961), Ricketts (1987), Witt (1987b), Loasby (1989), and Langlois (1991).

[66] The words "firm", "business enterprise" or substitute terms do not figure in the indices to Menger (1871), Mises (1949), and Lachmann (1956, 1986)

to tell a coherent story about why there should be firms in a market economy were present in Austrian theory long before they became standard fare in neoclassical economics. I have in mind concepts such as property rights (Mises 1936), specific and complementary assets (Hayek 1931), asymmetric information (Mises 1936; Hayek 1937), the distinction between planned and spontaneous orders (Hayek 1973), nonmaximizing modes of behavior (Mises 1936; Hayek 1973; Kirzner 1973), and a basic understanding of the principal-agent relationship (Hayek 1935a,b, 1940; Mises 1936).[67] These are among the concepts that have occupied center stage in recent attempts to place the theory of the firm on a solid economic footing (for example, Alchian & Demsetz 1972; Williamson 1985).

It is important to note what these observations mean and what they do not mean. I do not say that the Austrians – had they pieced the above concepts and theoretical insights together – would necessarily have arrived at something similar or very close to the contemporary theory of the firm. One reason may be that, whereas the modern theory of the firm has had a comparatively loyal relationship to mainstream neoclassical economics, the Austrians, beginning with Hayek and Mises' work in the 1930s, have consistently and continuously emphasized their differences from mainstream economics, particularly as it took shape after World War II. In particular, as modern Austrians like to emphasize, the concepts of *market process* and *entrepreneurship* are missing from neoclassical economics in general (Kirzner 1973), and, we may add, from the contemporary theory of the firm in particular. What this implies is that there may be a potential for a distinct Austrian theory of the firm.

The way the ensuing pages proceed is the following. In the next section, I shall present a brief overview of "Contemporary Theories of the Firm", concentrating on the mainstreams in the contemporary theory of the firm. In section 3, I shall present some prominent "Austrians on Economic Organization", and argue that the Austrians anticipated many important modern developments in the theory of the firm. But as I argue in section 4 and 5, the Austrians are more than merely precursors; not only is Austrian economics at variance with the modern theory of the firm in some important respects (section 4), but it is also possible to construct a distinct theory of why there should be firms on an Austrian basis (section 5). In other words, the purposes of this chapter are historical, critical and constructive,

[67] A principal-agent *relation* is said to obtain when a principal wants a task to be carried out by an agent on the principal's behalf. A principal-agent problem obtains when there some kind of conflict of interest among the two and when the principal either cannot observe the actions of the agent (hidden action/moral hazard) or cannot ascertain whether the agent has made the best use of the knowledge he possesses (hidden information/adverse selection).

respectively. But in all three tasks, I basically adopt a method of "*rational reconstruction*": the Austrians can be "reconstructed" as 1) anticipating modern developments, as 2) simultaneously providing a critique of these, and, finally, as 3) having their own distinct perspective on economic organization. That is why I maintain that the Austrians, somewhat paradoxically, can be seen as both precursors and critics of the modern theory of the firm. The Austrians I primarily have in mind in this chapter are, in addition to Hayek and Mises, Ludwig Lachmann and Israel Kirzner.

2. Contemporary Theories of the Firm[68]

2.1. The Firm in Economics

The defining characteristic of the market economy is usually taken to be the organization of production and distribution through the price system. But the primacy of exchange is characteristic not only of the market economy but also of how economists view their discipline (McNulty 1984: 233). In more specific terms, firms in neoclassical (perfect competition) price theory are often taken to be identical except in terms of the product markets they serve.[69] And not only are firms often presumed to be identical, the actual description of them is the most stylized or anonymous possible. They are merely production functions. Of course, this procedure is not wrong in itself; for the purpose of analysis of market level allocation it is perfectly appropriate (cf. Machlup 1967).

But, as many critics have argued, neoclassical price theory provides no rationale for the very existence of the firm, not to mention its boundaries and internal organization. This is not just a matter of the price system operating so efficiently that there is no need for, say, any vertically integrated enterprises; it is more fundamentally a matter of neoclassical perfect competition theory being inherently incapable of rationalizing anything called "the firm". All relevant knowledge is given, prices provide all other information, factors are totally mobile, there are no costs of ascertaining quality etc. This implies that the theory cannot explain why buyers of goods should not simply contract with owners of factor services instead of with firms.

[68] This section draws on material in Foss (1993b).

[69] As argued in Foss (1991) it was the breakthrough for the theory of monopolistic competition in the mid-nineteen-thirties that established this assumption of uniformity. For an Austrian comment on this episode, see Kirzner (1979: 133-135).

2.2. Coase and Post-Coasian Theory

According to the usual account, it was *Ronald Coase* who in 1937 realized that not only had the firm been neglected in economics but, more importantly, that it was in fact possible to use economic theory to provide a rationale of why there should be firms in a market economy.[70] Coase's (1937) answer, in broad outline, is that efficiency requires the substitution of firms for markets if the transaction costs of using markets becomes large relative to the costs of managing. Market *transaction costs* are the costs of discovering contractual partners, drafting and executing contracts. Beyond a central threshold of market transaction costs, hierarchical direction – what Williamson (1991b) calls "intentional governance" – of the movements of goods and services becomes more efficient to all involved parties than exchange of property rights through the price mechanism; what Williamson (1991b) following Hayek calls "spontaneous governance". This provides a rationale for the *existence* of the firm.

Applying conventional marginalist method, the *boundaries* of the firm are determined by the condition that the transaction costs of organizing an additional transaction using the market should equal the transaction costs of organizing that same transaction using the firm. And Coase finally hinted at the possibility of using transaction cost reasoning to explain the details of internal organization.

Another aspect of the standard account of the development of the contemporary theory of the firm is that the field lay dormant for about thirty years until Armen Alchian, Harold Demsetz and Oliver Williamson revitalized the Coasian analysis at the beginning of the 1970s (Alchian & Demsetz 1972; Williamson 1975). Indeed, almost all modern theories – most of which have taken their lead from the early seminal contribution of Alchian and Demsetz and Williamson – of the firm are considered post-Coasian in the sense that they view the firm as an efficient contract between a multitude of parties; efficient in the sense that it best facilitates exchange, given existing resource scarcities (including scarcity of information and rationality). In spite of the fact of a common Coasian origin, the contemporary theory of the firm is not monolithic (see, e.g., Holmstrom & Tirole 1989); in their attempts to operationalize, make more precise and understand the original Coasian insights, modern theories have given rather different answers.

70 This, of course, is not totally correct since Frank Knight in 1921 had provided economic rationales for the existence of the firm. For a comparison of Coase's and Knight's theories of the firm, and a ringing endorsement of Knight's theory, see Boudreaux and Holcombe (1989) (and for a moderator, see Foss 1993c).

In a recent article, Armen Alchian and Susan Woodward (1988) introduced a distinction between "a moral hazard approach" to economic organization, inspired by the original Alchian and Demsetz analysis (1972), and "an asset specificity approach", best represented by the work of Oliver Williamson (1975, 1985, 1991a,b). The moral hazard approach is usually referred to as "the nexus of contracts approach" (Jensen and Meckling 1976; Fama 1980; Cheung 1983), and I shall use that term here. At an overall level, what makes these two approaches different is their degree of adherence to neoclassical theory; whereas the nexus of contracts approach is a sort of generalized (property rights) neoclassical theory, the asset specificity approach – particularly in its Williamsonian manifestation – is characterized by the import of a number of nonneoclassical concepts, particularly Herbert Simon's concept of bounded rationality (Simon 1979). They have given correspondingly different answers to Coasian questions like, "What is the precise nature of transaction costs?", "How are they best to be operationalized?", "What determines the size of hierarchical costs?" etc.

2.3. The Nexus of Contracts Approach

In Alchian and Demsetz' (1972) original analysis the existence of the firm is explicable in terms of the incentive problems that arise when *team production* – production that involves inseparable production functions – is combined with *asymmetric information* and *moral hazard.* In this prisoners' dilemma-setting, shirkers do not bear the full consequences (costs) of their actions, and viable shirking is the result. The way the market system copes with such shirking is through the contractual entity, "the classical capitalist firm", characterized by the existence of one central agent, who is both a monitor who meters the performances of other agents and a residual claimant and with whom other agents enter into contracts. Market forces then guarantee efficient monitoring of team production via the incentive structure confronting the monitor-residual claimant. Viable firms are those that succeed in minimizing the costs involved in monitoring team production. A number of analytical addenda to this basic story have been presented. Jensen and Meckling (1976) recognized that the monitoring story as told by Alchian & Demsetz was not limited to team production. And Barzel (1987) demonstrated that the agent that was most likely to end up as monitor-residual claimant (principal) was the one whose contribution to the joint product was the most difficult to measure.

However, such refinements of the nexus of contracts approach came at a significant cost – at least from an Austrian influenced perspective.

Though the basic claim was present in Alchian and Demsetz' (1972) original discussion, it became clear that within this tradition the very concept of the firm as a planned order was difficult to uphold. What we ordinarily refer to as "a firm" is simply a complex set of market contracts (Cheung 1983), only distinguished from ordinary spot market contracts by the continuity of association among input owners. Given this, it comes as no big surprise that nexus-of-contracts theorists, Eugene Fama (1980) and Steven Cheung (1983), call for an abandonment of the concepts of "the entrepreneur" and "the firm", respectively. Since all allocation of resources – including those "inside" the firm – is ultimately governed by relative price movements, there can be no or little room for planned direction of resources as embodied in entrepreneurial plans.

2.4. The Asset Specificity Approach

In the same way that the nexus-of-contracts approach seems to have increasingly centered around one central analytical concept, namely the cost of metering quality of goods and services, the contractual approach associated with Williamson (1985) has increasingly focused attention on one central character: *asset specificity*. Asset specificity is said to exist when the opportunity cost of an asset is significantly lower than its value in present use. Often, asset specificity will involve a high degree of *complementarity* among the relevant assets. The difference between these two values is a Marshallian quasi-rent that can be appropriated through the exercise of opportunism. The tussle for rents in bilateral monopoly situations characterized by asset specificity, *opportunism* and bounded rationality, is the driving force behind firms' changing boundaries. It is, in other words, costly bargaining games that underlie the existence of the firm and its efficient boundaries.

As indicated by Grossman and Hart's (1986) refinement of this mode of analysis, it is not really the contractual "ink costs", and not even the appropriation potential relating to the rents from specific assets that underlies integration per se. It is rather the mutual desire to implement efficient investment incentives that determines to whom the ownership rights ("residual rights") – that is, the right to determine and control the use of (physical) assets in circumstances not spelled out in the contract – will be allocated.

One of the really recalcitrant problems in modern debates on economic organization has to do with specifying the costs of internal organization. In the absence of such a specification one cannot solve the puzzle of why the economy is not organized in one big firm (Coase 1937: 86). Indeed, Williamson (1985: 132) refers to this problem as a "chronic puzzle", and highlights it with his "problem of selective intervention": why cannot a merger of two firms not always do the same or better than two independent ones, since management in the merger can always intervene selectively?

One of the important attempts to identify the (incentive) costs of internal organization is Milgrom (1988) who basically asks why the hierarchical organization continues to survive in a competitive market economy despite its bureaucratic costs. Applying insights from rent-seeking literature, Milgrom identifies the sources of bureaucratic costs as subordinates' "influence activities", that is, their strategic attempts to change the actions of superiors in their own interest. Such influence activities produce influence costs that usually have a negative impact on firm profitability. As Milgrom argues, centralized authority is particularly vulnerable to influence activities; the decentralized market provides much fewer targets. The reason the hierarchy may survive after all is because the existence of strict bureaucratic rules have the beneficial function of damping the influence activities of subordinates.

Summing up, we may highlight the following *specific* concepts as those that are crucial to tell a story about why there should be firms in a market economy. *Asymmetric information* is absolutely crucial since in the absence of knowledge dispersion there would be no transaction costs; that is, economic organization would be indeterminate. Some notion of *linkage of resources* – either in the form of Williamson's notion of asset specificity or Alchian and Demsetz' concept of team production – seems also necessary, since in its absence there would be no rents to appropriate. Finally, a notion of *self-interest seeking* with guile (opportunism, moral hazard) also seems necessary, since in its absence there would be no need for the services of a monitor, hierarchical fiat, bureaucracy etc. Market contracts coupled with promises – that would always be credible – would be sufficient.

On a more *general theoretical level*, most modern theories of the firm bears an intellectual debt to property rights theory (Coase 1960; Demsetz 1967). The structure of contracts that constitutes the firm implies an allocation of property rights. Finally, on a *methodological level* modern theorists of the firm and economic organization are committed to a method of *comparative institutionalism* which implies that, for purposes of comparison, the relevant yardstick is not the unattainable ideal of general competitive equilibrium but real, attainable institutions or market outcomes (Demsetz 1969).

I have asserted that the Austrians in some important dimensions can be seen as precursors of modern theories of economic organization, including the theory of the firm. In the next section I shall attempt to substantiate that assertion. I shall concentrate attention on the points where the Austrians directly anticipate modern developments and neglect those where variance exists (they will be discussed in section 4).

3. Austrians on Economic Organization

Sifting through the pages of the works of prominent Austrians confirms that while they generally have had very little to say about the theory of the firm per se, economic organization and institutions have always occupied center stage. The kind of economic organization issues that the Austrians have been primarily interested in are issues of comparative systems, represented most notably by the socialist calculation debate (Mises 1920, 1936, 1949; Hayek 1935a,b, 1940, 1937; Lavoie 1985). It is certainly an anachronistic fallacy to criticize the Austrians for not discussing a subject matter that only became established in economics at the beginning of the 1970s. But, on the other hand, the Austrians had so many of the necessary ingredients of a theory of the firm that it is surprising why it was left to the non-Austrian Ronald Coase to raise the question of the existence, its boundaries and the internal organization of the firm. To locate some of these ingredients in the Austrian literature is the primary purpose of this section.

3.1. Kinds of Orders and their Governing Rules

Perhaps the most pertinent overall distinctions to be made in a discussion of economic organization are the ones between "pragmatic" and "organic" institutions (Menger 1883) and "planned" and "spontaneous orders" (Hayek 1973). While pragmatic institutions are the results of "socially teleological causes", organic institutions are "...the unintended result of innumerable efforts of economic subjects pursuing individual interests" (Menger 1883: 158). Menger's discussion is primarily oriented towards giving an explanation of the different ways in which institutions may arise; but not to the same extent towards explaining how they are preserved – and their principles of operation - once they are established. Hayek's (1973) distinction between planned and spontaneous orders supplements Menger's discussion in this regard, since his distinction is based on the different organizing rules they comprise. Rules supporting spontaneous orders are abstract, purpose-independent and general, while the rules (or commands) that support planned orders are designed and specific in nature.[71]

Although Hayek tends to dichotomize strictly not only spontaneous and planned orders but also the relevant rules that direct them – into "nomos" and "thesis", respectively – precise distinctions are in fact difficult to draw. This is because, for example, "thesis" may be of very different generality, planned orders may comprise elements of spontaneous orders, markets (spontaneous orders) may to some extent be said to be planned by business firms (as Marshall (1925) was well aware of) etc. I shall touch on these issues later on. For now I shall content myself with noting that the distinction between planned and spontaneous orders closely parallels the one between "markets and hierarchies" (Williamson 1975), or as Williamson (1991b) now says, between "spontaneous" and "intentional governance". Here are some of the meanings we may ascribe to the contrast between these two modes of organizing economic activities:

1. Full-scale comprehensive planning versus price-mediated exchange on the basis of private property rights.
2. Market socialism versus price-mediated exchange on the basis of private property rights.
3. Firm hierarchies versus price-mediated exchange.
4. Quasi-hierarchies (such as joint ventures) or decentralized organizations (such as franchising) versus price-mediated exchange.
5. Firm hierarchies versus government hierarchies.

The distinctions outlined in 1) and 2) were the themes discussed in the socialist calculation debate; 3) is the distinction examined by Coase (1937); 4) has been examined by the followers of Coase, particularly Williamson (1985), and 5) has been examined by property rights theorists and public choice theorists. It is only to theory about the distinctions in 1) and 2) that the Austrians have systematically and comprehensively contributed. But, as I shall briefly argue in the ensuing, the Austrian contributions to the cal-

[71] As Hayek (1973: 49,50) puts it: "..what distinguishes the rules which will govern action within an organization is that they must be rules for the performance of assigned tasks. They presuppose that the place of each individual in a fixed structure is determined by command and that the rules each individual must obey depend on the place which he has been assigned and on the particular ends which have been indicated for him by the commanding authority...the general rules of law that a spontaneous order rests on aim at an abstract order, the particular or concrete content of which is not known or foreseen by anyone; while the commands as well as the rules which govern an organization serve particular results aimed at by those who are in command of the organization"

culation debate provided a number of insights that are extremely pertinent when theorizing about the distinctions in points 3 to 5. This is a not a novel observation in itself. O'Driscoll and Rizzo (1985: 124) report that they find Coase's (1937) insights in economic organization "congenial" because they incorporate "...the essential conclusions of the economic calculation debate".[72] And many theorists of economic organization have noted the affinities of Austrian insights in the calculation debates to modern theory (for example, Williamson 1985: 8; Milgrom & Roberts 1992: 51). I shall, however, be somewhat more explicit and detailed about where the points of similarity are.

3.2. The Socialist Calculation Debate

The Austrian insights presented in the course of the calculation debate that are directly relevant to the theory of economic organization in the sense that they anticipate modern developments can be summarized in the following closely connected points:

1) the insight that welfare assessments of institutions and outcomes should not be based on a "Nirvana approach" (Demsetz 1969),
2) the importance of change to economic organization,
3) the understanding that economic organization should be sensitive to the knowledge and rationality that agents possess,
4) An understanding of the principal-agent relation and the importance of incentives more generally.

To start with the general methodological point, it is apparent already from Mises' (1920) opening salvo in the debate, from later Austrian contributions such as Hayek's "Use of Knowledge" article, to Mises' restatement of his position in "Human Action" (1949), that what really irritated the Austrians was their socialist opponents' use of unrealistic and unattainable social ideals – Nirvanas – as standards of comparison. Naturally, against such standards, capitalism would appear inefficient and wasteful: "The "anarchy" of production appears wasteful when contrasted with the plan-

[72] Coase does not seem, however, to have been directly inspired by the calculation debate, although his article contains a reference to Hayek's 1933 essay, "The Trend of Economic Thinking" (which marks Hayek's first involvement in the debate). As Coase has later reported (Coase 1988), he had the crucial insight already in 1931, well before the calculation debate in its Anglo-Saxon manifestation took place.

ning of the omniscient state" (Mises 1949: 692). Being the first to insist that socialist economic organization too should be approached with the tools of economic analysis, and that idealized, institutionless models should be banned as standards of comparison, the Austrians may be said to be the first economists consistently pursuing a program of comparative institutionalism. For example, the Austrians implicitly criticized models such as Oskar Lange's (1938) version of market socialism for not conforming to the stipulations of a method of comparative institutionalism. This is because 1) the socialist economists neglected the role of incentives (Mises 1936; Hayek 1940), 2) made unrealistic assumptions about the amounts of knowledge that agents can possess (particularly the plan authorities), and 3) formulated their reasoning within static models that obscured all significant economic problems. Or, in a more compact formulation, basing theory on the economics of the stationary state, market socialists such as Oskar Lange could suppress the knowledge and incentive problems of real economies.

Mises, on the other hand, insisted that "...the problem of economic calculation is of economic dynamics; it is no problem of economic statics " (1936: 121). And Hayek later seconded Mises when he made the observation that "economic problems arise always and only in consequence of change" (1945: 82). As Mises (1936, 1949) recognized, in a changeless stationary state, the political authorities could implement the existing allocation as its plan and everything would continue the way it was before. The lesson to be drawn from this Misesian insight is the general one that it is only when economic change is introduced that economic organization is determinate.[73] And the specific Austrian conclusion in the calculation debate was that in the presence of economic change, economic organization on the basis of private property and a price system was strictly superior on efficiency grounds. But the Austrian insight into how change and economic organization are related is of a wider applicability and can be given various interpretations, as we have seen in previous chapters.

In summary, one of these interpretations is the general Austrian one that we need the entrepreneurial market process to cope with the knowledge problems that economic change introduces (Kirzner 1973); and that market process performs most efficiently when fueled by well-defined and protected private property rights that provide appropriate incentives for

[73] It is precisely in such a context that Williamson (1985: 8, 1991: 162) praises Hayek (but not Mises). Misesian insights appear when Williamson discusses the adaptive properties of the hierarchy and in this context refers to Mises' (1949) distinction between "case probability" and "class probability" (Williamson 1985: 58).

entrepreneurial alertness (ibid.; Mises 1949). Another and perhaps more pertinent interpretation is to interpret the Austrian insight as anticipating the point that without change there would be no transaction and information costs; that is, in the absence of the knowledge problems introduced by a changing economic reality there would be no costs of discovering contractual partners, drafting and executing contracts, monitoring production, constructing contractual safeguards, judging quality etc. And in the absence of transaction cost, the choice between price-mediated market transactions and firm hierarchies would be indeterminate. As the Austrians recognized, in real world economies, institutions like markets and hierarchies perform the function of economizing on bounded rationality and dispersed information, precisely the factors that ultimately underlie transaction and information costs.

From a doctrinal perspective, this indicates a link between the Austrian insights in the calculation debate and the Coasian insights in economic organization, though not one that was recognized either by the Austrians or Coase, probably because they had concentrated attention on different institutions. Where Hayek (1945) praised "the marvel" of the price system, Coase had eight years earlier established that the reason firms existed was that the "telecommunications system" of prices did not perform costlessly. Indeed, some commentators have seen the analysis of Coase and that of Hayek as strongly opposed. Of course, they are not; it is only in the kind of dynamic economic reality visualized by the Austrians that Coase's argument acquires its full force.

At a more specific level, we can see several other ways in which Austrian insights presented in the course of the calculation debate anticipate or complement modern insights into economic organization. One of the most rapidly expanding areas in the theory of economic organization is agency theory. And in the course of the calculation debate, the Austrians anticipated several insights from this theory. As a general matter, they pointed out that it did not follow that under socialism, individual managers (agents) would act in the interest of the principals, that is, the planning authorities (e.g. Hayek 1940). And they identified the existence of a problem of risk allocation between principals and agents: under socialism, managers would be either inefficiently risk-averse or risk-loving in the face of career concerns and/the presence of an institution (the planning authorities) that could act as an insurance institution and take over the moral hazard of individual managers (Mises 1936: 122; Hayek 1940: 199).

Furthermore, socialist economic organization would supply a number of opportunities for rent-seekers (Mises 1936, 1945, 1949); that is, it would, in modern terminology (Milgrom 1988), provide a number of targets for influence activities and be associated with high levels of influence costs. The market socialists, in contrast, had no grasp of the principal-agent problem, or, if they had, assumed its disappearance. As has often been pointed out, Lange (1938) implicitly assumed continuous incentive compatibility between the individual managers and the planning authorities. One of the primary virtues of the market system organized on the basis of private ownership, as Mises saw it, was that it strongly mitigated potential agency problems. In the capitalist economy, the

> "operation of the market does not stop at the doors of a big business concern...[It] permeate[s] all its departments and branches...It joins together utmost centralization of the whole concern with almost complete autonomy of the parts, it brings into agreement full responsibility of the central management with a high degree of interest and incentive of the subordinate managers" (1945: 47).

Breaking the corporation up into separate profit centers is one way in which top management monitors subordinate managers. And anticipating Fama (1980), Mises (1945: 42-47) points to the existence of career concerns as important forces mitigating managers' shirking, that is, damping the potential agency problem. Agency theory, as well as the specific Austrian incentive arguments in the calculation debate, rests on more general property rights based reasoning. For example, it is fundamentally because agents usually do not have property rights to residual income streams from the productive activities they are engaged in that they may shirk their duties.

3.3. Property Rights

In chapter 5, I argued that although there are anticipations of modern property rights economics in the works of Menger and Böhm-Bawerk, it is in Mises' works that we find the most complete Austrian theory on the subject. For example, in "Human Action" there is a very clear statement of "tragedy of the commons" type problems (1949: 652), and the claim that more precise definitions of property rights – "...rescinding the institutional barriers preventing the full operation of private ownership" – will eliminate such problems. Mises also understood that property rights are composite rights. As he noted, rights to appropriate the rents and profits from assets (fructus) are crucial to the efficient working of the economy.

In fact, one of the reasons why "the artificial market" of market socialists will not work is precisely because the transfer of goods between socialist managers is not equivalent to the transfer of goods in a capitalist economy: under socialism it is not full property rights that are transferred; prices and incentives are accordingly perverse. On property rights grounds, it is inherently wrong to believe that "...the controllers of the different industrial units" in a socialist economy can be instructed "...to act as if they were entrepreneurs in a capitalistic state" (1936: 120; see also Mises 1949: 702-705).

Where Mises perhaps most explicitly anticipates modern developments - specifically the modern agency related work on how financial markets monitor management – is when he points out that for the efficient functioning of the economy, capital markets are absolutely crucial. They alone ensured that the calculation problems in a dynamic could be solved through "...dissolving, extending, transforming, and limiting existing undertakings, and establishing new undertaking" (1936: 215). Only unhampered capital markets and markets for corporate control could perform the two crucial tasks of monitoring management – a principal-agent problem – and pricing assets correctly. To the extent that the agency framework developed by, for example, Jensen and Meckling (1976) is seen as an integral part of the theory of the firm, Mises surely anticipated this theory.

3.4. Capital Theory and Business Cycle Theory

While the connection between the Austrian insights into socialist economic organization and theories of economic organization seems rather evident, capital theory and business cycle theory seem to be subjects much less connected to the theory of economic organization. The reason these theories are mentioned here is that they supply the last component in the set of concepts that are needed to give a coherent account of economic organization in general and the firm in particular. The relevant component has to do with the intertemporal structure of production highlighted in Austrian capital and business cycle theory (e.g. Hayek 1931, 1941; Lachmann 1956).

To say that the production process of the economy is a matter of a series of stages of production that bear a temporal relationship to final consumption (Menger 1871; Hayek 1931, 1941; Lachmann 1956) is equivalent to saying that the relevant productive activities are in a relation of *complementarity* to each other. And to say that expansion of credit may introduce maladjustment in the structure of production that has to be worked out over time (Hayek 1931) is equivalent to indicating that some activities may be *specific* to each other (see also Lachmann 1956). These relations can only be adequately understood in a temporal perspective such as the one in Austrian capital theory and business cycle theory (ibid.); they are obscured in the usual production function view of the productive process. And a phenomenon like vertical integration is much more easy to portray and comprehend within a sequential, stages of production framework such as the Austrian than it is within an atemporal framework such as the production function view. As recent work on the theory of the firm has demonstrated, the notions of complementarity between resources – for example, in the form of Alchian and Demsetz' (1972) team production – and specificity are necessary to tell a coherent story about firms.

3.5. Summing Up

In the preceding sections I have argued that the Austrians anticipated a number of insights that have become central in recent attempts to understand economic organization in general and the firm in particular. The roles of knowledge, incentives, and property rights were strongly in focus in Austrian theory, particularly in the context of the socialist calculation debate. This provides the opportunity to speculate about why the Austrians did not piece all these components together into something like the contemporary theory of economic organization in general and the theory of the firm in particular, and why that task was left to Ronald Coase. The candidates for explanation are many and very different.

One of them has to do with the allocation of research effort: the Austrians were always a rather tiny group of economists,[74] and the themes of the time, particularly in the 1930s, were very pressing; the subtle details of the economic organization of capitalist economies may have seemed to be of minor interest compared to debates with the market socialists on large-scale social reorganization, with Keynes on monetary policy, and with meeting the full-scale attack on Austrian capital theory that Frank Knight launched at almost the same time. But these debates meant the virtual elimination of the Austrians as a school.

Herein is a reason why the theory of economic organization in general

[74] Unless a very far-reaching definition of "Austrian" is adopted.

and the theory of the firm in particular had to await the beginning of the 1970s before it could start to blossom: the virtual elimination of the Austrian school and the increasing focus on institutionless, idealized, formal models following World War II meant that interest in the subject of institutions became regarded as the domain of Veblen-type "old" institutionalists which very few formal economists took seriously. However, developments in the 1960s in formal theory – for instance, the economics of information and uncertainty – together with developments in property rights theory increasingly implied that the theory of economic organization could be addressed with economic tools. But this rather slow process could have been speeded up had the earlier Austrian insights into economic organization not been so consistently neglected or misrepresented. Perhaps we may talk about a Kuhnian "loss of content" here.

It would be tempting in this context to say that Austrian theorizing simply was poorly articulated and "appreciative", not "formal" (in Nelson and Winter's (1982) terminology). In this interpretation, serious attention to the details of economic organization simply had to await developments in basic microeconomic tools. Now, this may be true at the levels of analytical precision and operationalization. But to obtain his seminal insight, Coase (1937) simply applied the economic tools of his day, that is, substitution at the margin, and added the concept of transaction costs. There is no inherent reason why Austrian theory would not have been able to present a similar insight. It is certainly not because it was too poorly articulated.

This is particularly so when it is recognized that the year of Coase's path-breaking paper (Coase 1937) was also the year of publication of Hayek's "Economics and Knowledge". The costs that Coase talk about are knowledge costs; they derive from the knowledge dispersion that Hayek had introduced simultaneously. Without this dispersion, there would be no "costs of using the price mechanism", no costs of discovering the relevant prices, negotiating contracts etc. So the two papers – "The Nature of the Firm" and "Economics and Knowledge" – are thematically twins – which makes it all the more surprising that no Austrian came forward with an explicit analysis of transaction costs.[75]

We shall have be content, it seems, with noting that the sort of intellectual creativity that produces new theoretical insights is a function of many factors, particularly a set of components that can be pieced together, a spe-

[75] Of course, Menger had been close to explicitly introducing transaction costs in his "Grundsätze" (Menger 1871: 192-193). For he had insisted that almost all exchange must be exchanges of unequal values – even at the margin. This "bid-asked" spread is of course a reflection of underlying transaction costs. Thanks to Brian Loasby for directing my attention to Menger's analysis.

cific context that indicates the existence of some important unexplained phenomenon, and finally a creative sparkle. As argued above, the components were there; but what may have been missing was probably the insight that these components could fruitfully be pieced together into something like a theory of the firm, as well as some intellectual context that could initiate such creativity.[76]

Here it is tempting to suggest that it was precisely the Austrian engagement in the calculation debate that blocked the application of general Austrian insights into the theory of the firm. Consider the following reasoning, akin to the one applied by Hayek (1945):

1) economically important knowledge is local and often tacit,
2) efficiency dictates that such knowledge be utilized by those who are closest to it,
3) the market allows this and is, therefore, efficient,
4) to stay in the market one has to perform efficiently,
5) some firms can observed to stay in the market. But we know that
6) the firm uses centralized decision-making.

And that violates statement 2 (cf. Minkler 1991: 9). Stated somewhat differently, what the Austrians did not supply was economic principles that could *discriminate* between firm and market on efficiency grounds. This was left to Ronald Coase, and his later followers.

4. An Austrian Critique of the Modern Theory of the Firm

In the discussion in the foregoing sections I have deliberately suppressed those points where Austrian theory is in conflict with the modern theory of economic organization in general and the theory of the firm in particular,

[76] The most comprehensive older Austrian discussion of economic organization within a capitalist economy appears in Mises' "Socialism" (1936), where vertical and horizontal integration and disintegration – among other things – is discussed in 7 pages (p.327-333). Here Mises explains that the firm's optimal size is determined "by the complementary quality of the factors of production", but does not, unfortunately, expand on this (p.328). The discussion is formulated in the context of the Smithian perspective on the progressive division of labor. Rothbard (1962: 544-550) discusses vertical integration and the size of the firm. Applying Austrian insights from the calculation debate, Rothbard argues that it is increasing calculation difficulties as the firm increases that set limits to the size of the firm. Despite a favorable reference to "the challenging article of R.H. Coase" (p.901), there is no mention of transaction costs.

and highlighted the points where the Austrians could be seen as precursors. But scattered among the Austrian literature there are critiques of contemporary economic orthodoxy that also have implications for the theory of the firm. The critiques of orthodoxy I have in mind are the strongly related standard Austrian critiques that neoclassical economics

1) is too prone to neglect the distinction between spontaneous and planned order (Hayek 1973; O'Driscoll & Rizzo 1985),
2) neglects the market process (Mises 1949; Hayek 1945; Kirzner 1973; O'Driscoll & Rizzo 1985; Lachmann 1986),
3) neglects the activities of the entrepreneur (ibid.), and
4) is too prone to introduce full information assumptions.

Let us see if these standard critiques can be applied to the theory of the firm.

4.1. Spontaneous and Planned Orders

With regard to the distinction between planned and spontaneous orders there are two fundamental overall errors one can commit on the level of economic organization. The first is to argue that what looks like a spontaneous market order is in fact the result of the plans of, typically, big enterprise, or more broadly to overlook spontaneous order altogether.[77] Historically, such arguments have been important to many proponents of socialism. The second error is to argue that spontaneous market forces are so pervasive that what look like planned orders are in reality spontaneous orders. If the first kind of error – the "undervaluation of spontaneous governance" (Williamson 1991b: 160) – was common in the days of the socialist calculation controversy, it is the second type of error we can see committed in modern contributions to the nexus-of-contracts perspective. As "nexus" theorists, Michael Jensen and William Meckling assert,

> "...it makes little or no difference to try to distinguish those things which are "inside" the firm (or any other organization) from those things that are "outside" of it.

[77] Simon's (1991: 27) parable of the "confused" mythical Martian is illustrative here: The Martian is approaching the Earth with a special telescope that reveals social structures. Boundaries of firms show up as green contours, and market transactions show up as red lines. Simon then avers that "A message is sent back home, describing the scene, would speak of "large areas bounded in green connected by a web of red lines". It would not speak of 'a network of red lines connecting green spots'."

> ...*The firm is not an individual.* It is a legal fiction which serves as a focus for a complex process in which the conflicting objectives of individuals...are brought into equilibrium within a framework of contractual relations...the behavior of the firm is like the behavior of the market; i.e. the outcome of a complex equilibrium process" (1976: 327).

Certainly, the firm may itself in a sense be said to incorporate aspects of an exchange process, besides being embedded in an overall societal exchange process; after all, firms' internal organization is characterized by various incentive schemes such as internal job ladders. But this does not make the firm a spontaneous order, as Jensen and Meckling seem to imply; the relevant exchange process is still subordinate to some overall purpose, which is sufficient to make it qualify as a planned order. Furthermore, conceptualizing the firm in the way Jensen and Meckling do basically disposes of the very problem that Coase set out to answer in 1937: why do firms as planned, hierarchical entities arise at all in a market economy? Since movements of relative prices in the nexus-of-contracts view of economic organization basically underlie all allocation – including that "inside" the firm – there can be no room for entrepreneurship and planned direction of resources (cf. Boudreaux & Holcombe 1989). This is the fundamental reason why "nexus"-theorists, Eugene Fama (1980) and Steven Cheung (1983) want to eliminate the concepts of the entrepreneur and the firm, respectively.

4.2. The Neglect of Process

The neglect of process is most acutely present in the most neoclassical of modern approaches to economic organization, the nexus-of-contracts approach. Although this approach is probably the one among modern approaches that most emphatically emphasizes the firm's (or, rather, "firm-like organization") embeddedness in a web of market transactions, no attention is given to the market process. All (contractual) outcomes are efficient equilibrium outcomes.

Much of this has to do with the way the nexus-of-contracts approach connects to property rights theory, and particularly the reasoning contained in the Coase theorem (Coase 1960).[78] A common but often im-

[78] In fact, the nexus of contracts approach is much closer to the reasoning in Coase's 1960 contribution than it is to Coase's 1937 contribution.

plicit interpretation of the Coase theorem is that if only property rights are well defined, reaching an optimal state is *unproblematic*; that is to say, automatic. Of course, this is not so. Neglecting problems of the empty core and trading under bilateral monopoly, it is obvious that agents need to *discover* opportunities for profitable trade before they can act on them (Kirzner 1973: 227). Entrepreneurial discovery of opportunities is temporally and logically prior to the (Robbinsian) realization of already discovered opportunities. But the process of entrepreneurial discovery is neglected in many versions of the Coase theorem and in the nexus-of-contracts approach as well.

Process arguments figure somewhat more prominently in the work of Williamson, particularly in the context of evolution of contract execution. Whereas contracting in the nexus of contracts is efficient on an ex ante basis, "the economics of time and ignorance" (O'Driscoll & Rizzo 1985) is present in Williamson's theory to the extent that he attempts to give a real-time account of contract execution (Williamson 1985). One consequence of this is that various ex post contracting institutions that exist to mitigate problems of ex post opportunism are given considerable attention (see further, Foss 1993b). And in seeking for the rationales of the existence of the firm, Williamson introduces the concept of "The Fundamental Transformation", that is, the semiprocess argument that in the course of contract execution, what was initially a "large numbers" situation with many contractors may turn into a "small numbers" situation (e.g. a bilateral monopoly). But this does not mean that Williamson systematically places the firm or other kinds of economic organization in a market process context. Markets that are "large numbers" are implicitly taken to be in continuous equilibrium.

4.3. The Neglect of the Entrepreneur

Neglect of the market process usually goes hand in hand with neglect of the entrepreneur. It is not surprising, then, that the approach that pays least attention to the market process, the nexus-of-contracts approach, is also the one that pays least attention to the activities of the entrepreneur; indeed, it explicitly attempts to dispose of the very concept (Fama 1980). The reason for this is, as argued, the inability within the nexus-of-contracts tradition to uphold the distinction between planned and spontaneous orders.

Furthermore, the services of the entrepreneur are equivalent to the services of all other factor owners, and can be bought on markets as well (ibid.).[79] Or, in other words, what may look like entrepreneurial services are in fact managerial services. And in the world portrayed in the nexus-of-contracts approach there is, in fact, no need for the services of the entrepreneur since all contracting is efficient on an ex ante basis, implying that all gains from trade have been discovered and that no reallocations of property rights during contract execution have to take place.

In spite of the fact that the account of agency in Williamson's theory is more dynamic than the one in the nexus-of-contracts literature,[80] no attention is given to entrepreneurship. An aspect of this is that questions of innovation and the creation of markets are (deliberately) suppressed (Williamson 1985: 142).

As Williamson 1985: 87) points out, it is a heuristic starting point for his theory that "in the beginning there were markets". And since markets are given, so are also inputs, outputs, and technology.[81] As it is the case with the nexus-of-contracts approach, the agents that occupy Williamson's attention are *managers* of *existing* transactions, shifting transactions over the boundaries of the firm. In Kirzner's (1973) terms, they are "Robbinsian maximizers"; not alert entrepreneurs.

Regarding the neglect of process and entrepreneurship in modern theories of the firm, we may observe that, in a sense, process arguments and entrepreneurship are necessary for modern theories. Austrian economics and modern theories of the firm can be seen as complementary for the same reason that Hayek's (1945) "The Use of Knowledge in Society" and Coase's (1937) "The Nature of the Firm" can be seen as complementary: it is precisely in the kind of dynamic economic reality envisaged by the Austrians that questions of economic organization become really pertinent. To update insights from the calculation debate, there would be no transaction or information costs in a stationary state; hence, economic organization would be indeterminate. So we need change to make sense of transaction costs and economic organization. In such an interpretation, modern theories of the firm implicitly appeal to a changing and dynamic reality (Foss 1993a). In such a "changing and dynamic reality" transaction costs arise because of the, among other things, need "to discover what

[79] This assertion goes back to Coase (1937). As he remarked in a critique of Knight (1921), Knight erred in seeing entrepreneurial judgment as a reason for the existence of the firm, since "..we can imagine a system where all advice or knowledge were bought as required" (1937: 92). Coase totally missed Knight's point: it is precisely because idiosyncratic entrepreneurial judgment cannot be "bought as required" that the firm is needed (see also Boudreau & Holcombe 1989) and Foss 1993acc).

[80] For example, Williamson's concept of "opportunism" is broader than the moral hazard assumption of the nexus of contract tradition.

[81] This is not strictly correct since Williamson's "Fundamental Transformation" is a story about changes in inputs and technology (Foss 1993a&c).

the relevant prices are" (Coase 1937: 83). But who will perform this act of discovery if not entrepreneurs?

At a more general level, it can be argued that the neglect of process and entrepreneurship has meant that the kind of knowledge and coordination problems emphasized in Austrian literature (Hayek 1937; Kirzner 1973) are not present in the contemporary theory of the firm. The firm does not exist because it solves coordination of knowledge type problems; the reason for its existence lies in incentive considerations. In the nexus-of-contracts approach, the existence of the firm has only to do with mitigating free-rider type problems; in Williamson's approach, the firm exists to dampen incentives to opportunism (see further, Foss 1993b). As I shall argue in section 5, the type of coordination problems that interest Austrians should be incorporated in a more complete theory of the firm.

4.4. Knowledge and Production

Harold Demsetz (1988b) has convincingly argued that while knowledge for management purposes is assumed scarce in the modern theory of the firm, knowledge for production purposes is assumed to be a free good. This is the reason why production costs are not allowed to influence the make or buy decision.

As Demsetz (1988b: 147) further explains:

> "The emphasis that has been given to transaction costs...- dims our view of the full picture by implicitly assuming that all firms can produce goods or services equally well"

This reflects the common simplifying assumption that productive knowledge is given in explicit form to everybody. But given the facts of the dispersion of knowledge (Hayek 1945), the tacit nature of much of the economically relevant knowledge (Hayek 1935b: 154-155; Nelson & Winter 1982), the distribution of entrepreneurial capabilities (Knight 1921), the Smithian benefits of specialization, and the positive costs of information, obviously this cannot be so. Even in equilibrium, production costs may differ (Lippman & Rumelt 1982). Furthermore, as Hayek (1940: 196) points out, low-cost methods of production have to be *discovered* "...and discovered anew, sometimes almost from day to day, by the entrepreneur".

What all this implies for the theory of economic organization is that production costs may in fact enter the make or buy decision; an entrepreneur may decide to bring some transactions under the corporate umbrella simply because the costs of production that relate to the relevant transaction are lower in his firm than they would be in other firms. From an Austrian perspective that places much emphasis on the tacitness and idiosyncrasy of knowledge, and on its local nature (Hayek 1945), it is quite natural to think of technology and therefore also production costs as extremely specific to individual firms. This also means that transferring knowledge over the boundaries of the firm may be very costly. For example, it may be quite costly to educate supplier firms, which may lead to some transactions being internalized. While specific technology, and therefore production costs are one side of the coin, such coordination failures are its other side. As I argue below, this reasoning may lead to a distinct Austrian theory of the firm.

It seems to me that the relation between modern theories of economic organization and Austrian economics is more encompassing than the issues of the Austrians as precursors and critics. In the corpus of Austrian economics, there are a vast number of insights that are not present in the contemporary theory of the firm. But there is also a constructive aspect to this, since it is possible to utilize specific Austrian insights not only to supplement existing theories of the firm, but also to construct a distinct Austrian theory of the firm. To briefly substantiate this is the purpose of the following section.

5. Towards an Austrian Theory of the Firm

> "Clearly, much more work needs to be done on a subjectivist or Austrian theory of firm behavior" (O'Driscoll & Rizzo 1985: 125)

5.1. A Toolbox

Our Austrian/contemporary theory of the firm toolbox now includes:

1) a grasp of the distinction between planned and spontaneous orders,
2) the market process as a process of entrepreneurial discovery,
3) property rights (incentives),
4) specificity and complementarity of assets,

5) the private and tacit nature of knowledge ("impactedness"), and
6) transaction and information costs.

As we have seen, all these concepts, with the exception of transaction/information costs, are explicitly to be found in Austrian literature. Let us first examine in which respects some of these Austrian insights may complement the contemporary theory of the firm.

5.2. Austrian Economics as Complementing the Contemporary Theory of the Firm

Where Austrian insights have most to offer to the contemporary theory of the firm is at the level of process and knowledge. To start with the knowledge issue, the Austrian insight that most economically relevant knowledge is local and tacit is not systematically incorporated in contemporary Coasian theories of the firm, at least with regard to production knowledge (Demsetz 1988b). In the non-Coasian work of Edith Penrose (1959) and more recently Nelson and Winter (1982), the firm is seem as possessing a set of "capabilities" – that is, a stock of knowledge that is idiosyncratic to the relevant firm – a view of the firm that clearly harmonizes with Hayekian insights about knowledge (Hayek 1945). Furthermore, in terms of the Austrian emphasis on capital structures and the modern distinction between general and firm-specific human capital, we may view the firm's capabilities as a particular structure of human capital. Furthermore, what makes the firm unique are the precise patterns of co-specialization and complementarity among these capital assets.

As O'Driscoll and Rizzo (1985: 124) put it, with reference to Nelson and Winter (1982), this view of the firm furthermore applies "...a Hayekian theory of rules and evolved market institutions to firm behavior", in the sense that firms are placed in an evolutionary setting, incorporating both selection through the market and conscious adaptation (though not maximization), and portraying the firm as equipped with a set of "genotypes" – "routines" – on which these effects ultimately operate. Like Hayek's (1973) rules, Nelson and Winter's (1982) routines are stable and mostly tacit patterns of social behavior that are followed – largely unconsciously – because they produced success in the past, that is, coordinated individual actions relatively successfully. It is from the firm's stock of routines or capabilities that its strategies and actions emerge.

However, not all routines or capabilities are equally efficient. This provides room for a view of the market as a continuous disequilibrium process in which, for example, certain routines are selected against, in the sense that their share of the overall pool of routines is falling; closely akin to the way that Hayek characterizes cultural evolution. Such a view is consistent with Kirzner's (1979: 134) point that

> "...under conditions of disequilibrium, when scope exists for entrepreneurial activity, there is no reason genuine disparities may not exist among different producers"

Summing up, the "evolutionary" or "capabilities" view of the firm is broadly consistent with Austrian theory since it incorporates decentralized tacit knowledge, learning, and a commensurate role for the entrepreneur.

However, as previously noted, is it not somewhat contradictory to apply insights from the theory of spontaneous order – such as evolved rules, coordination etc., – to a planned order; that is, the firm? The market/price system – the paradigmatic spontaneous order – was described by Hayek as

> "...a sort of discovery procedure which both makes the utilization of more facts possible than any other system, and which provides the incentive for constant discovery of new facts which improve adaptation to the ever-changing circumstances of the world in which we live" (1968: 236).

But may we not say that the firm, too, is a learning system in some sense? I think we can, and, in fact, should. But what saves us from committing the error of identifying what is ultimately a planned order – the firm – as a spontaneous order, is the notion that the firm, like the entrepreneur, learns about local facts. The firm is a local learning system, not a global one, such as the spontaneous order of the market.

To put forward such a view of the firm is to implicitly criticize the contemporary (Coasian) theory of the firm. For, as noted, this theory is largely a static affair that pays little or none attention to the creation of markets, and assumes that inputs, outputs and technology are given, so that the economic problem has only to do with combining these in a transaction cost minimizing manner. But it is also to suggest that the Coasian and Austrian/evolutionary/capabilities view of the firm may be fruitfully combined (see also Langlois 1991). Conceptualizing the firm as a learning, evolved entity implies that the transaction costs associated with, for example, the firm's governance of internal transactions may change over time, for example, fall.[82] And conceptualizing the market as a learning system, too, implies that transaction costs associated with market exchange will also change. Based on a processual view, it becomes conceptually possible, then, to theorize how the organization of transactions change over time, that is, how the boundaries of the firm change over time.

Summing up, we may conclude that Austrian insights complement the contemporary (Coasian) theory of the firm to the extent that one wants to go beyond merely addressing the efficient organization of existing inputs and outputs, and incorporate dynamic factors, such as learning. But it is also possible to construct a theory of the firm that is distinctively Austrian. To loosely indicate the character of such a theory is the purpose of the following section.

5.3. Elements of an Austrian Theory of the Firm

The Austrian concept that is most conspicuously neglected in the contemporary theory of the firm is probably that of the entrepreneur. Or rather, to the extent that "the entrepreneur" is mentioned, he is identified with the manager (see already Coase 1937). This simply continues a tendency in price theory to "...understand the notion of the entrepreneur as nothing more than the locus of profit-maximizing decision-making within the firm" (Kirzner 1973: 27). However, the role of the manager is distinct from that of the entrepreneur, since the entrepreneur – to be an entrepreneur – is always occupied with the set-up of new means structures. Neither is he *necessarily* to be identified with the owner/manager of the firm; what this last person maximizes *may* not be entrepreneurial profit, but rather Ricardian and Paretian rents from already acquired resources. This leads us back to the founding of firms as the relevant domain for exercising entrepreneurship.

As Kirzner (1973: 52) explains, the concept of the entrepreneur is primary to that of the firm to the extent that

> "The firm...is that which results *after* the entrepreneur has completed some entrepreneurial decision-making, specifically the purchase of certain resources".

[82] This would involve more than, for example, management's increased knowledge about the capabilities of the firm's employees. It would involve, for example, the formation of what business analysts call "corporate culture", that is, a set of stable firm-specific rules that delimits intra-firm behavior. Culture does more than solve Austrian-type coordination problems; it may also dampen various sorts of proclivities to moral hazard, and thus harmonize incentives. For a relevant early discussion, see Malmgren (1961).

But when we link this initial entrepreneurial purchase decision to the later existence of the firm, we may in a sense say that the entrepreneur continues his activities to the extent that he deploys the firm's resources in exceptionally profitable ventures.

What should interest us in this perspective is why the firm is needed at all? Why are the firm and entrepreneurial direction of resources necessary? Why is it necessary to make a distinction between "plan complementarity, the complementarity of [resources] within the framework of one plan, and structural complementarity, the overall complementarity of [resources] within the economic system", where the first type of complementarity "is brought about *directly* by entrepreneurial action", while the second kind is brought about by the operation of the market (Lachmann 1956: 54)? We could, of course, provide Coasian answers to such Coasian questions. But a more congenial, and in some respects also more interesting, way is to look for an explanation in the peculiar character of entrepreneurship.

We have it from Coase (1937) and Fama (1980) that entrepreneurship not only cannot provide a rationale for the firm but, more importantly, is largely an irrelevant concept since the entrepreneur's services can be purchased in the market. What some theorists insist on calling an "entrepreneur" is simply an owner of some specialized human capital, his services have a market price and an opportunity cost. To such assertions, we may invoke such questions as, who *decides* to hire entrepreneurs? Who discovers that some agents posses some superior stocks of human capital? etc. What such questions indicate is that we simply cannot avoid using the concepts of entrepreneur and alertness to hitherto undiscovered opportunities if we want to discuss market dynamics of almost any kind. And that is basically Kirzner's point (1973, 1979); to "move" the market, we have to transcend Robbinsian maximizing and add the category of entrepreneurial alertness. Furthermore, as Kirzner argues, entrepreneurship is – contra Coase and Fama – categorically different from all other factor services since it has no opportunity cost. Pure entrepreneurship is primarily an act of perception. What has all this to do with the firm?

What is noteworthy about Kirzner's argument is perhaps first of all that he argues that entrepreneurship is fundamentally noncontractable. One interpretation we may give this is that entrepreneurial alertness – or "judgment", as Frank Knight called the same behavioral quality – is so very much inside a given individual's head – that is, tacit – that it is too "impacted" to be traded. In exploiting pockets of ignorance in the market, the entrepreneur applies this knowledge when he discovers what the market did not realize was available or even needed at all. Kirzner's pure arbitraging entrepreneur can in principle do this. But sometimes the realization of the entrepreneur's idiosyncratic judgment will require the formation of a firm.

Fundamentally, there are three different economic ways in which one can utilize knowledge that is specific to oneself:

1) sell one's services through a contract,
2) utilize it for arbitrage purposes, or
3) start a firm.

The options that Kirzner considers are primarily 1) and 2). But 3) is also relevant; noncontractability of entrepreneurial judgment may lead to the formation of a new firm,[83] incorporating a new resource use. The economic reason? There is simply no relevant market through which the entrepreneur's idiosyncratic vision can be communicated; knowledge transmission costs are exorbitant (cf. Silver 1984). The "telecommunications system of prices" fails as a means of coordination; conscious entrepreneurial direction "supersedes" (Coase 1937) the market. Notice that this explanation of the existence of the firm has nothing to do with incentives; it is a story about market coordination that fails due to lack of necessary intersubjective points of orientation; that is, so-called "Schelling points".[84] The thing to note about this explanation is that it should appeal to those bent on Austrian subjectivism; it takes almost to an extreme (some would say, seriously) the Austrian notions that "different men know different things" (Hayek) and "different men have different thoughts" (Lachmann).

This explanation can be extended from the issue of the existence of the firm to the boundaries issue. As Lachmann (1956: 131) notes:

> "We are living in a world of unexpected change; hence, [resource] combinations...will be ever changing, will be dissolved and re-formed. In this activity we find the real function of the entrepreneur".

[83] In Foss (1993a&c) I argue that this was basically Knight's (1921) theory of the firm. It should be noted that in a Knightian context, there is also a moral hazard aspect to firm formation, since the entrepreneur's services – because of their tacitness – are particularly susceptible to moral hazard and adverse selection problems (on this, see Barzel 1987).

[84] As Malmgren (1961) argued the emergence of behavior-coordinating Schelling points were not only a characteristic of the market, but perhaps even more of the firm. Fundamentally, when business analysts talk about firms as possessing different "cultures", what they – in this interpretation – mean is that they come equipped with different Schelling points.

Now, in his attempt to carry out his plan, the entrepreneur will not bring all the economic activities that are complementary to the execution of his own under his own ownership. Many goods and services can be acquired through the market without problem. But "in a world of unexpected change" there will sometimes arise a need for new resource combinations, involving, for example, new kinds of inputs. Unexpected change will feed plan revisions. And such revisions may result in changes in the boundaries of the firm for the following reason. New combinations of resources will sometimes involve new inputs that are totally specific to the firm (Lachmann 1956). But it is often not possible to transmit precise knowledge about input requirements across the boundaries of the firm without high levels of information costs. Economizing on such costs may dictate internalization of production of the relevant input (Silver 1984).

Furthermore, the entrepreneur may decide to internalize the transaction simply because he thinks that his firm can produce the needed equipment in a more production cost-effective way than the market can (other firms). The opportunity costs of purchase in the market are prohibitive, not necessarily because of incentive problems because of opportunistic suppliers, but simply because – as the entrepreneur ascertains the situation – the firm can produce more cost-efficiently. The reason for this is that the firm, as an evolved entity with a bundle of various resources hold together by entrepreneurial direction and the rules that evolve within the framework of purpose defined by the entrepreneur, is fundamentally an entity that is specialized in *knowledge*. And such knowledge is costly to transfer (Demsetz 1988b). So whether we look at it from the angle of knowledge-transmission costs or from that of production costs, we are led to a dynamic theory of firm boundaries, one that takes seriously the Austrian notions of dispersal, subjectivity and tacitness of knowledge.

6. Conclusion

In the above, I have taken the theme of Austrian economics and economic organization through several variations. I first argued that, to some extent, the Austrians could be seen as precursors of the contemporary theory of the firm in the sense that some of the crucial insights were present in the Austrian literature long before they became standard fare in mainstream economics. Second, I argued that from an Austrian perspective, the modern theory of the firm could be criticized for being excessively static and for not paying particular attention to knowledge problems. However, precisely because of the Austrian perspective on process and knowledge dispersal, Austrian theorizing could be seen as consistent with some strands of the modern theory of the firm, particularly the evolutionary or capabilities view. Finally, implicit in Austrian economics was a distinct entrepreneurial perspective on firm organization. I should emphasize that most of this has been a matter of rational reconstruction. I have been interested in how far we can carry Austrian economics in a specific context, that of the theory of the firm. That Austrian economics may have much potential for further development, but that modern Austrians often seem reluctant to do so, will be argued in the following chapter.

9: Modern Austrian Economics and Scientific Progress[85]

1. Introduction: Examining Modern Austrian Economics

Previous chapters of this book have primarily been concerned with the Austrian economics of Friedrich von Hayek and Ludwig von Mises, while older Austrians such as Menger, Wieser and Böhm-Bawerk have been largely neglected. I have also made references to the work of Mises' pupil, Israel Kirzner. But Austrian economics did not die with Mises or Hayek, and Israel Kirzner is not its only living modern representative, although surely the most distinguished. In the United States in particular, Austrian economics has spread since the mid-1970s and gained an increasing number of supporters and converts (although its growth now seems to have come to a halt). It is this modern version of Austrian economics that is in focus in this chapter, and it will be examined from a largely methodological perspective. I shall ask to what extent modern Austrian economics has contributed significantly to the progress of economic science. Where this examination begins is with the philosophy of science.

2. Pluralism in Philosophy and in Economics

2.1. Pluralism in the Philosophy of Science

Among philosophers, as well as among practicing scientists, a leading idea seems to be that scientific progress within a discipline depends positively on the degree of pluralism and openness of the discipline. Traditionally, the idea that the growth of knowledge is best promoted within an open social structure has been an influential part of classical liberal philosophy. Its classic statement is made in John Stuart Mill's "On Liberty", and the most significant modern re-statement of the basic idea is probably Karl Popper's "The Open Society and Its Enemies" (1945). Of course, the idea is more than a matter of social philosophy; it also has methodological implications. The "open society idea", as it may be called, also applies to the society of scientists, and it is accordingly present in the

[85] This chapter to a large extent builds on previous work co-authored with Christian Knudsen (Foss & Knudsen 1993).

work of Popperian methodologists such as Hans Albert (1985) and Imre Lakatos (1970). Popper's arguments have also been strongly radicalized by the notorious Paul Feyerabend. His philosophy of anarchism, with its "counter-inductive principle", instructs scientists to suggest the most improbable propositions in order to challenge established theories and views. The rationale for this is that the disunity and inconsistency that new improbable theories imply, relative to existing theories, greatly improve the chances of scientific breakthroughs; a sort of "creative destruction" in the domain of ideas through radical and "impossible" intellectual innovations.

2.2. Pluralism, the Organization of Economics and Heterodoxy

It is not surprising that such views have often won the sympathy of heterodox economists. This is because economics for decades has been almost completely dominated by mainstream neoclassical economics or orthodoxy. According to the sociologist of science, Richard Whitley (1984), it is the presence of a unifying paradigm that separates economics from such fields as sociology, political science and management science. By comparison to the economist, other social scientists will be confronted with a higher degree of uncertainty in applying their disciplines, since the theoretical and methodological options in solving a specific problem are far greater. One of the reasons why this situation obtains is, according to Whitley, that mainstream economics is characterized by a certain way of organizing its research efforts.

Whitley suggests analyzing scientific disciplines as, what he calls, "reputational organizations". In the case of economics, he describes the structure of its reputational organization as a "partitioned bureaucracy".[86] Such a way of organizing research efforts consists of a core of formal theorizing and a number of peripheral fields of applied research where the formal models of the core are applied. However, the reason why Whitley uses precisely the term, a *partitioned* bureaucracy to characterize economics lies in the absence of a feedback *from* applied and empirical work in the periphery to the formal modelling and pure theory at the core. The reason why economics can be characterized as a rather hierarchical organization

[86] In terms of the typology of scientific fields constructed by Richard Whitley, the other social sciences may best be characterized as having flatter and less bureaucratic reputational organizations than the partitioned bureaucracy of economics. In fact, Whitley uses the term: fragmented adhocracy to characterize the way these fields are organized. That is, they are more fragmented, since new contributions are not being fully integrated into the existing structure of knowledge. Instead, they are merely tacked unto this structure in an ad hoc way.

lies in the existence of a mainstream tradition that makes it fairly easy to decide to what type of research high or low prestige is to be ascribed. In general, formal and theoretical research is seen as the most prestigious, while more applied and empirical research is given much less prestige. The heterodox critique has traditionally been that this kind of organization makes the formal core diverge more and more from the complexities of real economic life.

The almost complete monopoly of orthodoxy in economics seems hard to find parallels for in other sciences. The situation in economics for most of this century seems, according to the critics, always to have been a long way away from the methodological ideal of pluralism. Challenges to orthodoxy have been rather continuously and successfully eliminated, and the influence of heterodoxy been reduced to almost nothing. For example, historicism was influential in both the United States and Great Britain at the turn of the century, and institutionalism dominated many economics departments in the 1920s and 1930s. In central Europe, varieties of historicism continued to be strong well after Second World War. However, compared to their former glory, the modern significance of these schools is nil. From the modern heterodox perspective, this has not been a desirable development. And the explanation for the events that led to the suppression of the "old" heterodoxy is largely a matter of neoclassical economics gaining something close to a monopoly within the "reputational hierarchy" of the discipline (Whitley 1984). According to the heterodox economist, this is more than a mere matter of intellectual history. For heterodox critics have seen the orthodox monopoly as one of the dominant reasons for the alleged stagnation of the economics discipline, for example in its increasing inability to handle problems of a more practical, empirical nature (Hodgson 1992).

The not-so-surprising reaction of orthodox economists has been to argue that *if* heterodox traditions had really been better at solving the relevant problems (provided there are any), they surely would have achieved the influence within the discipline that they deserved. But, predictably, they have not. Furthermore, the sophisticated orthodox economists will argue that heterodoxy has been excessively critical of orthodoxy, as well as built on the naive belief that a negative critique is sufficient to found a viable alternative to orthodoxy. In a recent methodological contribution, Thomas Mayer (1993) quite explicitly points out that his critique of the practice of mainstream economics is an internal one, and *not* one from the perspective of post-Keynesianism, institutionalism etc. He is worth quoting more fully:

"[A] reason why many working economists have little use for books on methodology is that so many of these books consist of institutionalist and post-Keynesian attacks on classical theory couched in the language of Virtue Militant. Having been defeated on the battlefield of substantive research, they have retreated to the barren hills of methodology, from which they carry out guerrilla attacks on mainstream economics. This book is different...I like neoclassical theory" (1993: 5).

2.3. Whither Pluralism?

One lesson to learn from this brief sketch of the coexistence of different and competing theoretical traditions in economics is that the positive consequences of theoretical pluralism predicted by the philosophers mentioned above do not seem to have materialized. The society of economics has not been an open and tolerant one in which diverse, contradictory and competing ideas have been seriously compared and discussed as valuable contributions to the mutual effort of making knowledge grow. On the contrary, the existing rivalry has resulted in the contenders being locked into often stereotyped attitudes towards each other – as is, for example, the case with the relationship between orthodoxy and the modern Austrian school. The situation therefore seems to constitute something like a Kuhnian breakdown in communication, that is to say, a situation in which the dialogue has entirely disappeared or in which the parties have been talking past each other instead of conversing in a language that comprehends their conflicting paradigms (Kuhn 1970).

Again, the heterodox economist will typically complain that the heterodoxy he stands for has been consistently overlooked or ridiculed by orthodox economists. That there is something to such a complaint cannot be denied; but the case is not wholly clear-cut. With hindsight, I submit that responsibility for this breakdown of communication should be placed upon both orthodox and heterodox economists. Let me expand a bit on this assertion. On the one hand, the orthodox critique that heterodox economists have invested too many resources in negative criticism of orthodoxy and too little in building up viable theoretical alternatives is surely correct.[87] In their critiques of orthodoxy, heterodox economists have furthermore rather consistently underestimated the flexibility of orthodoxy.

[87] I neglect discussion and critique between heterodox groups; but see Boettke (1989) for an Austrian comment on classical institutionalism, Böhm (1987) for an attempt to establish "a better understanding" between Austrians and post-Keynesians, and Ionnanides (1992) for a Marxist critique of Austrian economics.

On the other hand, the heterodox critique that orthodoxy has suppressed a number of important phenomena cannot be easily rejected. There has been a tendency in orthodoxy to either neglect the significance of those empirical phenomena that could not be easily subordinated to formal theorizing, or to exhibit an excessive faith in the ability of orthodox theory to approach such phenomena in the long run (which may also excuse their contemporary neglect). And in their reactions to heterodoxy, orthodoxy has often displayed a certain "sponginess", that, in the words of two heterodox economists,

> "...enables it to absorb divergent elements around it without ever emphasizing their main points. These fringe ideas become footnotes to which theorists can refer as evidence that they have taken the ideas into account" (O'Driscoll and Rizzo 1985: 231).[88]

2.4. A Balanced Perspective on Pluralism

Until now, most existing attempts to analyze the problem of absence of the beneficial effects of theoretical pluralism in the economics discipline have been conducted from the perspective of a heterodox tradition. It is therefore hardly surprisingly that orthodox theory has been made responsible to a large extent for the fact that the predicted benefits of theoretical pluralism have not materialized in economics. In the ensuing pages I choose a different – and less traditional – starting point for my investigation of the prerequisites for theoretical pluralism in economics. Rather than placing the responsibility for the lack of interaction between orthodoxy and heterodoxy on the former, I shall begin with a brief discussion of a specific heterodox tradition in order to clarify some of the factors that block communication between paradigms. The case I shall consider is the modern Austrian school of economics (sections 2 and 3). I should like to strongly emphasize that my critical remarks about Austrian school theorizing and attitudes only pertain to its modern-day representatives. There can, in my eyes, be little doubt that the Austrian theorizing I have discussed in the preceding chapters was extremely innovative and important. For example, Austrian contributions to the socialist debate and to busi-

[88] For example, Austrian economists – those heterodox economists that I here focus on – would probably say that orthodoxy has sponged on the central Austrian concepts of the market process as an entrepreneurial process of discovery, prices as communication devices, the temporal structure of production etc. Assuredly, these ideas are known and mentioned (in footnotes) in orthodoxy, but their Austrian core is never taken seriously.

ness cycle theory are lasting testimony of the Austrian greatness that once was. Following the case of the modern Austrian School, I shall present an analysis of the relationship between theoretical pluralism and scientific progress in more general terms (section 4 and 5).

3. The Modern Austrian Research Programme

3.1. Core Propositions of Modern Austrian Economics

After the Austrian School was virtually eliminated at the end of the 1930s with the attacks of Keynes, Sraffa, Knight and Kaldor on Austrian capital and business cycle theory, and until the beginning of the 1970s, very few economists would apply the epithet "Austrian" to their work. Among the few practicing Austrians were two of Mises' students, Israel Kirzner and Murray Rothbard, and one of Hayek's students, Ludwig Lachmann. But after three decades of almost total neglect, the Austrian School has launched a major comeback since the mid-1970s, growing in number of associated economists, affiliations with academic institutions (at least three American universities have Austrian Ph.D. programs), journals, publishing series etc. Kirzner, Rothbard and Lachmann (until his death in 1991) have continued to carry the Austrian torch further, along with numerous younger Austrians.

Modern Austrians emphasize their intellectual indebtedness to older Austrians, particularly Mises. According to their own self-understanding, it is a thorough-going *subjectivism* that really sets Austrian economics apart from orthodoxy as well as from other heterodox traditions (see, for example, O'Driscoll and Rizzo 1985; Kirzner 1986; Böhm 1987; Boettke, Horwitz, & Prychitko 1986). I take this differentia to constitute *the Lakatosian "hard core"* of Austrian economics. That is, the unchanging and unchangeable component in the modern Austrian *"research program"*, tying successively developed Austrian theories together over time, and in a unified way.[89]

Somewhat more specifically, subjectivism is the Austrian code word for what is, in fact, a great many epistemological, methodological and ontological doctrines, encompassing, in arbitrary ranking, such things as me-

[89] For another Lakatosian interpretation – that differs from the present one, however – see Rizzo (1982). Somewhat in contrast to the way in which Lakatos' methodology is usually interpreted when applied to the social sciences, I shall put a bit more into the Austrian hard core than merely behavioral assumptions. Briefly, I take the Austrian hard core to be identical to what is later on called the "meta-physics" of Austrian economics, that is its ontological, epistemological, and methodological presuppositions.

thodological and ontological individualism, the claim that value is not something ontologically inherent in goods but is a relation between a good and a valuing person; the subjective character of costs; the empirical fact of the dispersion of knowledge in society ("different men know different things"); the claim that expectations will diverge (since the knowledge on which expectations are based is different over agents) ("different men have different thoughts"); the insistence that the proper approach to understanding human action is essentially an interpretive one; the claim that human action is not predictable (or at least only within very wide bounds); etc.[90] Some of these doctrines are part of orthodoxy -such as methodological individualism – while others are not, for example, the Shackle-Lachmann theme of the divergence of expectations.[91]

3.2. Austrian Heuristics

Closely associated with the doctrine(s) of subjectivism are the following *negative heuristics*, that is, the set of methodological prescriptions of the "do not" variety: do not practice macroeconomics or any other kind of economic theorizing involving aggregates; do not practice econometrics; do not explain economic phenomena in terms of equilibrium; avoid mathematical theorizing since this implies quantification and implies the illegitimate introduction of constants in the domain of human action; and a lot of other propositions directly derivable from the above-mentioned meanings of "subjectivism", such as "do not explain human action in causal terms", do not assume that costs are objectively given to an outside observer etc., etc. There is, in the Austrian methodological literature, some confusion here, since some of the elements of the Austrian negative heuristic do not follow of necessity from the central position on subjectivism: Austrians are simply not logically committed to antipathy towards, for instance, econometrics, provided it is only utilized in retrospective – historical -research. To sum up on the negative heuristics we may, however, note that this part of the Austrian program is indeed well developed. Even a favorable commentator, such as Richard Langlois (1982), noted that there "...remains a certain negative cast to Austrian methodological discussions" (p.75).

[90] For various presentations of these themes, consult Hayek (1948), Mises (1966), Dolan (1976), Spadaro (1978), Rizzo (1979), Kirzner (1982,1986). Loasby (1991) may well be the best overall and undogmatic introduction to Austrian economics.

[91] For a more comprehensive discussion of this, see O'Driscoll and Rizzo (1985), who distinguish between "static" and "dynamic" subjectivism, referring, respectively, to the subjectivity of preferences (standard in orthodoxy) and the radical subjectivism of Shackle and Lachmann.

On the level of *positive heuristics* (the Lakatosian methodological prescriptions of the "do" variety), we may single out the following: explain economic phenomena in invisible hand terms (also believed to follow from the central tenet of subjectivism, since the incompleteness of knowledge in action is thought to give room for phenomena that are neither intended nor foreseen by agents); when explaining economic phenomena, always give room for a certain amount of indeterminacy in human action; always explain in strict methodological individualist terms; focus analysis on process rather than equilibrium; etc.[92] What is conspicuously missing in the positive heuristic is what most orthodox economists would consider essential: recipes for actually *modelling* economic phenomena. To put it bluntly: there simply is no Austrian equivalent to the maximum principles of orthodoxy; metaphorically, there is no Austrian Samuelson. This implies that since the Austrian positive heuristics are very broad and general, they put very little structure on actual theorizing. What is, for example, the *precise* implication of the recommendation to focus on process rather than equilibrium? To a much larger extent than is the case in orthodoxy, such decisions are left to the individual Austrian scholar; his "task uncertainty" (Whitley 1984) is greater.

3.3. Austrian Methodology

At the level of *methodology*, all Austrians are committed – albeit to varying degrees - to a position of distinctly anti-positivistic content, ranging from hermeneutics to hard rationalism. In a general sense, almost all Austrians take their methodological cues from (rationalist or hermeneutic) Continental, rather than (analytic) Anglo-Saxon philosophies.[93] The rationalist bent seems to be the most prevalent. It is held, in short, that from the universal – and introspectively derivable – fact that man acts rationally, all the fundamental laws of pure economics can be deduced with absolute certainty. They are "apodictic", as Mises – who gave the classic statement of this rationalistic position – characterized the theorems of his "praxeology" (Mises 1949). This, of course, gives short shrift to the empiricist insistence that statements are either analytic or synthetic. This dichotomy is either rejected in an Aristotelian-Thomist fashion (Rothbard), or in a more Kantian mode supplemented by the category of statements that are a priori

[92] The most complete statement of Austrian positive heuristics is probably O'Driscoll and Rizzo (1985).

[93] Having endorsed aspects of Karl Popper's falsificationism, Hayek is a partial exception to this.

synthetic (Mises); that is, derivable from pure unassisted reason, having true and informative implications for reality nevertheless.

3.4. Kinds of Modern Austrian Economics

I should hasten to add that Austrians are not uniform in their commitment to the above-mentioned core positions and heuristics. At least three (partly overlapping) constellations of modern Austrians can be identified, differentiated by how they weigh the above principles and heuristics. These constellations may usefully be grouped around three central Austrian theorists: Mises, Hayek and Lachmann.[94]

The most self-proclaimed Misesian are a group of Austrian economists gathered around Murray Rothbard, who have recently displayed great discomfort with what they take to be deviations from the true Misesian teaching.[95] A prominent deviant is Hayek – considerably less rationalistic than his mentor Mises – who may be taken to be an important influence for the Austrians in New York University; for example, Israel Kirzner, and perhaps even more so Gerald P. O'Driscoll and Mario Rizzo[96]. Close to the New York Austrians is the third identifiable group, the one that is associated with the name of Lachmann and is gathered in George Mason University around Don Lavoie. What separates George Mason-Austrians from other Austrians is their relatively undogmatic stance, particularly in methodology: hermeneutics, rhetoric and other modern philosophical influences (fads, perhaps) are strong in their thinking (see Lavoie 1991). These are also the Austrians that have most enthusiastically endorsed the doctrines of George Shackle. What makes the association with Lachmann appropriate is that he is generally regarded as the most hermeneutically inclined Austrian, an open proponent of "hermeneutic interpretation of economic phenomena" (Lachmann 1991: 139).[97]

In spite of the above-mentioned intra-Austrian differences, I shall nevertheless take modern Austrian economics to constitute a Lakatosian research program. Undoubtedly, all three groups would subscribe to the above interpretations of subjectivism and the claim that it is the core theme of modern Austrian economics. I shall not, however, judge Aus-

[94] For various indications of the schisms in modern Austrian economics, see Böhm (1987), Rothbard (1989), and Vaughn (1992).

[95] See for example Herbener (1991) or Rothbard (1991). Herbener (1993) is very representative for the outlook of this group.

[96] See their joint 1985 book which contain surprisingly few references to Mises. (O'Driscoll has now left New York University).

[97] Albert (1988) subjects the Lachmann-inspired hermeneutic tendency among modern Austrians to a very detailed and well-argued critique.

trian economics by Lakatos' normative standards. That is, I shall not pronounce on whether Austrian economics is "theoretically" or "empirically" "progressive", has "excess empirical content" etc. My standard of judgment is more modest, and, I believe, more commonsense. I shall simply ask whether Austrian economics has been a good *problem-solver*, that is to say, has Austrian economics brought us further in the understanding of economic reality?[98] Such an exercise is, of course, a comparative one, and the standard of comparison chosen here is orthodoxy. My overall judgment is that against this standard of evaluation, the Austrians have not fared well. The Austrian program has, relatively speaking, been degenerating, emphasizing the negative aspects of its heuristics and committing too many resources to developing the hard core/metaphysics at the cost of theorizing based on its positive heuristics.[99] In the following section I detail this argument, and further argue that Austrian economics may have degenerated as a result of a too strict interpretation of Mises' methodology.

4. Modern Austrian Economics as Problem-Solver: a Critique

4.1. Economic Problems and Praxeology

Economic reality continually presents us with new problems to be handled and conceptualized. As Douglass North (1990) puts it, there is indeed "...a persistent tension in the social sciences between the theories we construct and the evidence we compile about human interaction in the world around us" (p.7). One consequence is of course that economic theory grows in response to these "tensions". As Mises puts it:

> "...it is quite obvious that our economic theory is not perfect. There is no such thing as perfection in human knowl-

[98] This perspective is more in line with that of Laudan (1977) than with Lakatos (1970).

[99] This observation is not novel with me. It was anticipated by the late Alan Coddington when he said, both jokingly and irritated, that "If subjectivist logic is followed to the point of becoming convinced that there is nothing for economists to do but to understand certain (praxeological) concepts, then the only problem that remain is that of subjugating one's conscience long enough to draw one's salary in exchange for imparting this piece of wisdom. One could, of course, having got into this state of mind, spend a good deal of time and energy in trying to convince those who engage in macroeconomics, econometric model building, mathematical economics, general equilibrium theory and so on, of the folly of their ways. But, that task accomplished, there would be nothing left but for the whole profession to shut up shop. This could become a real issue if the current revival of interest in Austrian economics should succumb to the messianic element that is to be found in some of the writings of Austrian subjectivists. We would then be faced with a situation akin to one in which there was an outbreak of Christian science among the medical profession, or a passion for telekinesis among airline pilots" (1983: 61-62).

> edge...Omniscience is denied to man. The most elaborate theory that seems to satisfy completely our thirst for knowledge may one day be amended or supplanted by a new theory. Science does not give us absolute and final certainty. It only gives us assurance within the limits of our mental abilities and the prevailing state of scientific thought. A scientific system is but one station in an endlessly progressing search for knowledge" (1949: 7).

The fallibility of science does not mean that intellectually we are completely footloose. For we can insist on the essential givenness and correctness of at least some "core" principles; principles which we take to be true and unchanging, and on which we may found our theorizing. In a radicalized way, this is precisely what Mises (1949) says with his praxeology: as long as man is man, praxeology – which is the logical analysis of the structure and implications of human action – will hold independently of spatio-temporal characteristics. Notice that this is more than the epistemic content that a Lakatos may put into his "hard cores";[100] Mises' position is vintage rationalist, explicitly Kantian, and clearly justificationist. Praxeology is more than a matter of convention in a community of scientists; it supplies the very categories *necessary* for understanding action (the Kantian ingredient). It is concerned with the basic transcendental element in the theory of action,[101] and it is – as such – "apodictically certain" (Mises 1949: 237) (the rationalist justificationist element).

This position may be seen as "a travesty", "so uncompromising that [it has] to be read to be believed" and "cranky and idiosyncratic", as the orthodox methodologist, Mark Blaug (1980: 92-93) in fact does. But I do not really think such characterizations are appropriate. This is partly because of their ahistorical flavor: that many of Mises positivist and historicist opponents were no less extremists should be taken into account. Furthermore, Mises' (1949) presentation of his methodological positions is in fact more carefully guarded and less extremist than it is usually taken to be (for instance, by Blaug). It is important to note that Mises did not claim that all of economics could be spun out of a few necessarily true theorems, although this is how he is usually interpreted. What he did say was that *praxeology* could be thus conceived. And praxeology is a theory of action,

[100] As Mises says: "The starting point of praxeology is not a choice of axioms and a decision about methods of procedure, but a reflection about the essence of action" (1949: 39).

[101] So in a sense we may understand Mises to derive his praxeology from both the transcendental argument in Kant's "Critique of Pure Reason" and the concern with our knowledge of human action in "Critique of Practical Reason".

and therefore more narrow in scope than economics (Mises 1949: 66). Economics and praxeology are not the same thing. What is, therefore, "cranky and idiosyncratic" is the position that unfettered application of praxeological reasoning is capable of handling all the theoretical economic problems that exist and may arise in the future. I think that interpreting Mises in this way is not only wrong; it is probably also mainly responsible for the lack of theoretical progress in modern Austrian economics. In other words, clinging to an uncompromising version of what praxeology implies for economic research will lead, and has led to theoretical sterility. I shall elaborate on this assertion below.

4.2. Uncompromising Praxeological Positions

Mises himself was well aware that for the fruitful and nontrivial application of praxeological reasoning to economic reality, one generally had to add empirical (contingent) auxiliary hypotheses.[102] This was in no way inconsistent with his Kantian starting-point since the distinction was crucial in Kant's own philosophy between a priori categories and empirical concepts; for example, the categories are necessary in order to possess empirical concepts at all. On this basis it may be argued that praxeological a priori concepts are necessary to conduct historical studies that utilize more contingent conceptual constructions. Mises would certainly subscribe to this view as would his modern-day followers. But the Kantian distinction between a priori concepts and empirical concepts does not allow one to claim that analysis that utilizes empirical concepts is not *theory*.

This is, however, what is being done by some of Mises' followers (such as Hoppe 1988). Here it is asserted in a most uncompromising rationalist fashion that analysis of the fact of human action is all that is needed for the generation of economic – not just praxeological – analysis.[103] The distinction that Mises in fact drew between praxeology and economics seems to

[102] As Mises says in a specific context: "The disutility of labor is not of a categorial and aprioristic character. We can without contradiction think of a world in which labor does not cause uneasiness, and we can depict the state of affairs prevailing in such a world. But the real world is conditioned by the disutility of labor. Only theorems based on the assumption that labor is a source of uneasiness are applicable for the comprehension of what is going on in this world" (1949: 65). This is simply a manifestation of the more general fact that "Economics does not follow the procedure of logic and mathematics. It does not present an integrated system of pure aprioristic ratiocination severed from any reference to reality. In introducing assumptions into its reasoning, it satisfies itself that the treatment of the assumptions concerned can render useful services for the comprehension of reality" (ibid.: 66).

[103] This view seems to have been first attacked by Hayek in his 1937 essay, "Economics and Knowledge" (Hayek 1948: chapter 2). Hayek claimed that in order to generate theory transcending "the pure logic of choice" (that is, praxeology) assumptions about the acquisition and dissemination of knowledge had to be made. Although this is often interpreted as an attack on Mises, it is not clear to me whether this interpretation really fits: Assuredly, among Misesian contingent "auxiliary hypotheses" are assumptions about knowledge.

have been missed by many of Mises' followers. Hoppe (1988), for example, interprets Mises as fully conflating the two, and explains that

> "It is this assessment of economics as an a priori science...- which distinguishes Austrians, or more precisely Misesians, from all other current economic schools. All the others conceive of economics as an empirical science" (p.8).

But so did Mises – in the sense that he emphasized the necessity of working with contingent hypotheses. For example, he engaged in debate on the role of the assumption of expectational elasticity for business cycle theory; but whether expectations are elastic or not, to which extent etc., are fundamentally contingent (Mises 1943).

It is hard to deny that the fact of human action (and its various implications) remains of little help alone; both with regard to empirical and to theoretical research, as Lachmann (1951) already pointed out in his review of Mises' "Human Action" (see also Witt 1993). To be useful, the praxeological analysis of human action must be supplemented by auxiliary and contingent hypotheses. Consider first the most obvious case, namely empirical/historical research. Analyzing a particular historical business cycle episode, we have to add historical facts about how agents reacted, how their expectations were formed etc. No Austrian economist would presumably deny this, pointing to Mises' careful distinctions between history and praxeology, and his discussions of the proper role of praxeological reasoning in historical research (Mises 1957). But in theoretical research, too, it is not at all clear that we can do with praxeological reasoning only. To stay with the business cycle example, the predictive and explanatory potential of a given theory may depend on the assumptions we make about the Hicksian elasticity of expectations. But praxeology has nothing to say in and of itself about elasticities of expectations; assumptions about these are essentially contingent.[104] However, a business cycle theory that utilizes contingent assumptions is definitely a *theory*, it is not history.

The underlying attitude among many present-day Austrians seems, however, to be that, in fact, praxeology is the last word in economics; that economic reasoning can somehow proceed without contingent hypotheses of any kind. To repeat, this is fundamentally un-Misesian, and it is also damaging. It is damaging in the sense that it restricts the problem-solving capacity of Austrian economics by unduly isolating it from economic real-

[104] An implication is that Hoppe (1988: 8) errs when he asserts that praxeological reasoning is sufficient to give "definite proof" for the specific Austrian theory of the business cycle.

ity, and thus hinders the progress of the Austrian research program. In other words, a too strict interpretation of the metaphysics of the Austrian program produces a heuristic that blocks the handling of a number of empirical phenomena. It is not only that modern Austrian economics asks different questions and gives different answers (O'Driscoll & Rizzo 1985); it is perhaps more fundamentally a matter of modern Austrian economics being unable to ask a number of interesting questions.

4.3. Modern Austrian Theorizing

To illustrate the claim that damage has already been done, consider the following important objects for economic analysis:

- the process of technological change, its organization and economic consequences,
- strategic interaction between duopolists, oligopolists etc.,
- the firm, its organization and activities.

These are fundamental and legitimate objects for economic analysis – in fact, the orthodox theorist probably would regard theorizing within them as defining the theoretical frontier of today's economics. The objects are of such empirical importance that presumably no economist would deny that theoretical knowledge about them is desirable. But what has Austrian economics told us about them? – nothing, or close to nothing (but for the case of the firm, see the preceding chapter). Is there a possible reason? Addressing most of them involves – *must* involve – hypotheses that are essentially contingent. The behavioral quality of "opportunism", for instance, which seems necessary to explain the existence of the *firm* (Williamson 1985), is not something that can be upheld as some universally valid a priori category. It may or it may not manifest itself at different times and places and with different intensity. In order to theorize meaningfully about *the process of technological change*, we have to add assumptions about, say, diffusion rates. These are contingent assumptions, not a priori categories. And the problem of *strategic interaction* is pre-eminently an explanandum that requires very specific assumptions about behavior. All the stories constructed for explaining these phenomena are fundamentally what we understand by theories. Dismissing them as "history" simply because they utilize contingent assumptions is to give an absurd twist to terminology.

All this may be taken to be a most unfair criticism; theories or series of theories (i.e., research programs) are simply not designed to explain everything at all levels of analysis etc. Neo-Ricardians have probably even less to say about the above explananda than Austrians do. Austrian economics, however, generally presents itself as a true alternative to orthodoxy (which has at least attempted to theorize about all the above-mentioned explananda) in particular (for example, O'Driscoll & Rizzo 1985). Particularly in the time period that has elapsed since the Austrians launched their comeback on the theoretical scene, orthodoxy has expanded tremendously in terms of the phenomena and problems it has conceptualized and theorized. Given the fact that Austrian economics presents itself as a genuine alternative, and given the fact that modern Austrian economics has now been in existence for nearly two decades, one seems justified in examining the problem-solving capacity of Austrian economics vis-à-vis that of orthodoxy. And it is simply quite evident that modern Austrian economics shows a sorry record here, not *necessarily* in the sense that Austrian explanations are on a lower analytical level,[105] but simply in the sense that modern Austrians have at best given scant attention to a great many important objects for economic analysis. This is the sense in which I claim the modern Austrian research program to be degenerating.

Which problems, then, have the Austrians theorized? Two types of articles seem to dominate Austrian scholarship. The first category is the historical/exegetical: what did an older Austrian think about a particular issue? The second is the critique-of-orthodoxy type, which is often constructed on the basis of the following algorithm: pick an arbitrary neoclassical theory about an arbitrary theme from an arbitrary journal, isolate its behavioral assumptions, show that it is an equilibrium theory, and contrast all this with Austrian theorizing. This kind of article easily degenerates into little more than taxonomic exercise. But there is a residue, however: the constructive, not overly exegetical Austrian scholarship of which Israel Kirzner's (for example, 1973) theory of the entrepreneur and the entrepreneurial element in the market process is probably the best representative. It is also this kind of work that *may* allow Austrians to respond to the charges of theoretical sterility, particularly relative to orthodoxy. For the modern Austrian complaint that the market process and the entrepreneur have received insufficient attention in orthodoxy is surely correct. One should perhaps have expected the Austrians to carry on their

[105] Although I think that this is in fact the case. The merits of formalization simply cannot be denied (see Suppes' (1968) classic discussion). The dominating part of the Austrian corpus is composed of rather loose "story-telling", that is, unformalized stories about e.g. disequilibrium behavior. That such "story-telling" is, however, a necessary part of any well-working scientific has been strongly argued by Nelson and Winter (1982). More on this in later sections.

honorable legacy in capital theory and business cycle theory, utilizing perhaps modern techniques for the formalization of these theories. However, most recent Austrian research in these areas (e.g. Skousen 1991) has added very little to Hayek's canonical work dating from the 1930s (Hayek 1931).

4.4. Possible Responses

In response to my critique, it may be argued that what we should look for is not problem-solving capacity, but quite simply *truth*. False theories, that is to say theories that proceed from demonstrably false assumptions, should be discarded. The problem with this is, again, that insisting on infallibility restricts us to the theorems of pure praxeology – and there really is a trade-off between certainty and applicability. There are different ways out of these dilemmas. One – a position to which Israel Kirzner seems close – is to argue that orthodoxy is not fundamentally and irreconcilably in conflict with Austrian economics. Orthodoxy is simply less general, more fallible, more contingent, than Austrian economics. In this perspective, praxeology may be seen as a kind of organizing intellectual superstructure, supplying the basic logic of action, which is made more narrow by interpreting the Misesian "man acts" as the neoclassical "man maximizes". Orthodox maximizing man, then, is simply a species of the larger Misesian genus, Homo agens – a genus that also incorporates entrepreneurship. The role of Austrian economics is then to "...supplement a largely correct but seriously incomplete neoclassical economics" (Vaughn 1992: 252).

The obvious problem with this interpretation is that it will more or less eliminate Austrian economics as an independent intellectual force, leaving behind only some loose discourse on the entrepreneur and methodology. A different approach is to keep insisting that, at the level of pure economic theory, praxeological reasoning is all that is needed. Austrian economics is then reduced to Mises exegesis or something even narrower.[106] History, I submit, will give a negative verdict on this position.

The third way out, and the one I recommend, is to link up with the many *constructive* criticisms levelled against orthodoxy by, in particular, neo-institutionalists (e.g. Langlois 1986a) and evolutionary theorists (for example, Nelson and Winter 1982). As I have repeatedly argued in this book, a whole body of subtle *new heterodox theories* exist that to a large ex-

[106] For contributions very close to this kind of Austrian economics, see Hoppe (1988), Gunning (1991) and Herbener (1993).

tent have taken up favorite Austrian themes. Linking up with the new heterodoxy, the older heterodoxy of Austrian economics may assure itself of a continued raison d'être.[107] It is to the new heterodoxy that Austrian economics is most similar, and new heterodox economists are probably those that are most likely to appreciate constructive modern Austrian theorizing such as Kirzner's work on the entrepreneur (And see Nelson & Winter (1982:41) for a new heterodox appreciation of precisely this.) Orienting towards heterodoxy would, however, seem to require a substantial change of outlook among modern Austrians. It must involve de-emphasizing often pointless critiques of other approaches, and it must involve getting out of the methodological trap that all theory involving contingent assumptions is beyond the research efforts of Austrian economists. The new heterodoxy and how it relates to old heterodoxy and orthodoxy is discussed in broader terms in the following section.

5. The Role of Heterodox Traditions in Economics

5.1. Kinds of Heterodoxy

As stated at the outset, many philosophers have regarded it as almost a self-evident truth that the more pluralistic a discipline is, the greater the chances will be of significant scientific breakthroughs. And this in turn has formed the basis for the heterodox assertion that orthodoxy's unrivalled position has constituted the major impediment to scientific progress in economics. The intention behind discussing the case of modern Austrian economics was to indicate, however, that not only orthodoxy, but also heterodoxy is to blame for the breakdown of communication. This was argued by pointing to the overdeveloped negative heuristic of the modern Austrian approach, and its correspondingly underdeveloped positive heuristic. The way that modern Austrian economics has developed has produced not only a very critical attitude towards orthodoxy but also an inability to engage with it in serious communication.

Within the last decade there has been a tendency towards improved communication between orthodoxy and the new heterodox economics, represented by neo-institutionalist economic thought and evolutionary ec-

107 In other words, I reject Vaughn's "very uncomfortable impasse", that is the proposition that "Austrian economics must either be an adjunct to neoclassical economics...or it must be a philosophically oriented account of the implications of time and uncertainty with no theoretical structure underpinning it" (1992: 271).

onomics. Characteristically, the new heterodoxy has been more sophisticated in its critique of orthodoxy than has modern Austrian economics. This is because its critical emphasis has shifted from a predominantly external to a more internal form. As a consequence, orthodoxy has not been able to dismiss such criticism as naive and unsophisticated – as it could justifiably do in the case of much traditional Austrian criticism – but has instead been compelled to meet explicitly the arguments of the new heterodoxy. Furthermore, there is an increasing appreciation in the new heterodoxy of the argument that viable alternatives to orthodoxy cannot merely be critique-based, but must be based fundamentally on positive theoretical contributions.

Furthermore, the new heterodoxy is also far more positively inclined towards the use of formal methods as research tools than are modern Austrian economists. In a Lakatosian reading, this means that the new heterodox traditions are far more complete, since they place more emphasis on the development of a positive heuristic. In the absence of the development of a positive heuristic, the diffusion of a research program in the scientific community would come to a halt. As argued in previous sections, the modern Austrian school (and classical institutionalism, as well) is a research tradition without, or with only a very weak positive heuristic. This is one of the reasons why Austrian economics is generally of little use in the concrete construction of models, and why its problem-solving capacity is correspondingly limited. It may be the recognition of this that seems to have now stopped the expansion of the Austrian school.

In this connection, it is interesting to note that several of these new heterodox traditions are based on an overall "Weltanschauung" that is quite akin to that of the Austrians. As an example, consider Andrew Schotter's (1981) and Robert Sugden's (1986) attempts to model the growth of "organic" institutions with game theoretic tools. Both theorists are explicitly inspired by Menger and Hayek's discussions of the nature of grown orders and institutions, the role of tacit knowledge, and the intergenerational transmission of rules of conduct (i.e., institutions). Further examples are evolutionary theorists, Richard Nelson and Sidney Winter's (1982), as well as transaction cost theorist, Oliver Williamson's, many favorable references to primarily Hayek's work; in fact, Hayek today is a standard reference in neo-institutionalist work on economic organization. What is interesting about the new heterodox traditions is, then, that they go one step further than the Austrians by not merely "theorizing" at a very general metaphysical level, but directly attempt to construct actual models on the basis of this metaphysic.

The sorry state of affairs – for the modern Austrians – is that the best theorizing on such favorite Austrian themes as the emergence of institutions (Schotter, Sugden), the efficiency properties of capitalist institutions (Williamson 1985), the market as a disequilibrium process (Nelson and Winter 1982) and so on has generally not come from Austrians but from modern unorthodox economists. This situation is the more ironic, since I have argued several times in this book that the true precursors of much evolutionary and neo-institutionalist economic thought are Hayek and Mises, the patron saints of the modern Austrians.

The improvement in communication between orthodoxy and heterodoxy alluded to above is furthermore explainable in terms of important changes in recent years in the interpretation of the crucial concept of maximization within orthodoxy, and the increasing willingness to work with conceptualizations of bounded rationality. Furthermore, concepts such as "selection equilibrium" or "path dependence" that ten years ago would have been strictly heterodox territory are today increasingly common ground within orthodoxy. All this implies that the fixed positions that previously characterized the relation between orthodoxy and heterodoxy, and almost ruled out any productive dialogue, are gradually disappearing. This prompts the question whether it is possible to identify something that resembles an "ideal" situation in terms of relations between research programs within a discipline? Or, phrased somewhat differently, is there an optimal degree of pluralism within a discipline? Answering these questions is the concern of the rest of this chapter.

5.2. Three Components of a Scientific Discipline

One possibility, and the first I shall consider, is to identify what constitutes a sensible balance between the different components of a scientific discipline. I propose the following distinction between important components among which there should exist a balance:

1. the metaphysical component (that is, ontological, epistemological, and methodological considerations),

2. the methodological component (development of theories and methods), and

3. the empirical component (application, testing and reaction to empirical anomalies).

In this context, different research traditions have historically placed different emphasis on alternative components. For example, in the discussion in sections 2 and 3, I have basically argued that the *Austrian school* has emphasized the metaphysical component at the expense of the methodological and empirical components.

Furthermore, it is this overcommitment to the metaphysical component that explains why Austrian economics is a comparatively inferior problem-solver. *Orthodoxy*, on the other hand, has emphasized the "methodological component" at the expense of the "metaphysical" and the "empirical" components. Here emphasis is placed on whether it is possible to formalize and design logically consistent models, while empirical and metaphysical questions are given lower priority. Finally, *the German historical school and classical institutionalism* emphasized the empirical and the metaphysical components at the expense of the methodological component. Exhibit 1 sums up.

Exhibit 1

	Metaphysical	Methodic	Empirical
Modern Austrian economics	+	–	-
Classical institutionalism/ German historicism	+	-	+
Orthodoxy	-	+	-

I submit that in a healthy discipline it is of central importance that a sensible *balance* is maintained between the above three components. It is something very close to this that heterodox (evolutionary) economists, Richard Nelson and Sidney Winter (1982) argue in the following quotation:

> "...in a well-working scientific discipline, the flow of influence is not only from formal to appreciative theorizing, but in the reverse direction as well. Phenomena identified in applied work that resist analysis with familiar models, and rather casual if perceptive explanations for these, become

> the grist for the theoretical mill...Somewhat informal explanations in the style of appreciative theory are abstracted, sharpened, and made more rigorous. These linkages also can be seen as constraints. In particular, if certain mathematical limitations prohibit formal theorizing from proceeding fruitfully in certain directions, appreciative theory tends to respond to the blockage too, and to be pulled where formal theory does proceed fruitfully" (p.47).

Nelson and Winter's case for a sensible balance between "appreciative" and "formal" theory corresponds nicely to my case for a reasonable balance and interdependence between the metaphysical, the methodological and the empirical components of a discipline. But how should it be achieved? I submit that in economics it can be achieved by a close dialogue between orthodoxy and heterodoxy, since the three components are given different emphasis within them. So pluralism may have its merit – provided research programs within a discipline can communicate.

6. Concluding Comments

On the basis of the above discussion, it is possible to be a bit more precise about the relations between the degree of pluralism in a discipline, its organization and its possibilities of scientific progress. As noted, conventional wisdom in philosophy has it that the more theoretical alternatives in existence, the larger will be the chances for scientific breakthroughs and progress. This thesis, we have seen, neglects the way in which a discipline and its historically accumulated knowledge is organized and structured. It is convenient to continue with the analogy of the sciences as organizations, and draw on some insights from organization theorist James March (1991). As he argues:

> "Organizations that engage in exploration to the exclusion of exploitation are likely to find that they suffer the cost of experimentation without gaining many of its benefits. They exhibit too many undeveloped new ideas and too little distinctive competence. Conversely, (organizations) that engage in the exploitation to the exclusion of exploration are likely to find themselves trapped in suboptimal stable equilibria" (p.1).

In terms of the metaphor about the sciences, for optimal scientific development to take place, there has to be some balance between the generation of new theoretical alternatives and the selection among them. The other side of the coin is, of course, that numerous imbalances may develop. Here I shall focus on the two most obvious.

> *Imbalance number 1: too much pluralism.* This kind of imbalance exists when a system – biological or scientific – is bombarded with new variations at such a speed that the selection mechanism cannot function in such a way that those most fit for survival are selected. On the contrary, variations that under normal circumstances would have been rejected are accepted. Applying this analogy to the sciences, this imbalance will develop under conditions of too much pluralism. Typically, such circumstances characterize disciplines where the hierarchy of reputation is very flat, or where acceptance depends only on a few hierarchical levels. For the same reason, new variations will not be absorbed in an adequate manner into the background knowledge of the discipline, but will only be tacked onto the discipline in the form of ad hoc hypotheses.

> *Imbalance number 2: too little pluralism.* This kind of imbalance is the radical opposite, and consists of a system producing too few variations. Applied to the sciences this implies that too few theoretical alternatives are put forward, leading to a stagnation in the relevant discipline. In that case, there will be too little theoretical pluralism within the discipline. Such an imbalance may develop in disciplines characterized by very hierarchical reputational organization. This is also the kind of discipline where theoretical novelties have to be accepted by several layers in this hierarchy, which implies that the chance of such novelties being accepted will be mediocre.

We may conclude that disciplines characterized by a too low as well as too high a degree of theoretical pluralism will be confronted with a string of specific problems. In disciplines characterized by a *too high degree of pluralism,* scientists become unable to make "correct" choices between competing theories, implying a gradual fragmentation of the knowledge structure of the discipline. One important consequence of this fragmentation is that it will become increasingly difficult to absorb consistently new knowledge in such a discipline, since new contributions to knowledge will simply be tacked onto the existing structure of knowledge in a basically ad hoc manner. And the low absorptive capacity in fragmented disciplines will, in the longer run, make it increasingly difficult to produce new and deeper knowledge. Conversely, disciplines characterized by a *too low degree of pluralism* will experience a number of empirical phenomena that are difficult to rationalize and harmonize with the relevant background knowledge. Typically, this will produce so-called "appreciative theory" or "storytelling" in an attempt to glue together relatively abstract models with empirical phenomena. If the formal theoretical core of the discipline is not adapted in the longer run to the "appreciative" theory, the discipline will be kept in its partitioned bureaucracy with a core of formal theory on the one hand and empirical and applied research on the other. As I have argued in this chapter, the mushrooming of a new generation of heterodox traditions implies that economics as a discipline is transcending this state of affairs.

9: Concluding Comments

This book has mainly been about the history of the Austrian school, and particularly about that Austrian theory which can, in certain respects, be seen as anticipating recent neo-institutionalist and evolutionary themes in economics. Thus, to recapitulate, we saw in chapters 2 and 3 that the early Hayek should be included in the history of the general equilibrium approach in general and new classical economics in particular. Further, I argued that Hayek and Mises together anticipated numerous insights into modern neo-institutional and evolutionary economics (chapters 5 to 8). Turning to the modern representatives of the Austrian school, I argued in chapter 9 that they could not match their patron saints, Mises and Hayek, in terms of innovativeness and depth of insight.

To observe that the insights of Hayek and Mises in particular are reflected in modern economics may lead to several reactions. For instance, the mainstream economist may believe that all that which was of quality in the Austrian approach has been absorbed into mainstream economics. As I have argued in several previous chapters, however, it is rather modern heterodox economists of the neo-institutional or evolutionary variety who may, with some justice, claim this. It is not with the patched-up Walrasianism of modern mainstream economists that the kind of Austrian economics that has figured in this book should be associated, but rather with modern Schumpeterian and Coasian theories. As I have tried to tell the story, the following themes were crucially important to the theories of Mises and Hayek, themes that largely set them apart from the Walrasian tradition, but not from modern neo-institutionalist and evolutionary economics:

1) a strong emphasis on intertemporal trade and the problems of intertemporal trade. Thus, in chapters 2 and 3 Hayek's focusing of this theme in terms of Austrian capital theory was discussed as a unique perspective on intertemporal allocation (although we should not forget that the young Hayek tried to couch this perspective in Walrasian terms). The focus on intertemporal trade is also present in, for example, Mises' discussions of speculation and the entrepreneur,

2) the emphasis on intertemporal trade, expectations, and speculation is clearly related to the Austrian view of the future as inherently uncertain,

and of unexpected change as an important feature of the economic landscape. This was one of the insights that made the Austrians eschew the Nirvana-based assessments of the market put forward by market socialists and other orthodox neoclassical economists,

3) the view of the future as uncertain and the emphasis on unexpected change, in their turn, support a view of the market as an ongoing evolutionary process, what Hayek later called "a discovery procedure". The modern Austrian interpretation of the market process as a process of alert entrepreneurial discovery (such as in Israel Kirzner's works) is one possible interpretation of Hayek and Mises' process view of the market. As I have emphasized (chapters 4,6,7), both Hayek and Mises also had another, more evolutionary, understanding of the market process at the back of their minds, one in which it is "the market" just as much as individual entrepreneurs that carries out the discovery,

4) the process view of the market and the attendant emphasis on unexpected change underlie an understanding of institutions as not only efficient responses to various incentive related problems introduced by scarcity (chapter 5), but also as evolved entities for efficiently adapting to unforeseen change (chapters 4, 6,7).

What is, as I read them, unique about the contributions of Hayek and Mises in particular is not only that they were the first economists to consistently develop a process view of market activity. It is also that they linked this process view of the market to an economic approach to institutions. In effect, they argued that when looking for the rationales of institutions, a process view of market activity contained a number of pertinent insights. This explicit weaving together of the themes of process and institutions is something that modern neo-institutionalist and evolutionary thought still has to achieve. And it is perhaps here that modern theorists may gain particular inspiration from Mises and Hayek's theories.

My reading of the theories of Mises and Hayek may of course lead one to speculate along counterfactual lines (cf. also Loasby 1994). What were the opportunity costs of the economics professions settling on some sort of Walrasianism as the analytical core? What would have happened to economics if Keynes, Sraffa and Knight had not virtually eliminated the Austrian School in the 1930s, if Walrasianism had not spread among English and American economists to the extent it did, if Keynes had not written "The General Theory" etc. Well, the "ifs" are almost too many and the abstractions too severe to make much sense of such a Gedankenexperiment, but we may nevertheless venture a few guesses.

Abstracting from Walras and his followers, the two remaining marginalist traditions of importance at the turn of the century would be the English (Marshallian) and the Austrian traditions, both of which were concerned with understanding economic change, process and institutions (although in other respects they were very far apart indeed). In both these traditions, the primary motive for developing the abstract categories of economic analysis was the comprehension of reality, and they both (though particularly the Marshallian tradition) emphasized the need to let reality influence theorizing. What they would *not* have developed into, then, would be the kind of institution and process-less formalism that long dominated the mainstream of economics.

As a result, it would, in our brief counterfactual story, have been a top priority on the agenda of economists to understand the workings of real processes and institutions with the use of economic theory. For example, the economics of socialism would not have been couched in terms of what was essentially variations on Oskar Lange's Walrasian market socialism but rather, for example, in terms of Mises' property rights approach and the Mises/Hayek emphasis on institutions as devices for adapting to change. Marshall's insights in business organization and the Austrians' insights in the efficiency properties of institutions could have combined to emerge as a theory of economic organization that would have been less static than modern transaction cost economics. Competition would not have been (mis)represented as a matter of logical consistency between a set of relations, but would be represented in terms of active rivalry. Welfare economics would not have been plagued by the economics of Nirvana. In short, we would, on this extremely speculative reading, not have to wait until the mid-1970s to arrive at a realistic economic theory of institutions and an evolutionary theory of economic change. We would have had something like them much earlier.

That has not been the fate of economics. But the development from Walrasian formalism has not, it now seems, been a *completely* rigid and path-dependent affair. For the mainstream tradition itself may have slowly begun to change, in the crucial sense that its core propositions are gradually becoming questioned. For many years, mainstream economics simply "assimilated" new empirical problems and the insights of adjacent theoretical approaches in terms of the fundamental apparatus of equilibrium, maximization and stable preferences. However, the essence of neither the empirical problems nor the relevant theoretical approaches were taken seriously. The approach pioneered at Chicago University, and best associated with Gary Becker, is probably the prime example of the attempt to assimilate numerous new phenomena, without letting conceptualizations of these new phenomena in any way influence the fundamental explanatory apparatus.

By contrast, the recent decade (perhaps, decades) seems to have witnessed a growing willingness among many other mainstream economists to increasingly let conceptualizations of empirical phenomena significantly influence theorizing. The fact that bounded rationality, path dependence, and genuine uncertainty are now taken seriously by many mainstream economists, that "custom", "norms" and "rules" figure prominently in economic discourse etc., is evidence of this changed orientation. And this attitude was, I have argued, precisely characteristic of the Austrians of the mid-war period. Perhaps the open-minded mainstream economist will, in a few years, even begin to let concepts such as the entrepreneur and the market process influence his theorizing. In that case, there will be very little substantive difference between "open" mainstream economics and Austrian economics.

It seems traditionally to have been the fate of the Austrians to stand outside the mainstream, their ideas later on being absorbed – though incompletely absorbed - into this mainstream. However, one *may* argue that the mainstream does not just "sponge" on Austrian ideas anymore, but may be on the brink of coming to grips with their essence. A diehard modern Austrian may deny that, of course; however, it is harder to deny that what was called in chapter 9 "the new heterodoxy" of neo-institutionalist and evolutionary thought has incorporated and theorized numerous Austrian themes in terms of a "metaphysics" that is broadly similar to the one underlying Austrian economics. In fact, this has been one of the main messages of this book.

This does not necessarily exclude the possibility of still calling oneself "an Austrian". To paraphrase what Paul Samuelson once said about the Chicago school, Austrian economics is in some sense "a state of mind", rather than a distinct and coherent research program; it is, as discussed in chapter 9, primarily a "metaphysical" affair. But the profession may probably benefit from being continually reminded by a few eccentrics arguing, on a "metaphysical" basis, that genuine uncertainty should not be suppressed, that competition is a dynamic affair, that expectations normally diverge, that rational expectations strain credulity, that entrepreneurship is of paramount importance, that the subjective nature of costs renders cost/benefit analysis in the public domain problematic etc. In this scenario, modern Austrian economics may serve as a sort of continuous reminder that in a number of dimensions, neoclassical economics and perhaps even neo-institutionalist and evolutionary economics do not dig deeply enough.

That is probably the future role of Austrian economics, and it is an honorable one, *provided* the Austrians are willing to engage in dialogue with mainstream economists and with the new heterodoxy of neo-institutionalist and evolutionary economics. That this dialogue may slowly be starting is marked by the recent publication of such open-minded books as Karen Vaughn's (1994) "Austrian Economics in America: the Migration of a Tradition", and the anthology edited by Bruce Caldwell and Stephan Böhm (1993), "Austrian Economics: Tensions and New Directions", in which numerous Austrian fellow-travellers are brought together in an attempt to broaden the scope of Austrian economics and begin the dialogue. To the extent that a dialogue will successfully begin, the prediction of chapter 9 that the Austrian research program will continue to degenerate may yet prove false.

References

Abernathy, W.J. & J.M. Utterback (1978): Patterns of Industrial Innovation. In M.L. Tushman & W.L. Moore (eds.) (1988): *Readings in the Management of Innovation. Cambridge, MA: Ballinger.*

Albert, H. (1985): *A Treatise on Critical Reason*. Princeton: Princeton University Press.

Albert, H. (1988): Hermeneutics and Economics: A Criticism of Hermeneutical Thinking in the Social Sciences. *Kyklos* 41: 573-602.

Alchian, A.A. (1950): Uncertainty, Evolution and Economic Theory. In *idem*. (1977).

Alchian, A.A. (1965): Some Economics of Property Rights. In *idem*. (1977).

Alchian, A.A. (1969): Corporate Management and Property Rights. In *idem*.(1977).

Alchian, A.A. (1977): *Economic Forces at Work*. Indianapolis: Liberty Press.

Alchian, A.A. (1984): Specificity, Specialization and Coalitions. *Zeitschrift für die gesamte Staatswissenschaft 140: 34-49.*

Alchian, A.A. & W. Allen (1964): *University Economics*. Belmont: Wadsworth.

Alchian, A.A. & H. Demsetz (1972): Production, Information Costs, and Economic Organization. In *Demsetz*, H. (1988).

Alchian, A.A. & S. Woodward (1988): The Firm is Dead; Long Live the Firm. *Journal of Economic Literature 26*: 65-79.

Alessi, L.D. (1969): Implications of Property Rights for Government Investment Choices. *American Economic Review 59*: 13-24.

Alessi, L.D. (1980): The Economics of Property Rights: A Review of the Evidence. *Research in Law and Economics 2*: 1-47.

Alessi, L.D. (1983): Property Rights, Transaction Costs, and X-Efficiency: An Essay in Economic Theory. *American Economic Review* 73: 64-81.

Alessi, L.D. (1987): Property Rights and Privatization. In S.H. Hanke (ed.) (1987): Prospects for Privatization. New York: APS.

Arrow, K.J. (1987a): Reflections on the Essays. In G. Feiwel (ed.) (1987): *Arrow and the Foundations of the Theory of Economic Policy*. New York: New York University Press.

Arrow, K.J. (1987b): Rationality of Self and Others in an Economic System. *In R.M. Hogarth & M.W. Reder* (1987).

Barnard, C. (1938): *The Functions of the Executive.* Reprint 1962. Cambridge, MA.: Harvard University Press.

Barone, E. (1908): The Ministry of Production in the Collectivist State. In *A. Nove and D.M. Nuti (1972)*.

Barzel, Y. (1974): A Theory of Rationing by Waiting. *Journal of Law and Economics 17*: 73-96.

Barzel, Y. (1987): The Entrepreneur's Reward for Self-Policing. *Economic Inquiry 25:* 103-116.

Barzel, Y. (1989): *Economic Analysis of Property Rights.* Cambridge: Cambridge University Press.

Bauer, T. (1978): Investment Cycles in Planned Economies. *Acta Oeconomica*: 243-260.

Baumol, W.J. (1977): *Economic Theory and Operations Analysis*. Englewood Cliffs: Prentice Hall.

Baumol, W.J. (1982): Contestable Markets: An Uprising in the Theory of Industry Structure. *American Economic Review* 72: 1-15.

Baumol, W.J., J.C. Panzar, & R.D. Willig (1982): *Contestable Markets and the Theory of Industry Structure.* New York: Harcourt, Brace, Jovanovich.

Bergson, A. (1948): Socialist Economics. In H.S. Ellis (ed.) (1948): *A Survey of Contemporary Economics*. Homewood: Richard Irwin.

Bhaskar, R. (1978): *A Realist Theory of Science.* London: Harvester Wheatsheaf.

Binmore, K. (1989): *Foundations of Game Theory*. Cambridge: Cambridge University Press.

Blaug, M. (1980): *The Methodology of Economics or How Economists Explain*. Cambridge: Cambridge University Press.

Boettke, P.J. (1989): Evolution and Economics: Austrians as Institutionalists. *Research in the History of Economic Thought and Methodology 6:* 73-89.

Boettke, P., S. Horwitz, & D. Prychitko (1986): Beyond Equilibrium Economics: Reflections on the Uniqueness of the Austrian Tradition. *Market Process* 4: 6-9

Boudreaux, D. & R.G. Holcombe (1989): The Coasian and Knightian Theories of the Firm. *Managerial and Decision Economics 10*: 147-154.

Buchanan, J.M. (1969): *Cost and Choice*. Chicago: Markham Publishing Company.

Buchanan, J.M. (1975): *The Limits of Liberty*: Between Anarchy and Leviathan. Chicago: University of Chicago Press.

Böhm, S. (1987): Subjectivism and Post-Keynesianism: Towards a Better Understanding. In J. Pheby (ed.) (1987): *New Directions in Post-Keynesian Economics*. Aldershot: Edward Elgar.

Böhm-Bawerk, E.v. (1881): Whether Legal Rights and Relationships are Economic Goods. In H. Sennholz (ed.) (1962): *Shorter Classics of Böhm-Bawerk*. South Holland: Libertarian Press.

Böhm-Bawerk, E.v. (1891): *Positive Theory of Capital*. London: Macmillan.

Böhm-Bawerk, E.v. (1898): Rezension: Bergmann, E.v. (1895): Die Wirtschaftskrisen. *Zeitschrift für Volkswirtschaft, Sozialpolitik und Verwaltung*: 132-133.

Böhm-Bawerk, E.v. (1901): The Function of Savings. *Annals of the American Academy of Political and Social Science*: 59-69.

Caldwell, B. (1982): *Beyond Positivism: Economic Methodology in the Twentieth Century*. Cambridge: Cambridge University Press.

Caldwell, B.J. (1984): Praxeology and Its Critics: An Appraisal. *History of Political Economy 16*: 363-379.

Caldwell, B. (1988): Hayek's Transformation. *History of Political Economy 20*: 513-542.

Caldwell, B.J. & S. Böhm (eds.) (1993): *Austrian Economics: Tensions and New Directions*. Boston: Kluwer.

Casson, M. (1982): *The Entrepreneur: An Economic Theory*. Oxford: Martin Robertson.

Chandler, A.D. (1977): *The Visible Hand: The Managerial Revolution in American Business*. Cambridge: Harvard University Press.

Chandler, A.D. (1992): Organizational Capabilities and the Economic History of the Industrial Enterprise. *Journal of Economic Perspectives 6*: 79-100.

Cheung, S.N.S. (1974): A Theory of Price Control. *Journal of Law and Economics 17*: 53-71.

Cheung, S.N.S. (1983): The Contractual Nature of the Firm. *Journal of Law and Economics 26*: 1-22.

Cheung, S.N.S. (1992): On the New Institutional Economics. In *Werin, L. & H. Wijkander (1992)*.

Coase, R. (1937): The Nature of the Firm. *Economica 4*: 386-405.

Coase, R. (1960): The Problem of Social Cost. *Journal of Law and Economics 3*: 1-44.

Coase, R.H. (1988): The Nature of the Firm: Origin. *Journal of Law, Economics and Organization 4*: 3-17.

Coddington, A. (1983): *Keynesian Economics: The Search for First Principles*. London: George Allen and Unwin.

Debreu, G. (1959): *Theory of Value*. New York: Wiley.

Demsetz, H. (1964): The Exchange and Enforcement of Property Rights. In *idem*. (1988).

Demsetz, H. (1967): Toward a Theory of Property Rights. In idem. (1988a): *Ownership, Control, and the Firm*. Oxford: Basil Blackwell.

Demsetz, H. (1969): Information and Efficiency: Another Viewpoint. *Journal of Law and Economics 10*: 1-22.

Demsetz, H. (1982): *Economic, Legal and Political Dimensions of Competition*. Amsterdam: North-Holland.

Demsetz, H. (1988a): *Ownership, Control and the Firm*. Oxford: Basil Blackwell.

Demsetz, H. (1988b): The Theory of the Firm Revisited. *Journal of Law, Economics and Organization 4:* 141-162.

Dickinson, H.D. (1933): Price Formation in a Socialist Community. *Economic Journal 43*: 237-250.

Dickinson, H.D. (1937): Book Review: "Socialism. By Ludwig von Mises". *Economic Journal 47*: 96-97.

Dolan, E. (ed.) (1976): *The Foundations of Modern Austrian Economics*. Kansas City: Sheed Andrews and Macneel.

Dosi, G. et al. (eds) (1988): *Technological Change and Economic Theory*. London: Pinter.

Dosi, G., D.J. Teece, S.G. Winter, R.P. Rumelt (1993): Toward A Theory of Corporate Coherence. *Unpublished working paper*.

Dostaler, G. (1991): The Debate Between Hayek and Keynes. In W.J. Barber (ed.) (1991): *Perspectives on the History of Economic Thought, Vol. 6: Themes in Keynesian Criticism and Supplementary Modern Topics*. Brookfield: Edward Elgar.

Douma, S. & H. Schreuder (1991): *Economic Approaches to Organizations*. New York: Prentice Hall.

Dow, G. (1987): The Function of Authority in Transaction Cost Economics. *Journal of Economic Behavior and Organization 8*: 13-38.

Durbin, E.F.M. (1935): *The Problem of Credit Policy*. London: Chapman and Hall.

Ebeling, R.M. (1993): Economic Calculation Under Socialism: Ludwig von Mises and His Predecessors. *In J.M., Herbener* (1993).

Eggertson, T. (1990): *Economic Behavior and Institutions*. Cambridge: Cambridge University Press.

Ellis, H.S. (1934): *German Monetary Theory, 1905-1933*. Cambridge: Harvard University Press.

Elster, J. (1983): *Explaining Technical Change*. Cambridge: Cambridge University Press.

Fama, E. (1980): Agency Problems and the Theory of the Firm. *Journal of Political Economy 88*: 288-307.

Fisher, F.M. (1983): *Disequilibrium Foundations of Equilibrium Economics*. Cambridge: Cambridge University Press.

Fisher, F.M., J.J. McGowan, & J.E. Greenwood (1983): *Folded, Spindled and Mutilated: Economic Analysis and U.S. v. IBM*. Cambridge, MA: MIT Press.

Fitoussi, J.-P. & K. Velupillai (1987): Studies in Business Cycle Theory: A Review Essay. *Journal of Money, Credit and Banking 19*: 122-130.

Foss, N.J. (1991): The Suppression of Evolutionary Approaches in Economics: The Case of Marshall and Monopolistic Competition. *Methodus 3*: 65-72. (Reprinted in G. Hodgson (ed.) (1994): *Economics and Biology*. Cheltenham: Elgar).

Foss, N.J. (1993a): Theories of the Firm: Contractual and Competence Perspectives. *The Journal of Evolutionary Economics 3*: 127-144.

Foss, N.J. (1993b) : The Two Coasian Traditions. *Review of Political Economy 5*: 508-532.

Foss, N.J. (1993c): More on Knight and the Theory of the Firm. *Managerial and Decision Economics 14*: 269-276.

Foss, N.J. (1994): Realism and Evolutionary Economics. *Journal of Social and Evolutionary Systems 17*: 21-40.

Foss, N.J. (1995): More on "Hayek's Transformation". Forthcoming in *History of Political Economy*.

Foss, N.J. & C. Knudsen (1993): Pluralism and Scientific Progress. *Working Paper 93-8*, Institute of Industrial Economics and Strategy, Copenhagen Business School.

Friedman, M. (1953): The Methodology of Positive Economics. In idem. *Essays in Positive Economics*. Chicago: University of Chicago Press.

Frydman, R. (1984): Individual Rationality and Decentralization. In R. Frydman & E.S. Phelps (eds.) (1984): *Individual Forecasting and Aggregate Outcomes*. New York: New York University Press.

Furubotn, E.G. (1991): General Equilibrium Models, Transaction Costs, and the Concept of Efficient Allocation in a Capitalist Economy. *Journal of institutional and Theoretical Economics 147*: 662-686.

Furubotn, E.G. & S. Pejovich (1972): Property Rights and Economic Theory: A Survey of Recent Literature. *Journal of Economic Literature 10*: 1137-1162.

Gamble, A. (1985/1986): Capitalism or Barbarism: The Austrian Critique of Socialism. *The Socialist Register*. Ed. by R. Miliband, J. Saville, M. Liebman, & L. Panitch. pp. 355-372.

Garrison, R.W. (1985): Intertemporal Coordination and the Invisible Hand. History of *Political Economy 17*: 309-319.

Garrison, R.W. (1993): Mises and His Methods. In *Herbener, J.* (1993).

Grossman, S.J. & O.D. Hart (1986): The Costs and Benefits of Ownership. *Journal of Political Economy 94*: 671-719.

Gunning, J.P. (1991): *The New Subjectivist Revolution*. Savage: Rowman & Littlefield.

Hahn, F.H. (1973): *On the Notion of Equilibrium in Economics*. Oxford: Oxford University Press.

Hahn, F.H. (1982): Reflections on the Invisible Hand. *Lloyd's Bank Review 144*: 1-21.

Hahn, F.H. (1984): *Equilibrium and Macroeconomics*. Cambridge: Cambridge University Press.

Hahn, F.H. (1987): Information, Dynamics and Equilibrium. *Scottish Journal of Political Economy 34*: 321-334.

Hahn, F. (1990): On Some Economic Limits in Politics. In J. Dunn (ed.) (1990): *The Economic Limits to Modern Politics*. Cambridge: Cambridge University Press.

Hansen, A.H. (1933): Review: "Prices and Production". *American Economic Review 23*: 332-335.

Hawtrey, R.G. (1932): Review: "Prices and Production". *Economica 12*: 119-125.

Hayek, F.A.v. (1928): Intertemporal Price Equilibrium and Movements in the Value of Money. In idem. (1984): *Money, Capital and Fluctuations*. London: Routledge and Kegan Paul.

Hayek, F.A.v. (1931a): Reflections on the Pure Theory of Money of Mr. J.M. Keynes (Part I). *Economica 11*: 270-295.

Hayek, F.A.v. (1931b): A Rejoinder to Mr. Keynes. *Economica 11*: 398-403.

Hayek, F.A.v. (1932a): Reflections on the Pure Theory of Money of Mr. J.M. Keynes (Part II). *Economica 12*: 22-44.

Hayek, F.A.v. (1932b): Money and Capital – A Reply. Economic Journal 42: 237-249.

Hayek, F.A.v. (1932c): Review: "Trade Depression and the Way Out", by R.G. Hawtrey. *Economica 12*: 126-127.

Hayek, F.A.v. (1933a): *Monetary Theory and the Trade Cycle* (German original 1929). Reprint 1966. New York: Augustus M. Kelley.

Hayek, F.A.v. (1933b): Price Expectations, Monetary Disturbances and Malinvestments. In *idem.* (1939).

Hayek, F.A.v. (1935a): *Prices and Production* (1st ed. 1931). London: George Routledge.

Hayek, F.A.v. (ed.) (1935b): *Collectivist Economic Planning.* London: Routledge.

Hayek, F.A.v. (1935c): The Nature and History of the Problem. In *idem.* (1948).

Hayek, F.A.v. (1935d): The State of the Debate. In *idem.* (1948).

Hayek, F.A.v. (1935e): Maintaining Capital Intact. In *idem.* (1939).

Hayek, F.A.v. (1937): Economics and Knowledge. In *idem.* (1948).

Hayek, F.A.v. (1939): *Profits, Interest and Investment.* Reprint 1975. Clifton: Augustus M. Kelley.

Hayek, F.A.v. (1940): The Competitive "Solution". In *idem.* (1948).

Hayek, F.A.v. (1941): *The Pure Theory of Capital.* Reprint 1975. Chicago: University of Chicago Press.

Hayek, F.A.v. (1943): A Commodity Reserve Currency. *Economic Journal 53*: 176-184.

Hayek, F.A.v. (1944) : The Road to Serfdom. Chicago: University of Chicago Press.

Hayek, F.A.v. (1945): The Use of Knowledge in Society. In *idem.* (1948).

Hayek, F.A.v. (1946): The Meaning of Competition. In *idem.*(1948).

Hayek, F.A.v. (1948): *Individualism and Economic Order.* Chicago: University of Chicago Press.

Hayek, F.A.v. (1952): *The Counter-Revolution of Science: Studies in the Abuse of Reason.* Reprint 1979. Indianapolis: Liberty Press.

Hayek, F.A.v. (1967): *Studies in Philosophy, Politics and Economics.* London: Routledge and Kegan Paul.

Hayek, F.A.v. (1968): Competition as a Discovery Procedure. In *idem.* (1978).

Hayek, F.A.v. (1973): *Law, Legislation and Liberty, Vol. 1.: Rules and Order.* Chicago: University of Chicago Press.

Hayek, F.A.v. (1974): The Pretence of Knowledge. In *idem.* (1978).

Hayek, F.A.v. (1978): *New Studies in Philosophy, Politics, Economics and the History of Ideas*. London: Routledge and Kegan Paul.

Herbener, J.M. (1991): Ludwig von Mises and the Austrian School of Economics. *Review of Austrian Economics 5*: 33-50.

Herbener, J.M. (ed.) (1993): *The Meaning of Ludwig von Mises*. Norwell: Kluwer.

Hicks, J.R. (1933): Equilibrium and the Cycle. In *idem*. (1982).

Hicks, J.R. (1935): A Suggestion for Simplifying the Theory of Money. In *idem*. (1982).

Hicks, J.R. (1967): The Hayek Story. In idem. (1967): *Critical Essays in Monetary Theory*. Oxford: Oxford University Press.

Hicks, J.R. (1982): *Money, Interest and Wages: Collected Essays, Vol. 2*. Oxford: Basil Blackwell.

Hill, M. (1933): The Period of Production and Industrial Fluctuations. *Economic Journal 43*: 599-610.

Hodgson, G. (1988): *Economics and Institutions*. Oxford: Polity Press.

Hodgson, G. (1992): The Reconstruction of Economics: Is There Still a Place for Neoclassical Theory? *Journal of Economic Issues 26*: 749-767.

Hoff, T.J. (1948): *Economic Calculation in the Socialist Society*. Originally Norwegian 1938. London: William Hodge.

Hogarth, R.M. & M.W. Reder (1987): *Rational Choice: The Contrast between Economics and Psychology*. Chicago: University of Chicago Press.

Holmstrom, B.R. & J. Tirole (1989): The Theory of the Firm. In R. Schmalensee & R.D. Willig (eds.) (1989): *Handbook of Industrial Organization*. Amsterdam: North-Holland.

Hoppe, H.-H. (1988): *Praxeology and Economic Science*. Auburn: Ludwig von Mises Institute.

Hurwicz, L. (1971): Centralization and Decentralization in Economic Processes. In O. Eckstein (ed.) (1971): *Comparison of Economic Systems: Theoretical and Methodological Approaches*. Berkeley: University of California Press.

Hurwicz, L. (1973): The Design of Resource Allocation Mechanisms. In K.J. Arrow & L. Hurwicz (eds.) (1979): *Studies in Resource Allocation Processes*. Cambridge: Cambridge University Press.

Hurwicz, L. (1984): Economic Planning and the Knowledge Problem: A Comment. *Cato Journal 4*: 419-425.

Ikeda, S. (1990): Market Process Theory and "Dynamic" Theories of the Market. *Southern Economic Journal 57*: 75-92.

Ingrao, B. & G. Israel (1990): *The Invisible Hand: Economic Equilibrium in the History of Science.* Cambridge: MIT Press.

Ionnanides, S. (1992): *The Market, Competition, and Democracy: A Critique of Neo-Austrian Economics.* Cheltenham: Edward Elgar.

Jensen, M.C. & W.H. Meckling (1976): Theory of the Firm: Managerial Behavior, Agency Costs, and Ownership Structure. *Journal of Financial Economics 3*: 305-360.

Jensen, M.C. & W.H. Meckling (1992): Specific and General Knowledge and Organizational Structure. In *L. Werin & H. Wijkander* (1992).

Keizer, W. (1987): Two Forgotten Articles by Ludwig von Mises on the Rationality of Socialist Economic Calculation. *Review of Austrian Economics 1*: 109-122.

Keizer, W. (1989): Recent Reinterpretations of the Socialist Calculation Debate. *Journal of Economic Studies 16*: 63-83.

Keynes, J.M. (1914): Review of L. von Mises and F. Bendixen. *Economic Journal 24*: 417.

Keynes, J.M. (1930): *A Treatise on Money: Vol. 1.: The Pure Theory of Money.* London: Macmillan.

Keynes, J.M. (1931): The Pure Theory of Money: A Reply to Dr. Hayek. *Economica 11*: 387-397.

Keynes, J.M. (1936): *The General Theory of Employment, Interest and Money.* London. Macmillan.

Keynes, J.M. (1944): A Note by Lord Keynes. *Economic Journal 54*: 429-430.

Keynes, J.M. (1973): *The General Theory and After. Part I: Preparations* (Collected Writings, vol. 13). London: Macmillan.

Kirman, A. (1989): The Intrinsic Limits of Modern Economic Theory: The Emperor has no Clothes. *The Economic Journal 99*: 126-139.

Kirman, A.P. (1992): Whom or What Does the Representative Individual Represent? *Journal of Economic Perspectives 6*: 117-136.

Kirzner, I.M. (1962): Rational Action and Economic Theory. *Journal of Political Economy 70*: 380-385.

Kirzner, I.M. (1973): *Competition and Entrepreneurship.* Chicago: University of Chicago Press.

Kirzner, I.M. (1979): *Perception, Opportunity and Profit.* Chicago: University of Chicago Press.

Kirzner, I.M. (ed.) (1982): *Method, Process and Austrian Economics.* Lexington: Lexington Books.

Kirzner, I.M. (1983): Book Review: Schumpeterian Economics, edited by Helmut Frisch. *Journal of Economic Literature 21*: 1501-1502.

Kirzner, I.M. (1984): Economic Planning and the Knowledge Problem. *Cato Journal 4*: 407-418.

Kirzner, I.M. (ed.) (1986): *Subjectivism, Intelligibility and Economic Understanding*. London: Macmillan.

Kirzner, I.M. (1988): The Economic Calculation Debate: Lessons for Austrians. *Review of Austrian Economics 2*: 1-18.

Kirzner, I.M. (1992): Knowledge Problems and Their Solutions: Some Relevant Distinctions. In idem. (1992): *The Meaning of Market Process: Essays in the Development of Modern Austrian Economics*. London: Routledge.

Knight, F.H. (1921): *Risk, Uncertainty and Profit*. Reprint 1965. New York: Augustus M. Kelley.

Knight, Frank H. (1924): Some Fallacies in the Interpretation of Social Cost. In G.J. Stigler & K.E. Boulding (eds.) (1952): *Readings in Price Theory*. Chicago: Richard D. Irwin.

Koopmans, T.C. (1951): *Activity Analysis of Production and Allocation*. New York: John Wiley.

Koopmans, T.C. (1957): *Three Essays on the State of Economic Science*. New York: McGraw-Hill.

Koppl, R. (1992): Invisible-Hand Explanations and Neoclassical Economics: Towards a Post Marginalist Economics. *Journal of Institutional and Theoretical Economics 148*: 292-313.

Kreps, D.M. (1990): *A Course in Microeconomic Theory*. New York: Harvester Wheatsheaf.

Kreps, D. (1992): Static Choice in the Presence of Unforeseen Contingencies. In P. Dasgupta et al. (eds.) (1992): *Economic Analysis of Markets and Games: Essays in Honor of Frank Hahn*. Cambridge: Cambridge University Press.

Kuhn, T. (1970): *The Structure of Scientific Revolutions*. 2nd ed. Chicago: University of Chicago Press.

Kuznets, S. (1930): Equilibrium Economics and Business Cycle Theory. *Quarterly Journal of Economics 44*: 381-415.

Lachmann, L.M. (1951): The Science of Human Action. In idem. (1977): *Capital, Expectations, and the Market Process*. Kansas City: Sheed Andrews and McNeel.

Lachmann, L.M. (1971): *The Legacy of Max Weber*. London: Heinemann.

Lachmann, L.M. (1973): *Macroeconomic Thinking and the Market Economy*. London: Institute of Economic Affairs.

Lachmann, L.M. (1976): From Mises to Shackle: An Essay on Austrian

Economics and the Kaleidic Society. *Journal of Economic Literature 14*: 54-62.

Lachmann, L.M. (1982): The Salvage of Ideas. *Zeitschrift für die gesamte Staatswissenschaft 138*: 629-645.

Lachmann, L.M. (1986): *The Market as an Economic Process*. Oxford: Basil Blackwell.

Lachmann, L. (1991): Austrian Economics: A Hermeneutic Approach. In *Lavoie, D.* (1991).

Laidler, D. (1981): Monetarism: An Interpretation and an Assessment. *Economic Journal 91*: 1-25.

Laidler, D. (1991): The Austrians and the Stockholm School: Two Failures in the Development of Modern Macroeconomics? In L. Jonung (ed.) (1991): *The Stockholm School of Economics Revisited*. Cambridge: Cambridge University Press.

Lakatos, I. (1970): Falsification and the Methodology of Scientific Research Programmes. In idem. (1978): *The Methodology of Scientific Research Programmes*. Cambridge: Cambridge University Press.

Lange, O. (1936/1937): On the Economic Theory of Socialism. In *B.E. Lippincott (1938)*.

Langlois, R.N. (1982): Austrian Economics as Affirmative Science: Comment on Rizzo. In *I.M. Kirzner (1982)*.

Langlois, R.N. (ed.) (1986a): *Economics as a Process: Essays in the New Institutional Economics*. Cambridge: Cambridge University Press.

Langlois, R.N. (1986b): The New Institutional Economics: An Introductory Essay. In *idem. (1986a)*.

Langlois, R.N. (1991): Transaction Cost Economics in Real Time. *Industrial and Corporate Change 1*: 99-127.

Langlois, R.N. (1993): Institutions. In B. Caldwell & Stephan Böhm (1973).

Langlois, R.M. & R. Koppl (1991): Fritz Machlup and Marginalism. *Methodus 3*.

Laudan, L. (1977): *Progress and Its Problems*. Berkeley: University of California Press.

Lavoie, D. (1981): A Critique of the Standard Account of the Socialist Calculation Debate. *Journal of Libertarian Studies 5:* 41-87.

Lavoie, D. (1985): *Rivalry and Central Planning: The Socialist Calculation Debate in Perspective*. Cambridge: Cambridge University Press.

Lavoie, D. (1986): Between Institutionalism and Formalism: The Rise and Fall of the Austrian School's Calculation Argument: 1920-1950.

Working Paper, Center for the Study of Market Processes, George Mason University.

Lavoie, D. (ed.) (1991): *Hermeneutics and Economics*. London: Routledge.

Lawlor, M.S. and B.L. Horn (1992): Notes on the Hayek-Sraffa Exchange. *Review of Political Economy 4*: 317-340.

Leijonhufvud, A. (1981): The Wicksell Connection. In idem. (1981): *Information and Coordination.* New York: Oxford University Press.

Lerner, A. (1944): *The Economics of Control: Principles of Welfare Economics*. New York: Macmillan.

Lippincott, B.E. (ed.) (1938): *On the Economic Theory of Socialism*. Reprint 1964. New York: McGraw-Hill.

Lippman, S.A. & R.P. Rumelt (1982): Uncertain Imitability: An Analysis of Interfirm Differences in Efficiency under Competition. *Bell Journal of Economics 13*: 418-438.

Littlechild, S.C. (1979): An Entrepreneurial Theory of Games. *Metroeconomica 31*: 145-165.

Littlechild, S.C. (1986): Three Types of Market Process. *In R.N. Langlois (1986a)*.

Loasby, B.J. (1976): *Choice, Complexity, and Ignorance*. Cambridge: Cambridge University Press.

Loasby, B.J. (1989): *The Minds and Methods of Economists*. Cambridge: Cambridge University Press.

Loasby, B.J. (1991): The Austrian School. In D.M. & A.G. Miller (eds.) (1991): *A Modern Guide to Economic Thought*. Aldershot: Edward Elgar.

Loasby, B.J. (1994): Missed Connections and Opportunities Forgone: A Counterfactual History of Twentieth Century Economics. *Unpublished working paper*.

Lucas, R.E. (1975): An Equilibrium Model of the Business Cycle. In *idem*. (1981).

Lucas, R.E. (1977): Understanding Business Cycles. In *idem*. (1981).

Lucas, R.E. (1978): On the Size Distribution of Business Firms. *Bell Journal of Economics 9*: 508-523.

Lucas, R.E. (1980): Methods and Problems in Business Cycle Theory. I *idem*. (1981).

Lucas, R.E. (1981): *Studies in Business Cycle Theory*. Cambridge, Mass.: MIT Press.

Lucas, R.E. (1987a):.*Models of Business Cycles*. London: Basil Blackwell.

Lucas, R.E. (1987b): Adaptive Behavior and Economic Theory. In *Hogarth, R.M. and M.W. Reder (1987)*.

Lucas, R.E. & T. Sargent (1979): After Keynesian Macroeconomics. In *idem.* (1981).

Lucas, R.E. & T. Sargent (eds.) (1981): *Rational Expectations and Econometric Practice.* London: George Allen and Unwin.

Lutz, F. (1932): *Das Konjunkturproblem in der Nationalökonomie.* Jena: Gustav Fischer.

Löwe, A. (1926): Wie ist ein Konjunkturtheorie Überhaupt Möglich? *Weltwirtschaftliches Archiv 24*: 165-197.

McCloskey, D.N. (1985): *The Rhetoric of Economics.* Madison: University of Wisconsin Press.

Machlup, F. (1959): Static and Dynamics: Kaleidoscopic Words. In idem. (1963): *Essays in Economic Semantics.* Englewood Cliffs: Prentice Hall.

Machlup, F. (1963a): *Essays on Economic Semantics.* Englewood Cliffs: Prentice Hall.

Machlup, F. (1963b): Equilibrium and Disequilibrium. In *idem. (1963a).*

Machlup, F. (1967): Theories of the Firm: Marginalist, Behavioral, Managerial. In idem. (1978): *Methodology of Economics and Other Social Sciences.* New York: Academic Press.

Machlup, F. (1983): The Rationality of "Rational Expectations". *Kredit und Kapital*: 172-183.

McNulty, P.J. (1984): On the Nature and Theory of Economic Organization: The Role of the Firm Reconsidered. *History of Political Economy 16*: 233-253.

Malmgren, H.B. (1961): Information, Expectations and the Theory of the Firm. *Quarterly Journal of Economics 75*: 399-421.

Manne, H. (1965): Mergers and the Market for Corporate Control. *Journal of Political Economy 73*: 110-120.

March, J.G. & H.A. Simon (1958): *Organizations.* New York: John Wiley.

March, J.G. (1991): Exploration and Exploitation in Organizational Learning. *Organization Science 2*: 1-19.

Marshall, A. (1925): *Principles of Economics.* London: Macmillan.

Mayer, H. (1932): Der Erkenntniswert der funktionellen Preistheorien. In idem. (ed.) (1932): *Die Wirtschaftstheorie der Gegenwart, Vol. 2.* Wien: Julius Springer.

Mayer, T. (1993): *Truth versus Precision in Economics.* Aldershot: Edward Elgar.

Ménard, C. (1990): The Lausanne Tradition: Walras and Pareto. In K. Hennings & W. Samuels (eds.) (1990): *Neoclassical Economic Theory, 1870 to 1930.* Boston: Kluwer.

Menger, C. (1871): *Principles of Economics*. Reprint 1976. New York: New York University Press.

Menger, C. (1883): *Problems of Economics and Sociology*. 1963 edition. Urbana: University of Illinois Press.

Milgate, M. (1979): On the Origin of the Notion of "Intertemporal Equilibrium". *Economica 46*: 1-10.

Milgrom, P. (1988): Employment Contracts, Influence Activities and Efficient Organization Design. *Journal of Political Economy 96*: 42-60.

Milgrom, P. & J. Roberts (1992): *Economics, Organization, and Management*. New York: Prentice-Hall.

Minkler, A.P. (1991): The Problem With Knowledge: An Essay on the Theory of the Firm. *Working paper.*

Mises, L.v. ([1912], 1981): *The Theory of Money and Credit*. Reprint 1981. Indianapolis: Liberty Press.

Mises, L.v. ([1920], 1990): *Economic Calculation in the Socialist Commonwealth*. Auburn: Ludwig von Mises Institute.

Mises, L.v. ([1933], 1960): *Epistemological Problems of Economics*. Princeton: Van Nostrand.

Mises, L.v. ([1936], 1981): *Socialism: An Economic and Sociological Analysis*. Indianapolis: Liberty Press.

Mises, L.v. (1943): "Elastic Expectations" and the Austrian Theory of the Business Cycle. *Economica 10*: 251-253.

Mises, L.v. (1945): *Bureaucracy*. London: William Hodge.

Mises, L.v. (1949): *Human Action: A Treatise on Economics*. London: William Hodge.

Mises, L.v. (1957): *Theory and History*. London: Jonathan Cape.

Mises, L.v. (1974): *Planning for Freedom*. Illinois: Libertarian Press.

Mitchell, W.C. (1927): *Business Cycles*. New York: National Bureau of Economic Research.

Moore, H.L. (1929): *Synthetic Economics*. New York: Macmillan.

Morgenstern, O. (1935): Perfect Foresight and Economic Equilibrium. In Schotter, A. (ed.) (1976): *Selected Economic Writings of Oskar Morgenstern*. New York: New York University Press.

Murrell, P. (1983): Did the Theory of Market Socialism Answer the Challenge of Ludwig von Mises? A Reinterpretation of the Socialist Controversy. *History of Political Economy 15*: 92-105.

Muth, J.F. (1961): Rational Expectations and the Theory of Price Movements. *In Lucas, R.E. & Sargent. (1981).*

Myrdal, G. (1933): Die Gleichgewichtsbegriff als Instrument der geldtheoretischen Analyse. In F.A.v. Hayek (ed.) (1933): *Beiträge zur Geldtheorie.* Wien: Julius Springer.

Mäki, U. (1987): Review of Richard N. Langlois (ed.), "Economics as a Process". *Economics and Philosophy 3*: 367-373.

Mäki, U. (1993): The Market as an Isolated Causal Process: A Metaphysical Ground for Realism. In *Böhm, S. & B. Caldwell (1993)*.

Nelson, R.R. (1981): Assessing Private Enterprise: An Exegesis of Tangled Doctrine. *Bell Journal of Economics 12:* 93-111.

Nelson, R.R. (1987): *Understanding Technical Change as an Evolutionary Process*. Amsterdam: North-Holland.

Nelson, R.R. & S.G. Winter (1982): *An Evolutionary Theory of Economic Change*. Cambridge, Mass.: Belknap Press.

Nove, A. (1983): *The Economics of Feasible Socialism*. Boston: Allen and Unwin.

Nove, A. & D.M. Nuti (eds.) (1972a): *Socialist Economics*. Middlesex: Penguin Books.

Nove, A. & D.M. Nuti (1972b): Introduction. In *idem. (1972a)*.

Nutter, G.W. (1967): Markets without Property: A Grand Illusion. In idem. (1983): *Political Economy and Freedom*. Indianapolis: Liberty Press.

O'Driscoll, G.P. & M. Rizzo (1985): *The Economics of Time and Ignorance.* Oxford: Basil Blackwell.

Pejovich, S. (1982): Karl Marx, Property Rights School and the Process of Social Change. *Kyklos 35*: 383-307.

Pelikan, P. (1988): Can the Innovation System of Capitalism be Outperformed? In G. Dosi et al. (eds.): *Technical Change and Economic Theory.* London: Pinter.

Penrose, E.T. (1959: *The Theory of the Growth of the Firm*. Oxford: Oxford University Press.

Polanyi, M. (1958): *Personal Knowledge: Towards a Post-Critical Philosophy*. Chicago: University of Chicago Press.

Popper, K.R. (1945): *The Open Society and Its Enemies*. 1962 ed. New York: Harper & Row.

Popper, K.R. (1965): *Conjectures and Refutations: The Growth of Scientific Knowledge*. New York: Harper Colophon.

Pratt, J.W. & R.J. Zeckhauser (1985): *Principals and Agents*. Boston: Boston Business School Press.

Prychitko, D. (1987): Ludwig Lachmann and the Farther Reaches of Austrian Economics. *Critical Review 1*: 63-76.

Ricketts, M. (1987): *The Economics of Business Enterprise*. Brighton: Wheatsheaf Books.

Rizzo, M. (ed.) (1979): *Time, Uncertainty and Disequilibrium*. Lexington: Lexington Books.

Rizzo, M. (1982): Mises and Lakatos: A Reformulation of Austrian Methodology. In *I.M. Kirzner* (1982).

Robertson, D.H. (1926): *Banking Policy and the Price Level*. London: King & Son.

Robertson, D.H. (1934): Industrial Fluctuation and the Natural Rate of Interest. In idem. (1940): *Essays in Monetary Theory*. London: Staples Press.

Robinson, J. (1933): A Parable on Savings and Investment. *Economica 13*: 75-84.

Robbins, L. (1934): *The Great Depression*. London: Macmillan.

Rothbard, M.N. (1962): *Man, Economy and State*, Vol. I & II. Los Angeles: Nash.

Rothbard, M.N. (1989): The Hermeneutical Invasion of Philosophy and Economics. *Review of Austrian Economics 3*: 45-60.

Rothbard, M.N. (1991): The End of Socialism and the Calculation Debate Revisited. *Review of Austrian Economics 5*: 51-76.

Russell, B. (1931): *The Scientific Outlook*. New York.

Salerno, J.T. (1990): Ludwig von Mises as Social Rationalist. *Review of Austrian Economics 4*: 26-54.

Samuelson, P.A. (1947/1983): *Foundations of Economic Analysis*. Cambridge, Mass.: Harvard University Press.

Samuelson, P. (1983): Marx, Keynes and Schumpeter. *Eastern Economic Journal 9*: 166-179.

Schaffer, M.E. (1989): Are Profit-Maximisers the Best Survivors? *Journal of Economic Behavior and Organization 12*: 29-45.

Schelling, T.C. (1978): *Micromotives and Macrobehavior*. New York: Norton.

Schotter, A. (1981): *The Economic Theory of Social Institutions*. Cambridge: Cambridge University Press.

Schumpeter, J.A. (1912): *The Theory of Economic Development*. Oxford: Oxford University Press.

Schumpeter, J.A. (1942): *Capitalism, Socialism and Democracy*. 1963 ed. New York: Harper & Row.

Schumpeter, J.A. (1952): *History of Economic Analysis*. Oxford: Oxford University Press.

Shackle, G.L.S. (1933): Some Notes on Monetary Theories of the Trade Cycle. *Review of Economic Studies 1*: 27-38.

Shackle, G.L.S. (1972): *Epistemics and Economics*. Cambridge: Cambridge University Press.

Silver, M. (1984): *Enterprise and the Scope of the Firm*. Aldershot: Martin Robertson.

Simon, H.A. (1976): From Substantive to Procedural Rationality. In S. Latsis (ed.) (1976): *Method and Appraisal in Economics*. Cambridge: Cambridge University Press.

Simon, H.A. (1979): Rational Decision Making in Business Organizations. *American Economic Review 69*: 493-513.

Simon, H.A. (1991): Organizations and Markets. *Journal of Economic Perspectives 5*: 25-44.

Skousen, M. (1991): *The Structure of Production*. New York: New York University Press.

Smith, A. (1776): *An Inquiry Into the Causes of the Wealth of Nations*. Indianapolis: Liberty Press.

Spadaro, L. (ed.) (1978): *New Frontiers in Austrian Economics*. Kansas City: Sheed Andrews and McNeel.

Sraffa, P. (1932): Dr. Hayek on Money and Capital. *Economic Journal 42*: 42-53.

Steele, D.R. (1981): Posing the Problem: The Impossibility of Economic Calculation under Socialism. *Journal of Libertarian Studies 5*: 7-22.

Stiglitz, J.E. (1975): Incentives, Risk and Information: Notes Towards a Theory of Hierarchy. *Bell Journal of Economics 6*: 552-579.

Streissler, E. (1972): To What Extent Was the Austrian School Marginalist? *History of Political Economy 4*: 426-441.

Szamuely, L. (1974): *First Models of the Socialist Economic Systems*. Budapest: Akademiai Kiado.

Sugden, R. (1986): *The Economics of Rights, Cooperation and Welfare*. Oxford: Basil Blackwell.

Suppes, P. (1968): The Desirability of Formalization in Science. *Journal of Philosophy 65*: 651-664.

Taylor, F.M. (1928): The Guidance of Production in a Socialist State. In *B.E. Lippincott (1938)*.

Teece, D.J. (1986): Profiting from Technological Innovation: Implications for Integration, Collaboration, Licensing. In M.L. Tushman & W.L. Moore (eds.) (1988): *Readings in the Management of Innovation*. Cambridge: Ballinger Publishing Company.

Thomsen, E.F. (1989): *Prices and Knowledge: A Market-Process Perspective*. Dissertation, New York University.

Ullman-Margalitt, E. (1978): Invisible Hand Explanations. *Synthese 39*: 282-296.

Vaughn, K.I. (1980): Economic Calculation Under Socialism: The Austrian Contribution. *Economic Inquiry 18:* 535-554.

Vaughn, K.I. (1992): The Problem of Order in Austrian Economics: Kirzner vs. Lachmann. *Review of Political Economy 4*: 251-274.

Vaughn, K.I. (1994): *Austrian Economics in America*: The Migration of a Tradition. Forthcoming.

Ward, B. (1972): *What's Wrong With Economics?* London: Macmillan.

Werin, L. & H. Wijkander (1992): *Contract Economics*. Oxford: Blackwell.

Whitley, R. (1984): *The Intellectual and Social Organization of the Sciences*. Oxford: Clarendon Press.

Wicksell, K. (1934): *Lectures I: General Theory*. (Originally in Swedish 1901). London: George Routledge.

Wicksell, K. (1936): *Interest and Prices*. (Originally in German 1898). London: Macmillan.

Wilczynski, J. (1970): *The Economics of Socialism*. London: Allen and Unwin.

Williamson, O.E. (1975): *Markets and Hierarchies*. New York: Free Press.

Williamson, O.E. (1981): The Modern Corporation: Origins, Evolution, Attributes. *Journal of Economic Literature 19*: 1537-1568.

Williamson, O.E. (1985): *The Economic Institutions of Capitalism*. New York: Free Press.

Williamson, O.E. (1987): The Economics and Sociology of Organization: Promoting a Dialogue. In G. Farkas & P. England (eds.) (1987): *Industries, Firms, and Jobs: Sociological and Economic Approaches*. New York: Plenum Press.

Williamson, O.E. (1991a): Comparative Economic Organization: The Analysis of Discrete Structural Alternatives. *Administrative Science Quarterly 38:* 269-296.

Williamson, O.E. (1991b): Economic Institutions: Spontaneous and Intentional Governance. *Journal of Law, Economics, and Organization 7*: 159-187.

Winter, S.G. (1964): Economic Natural Selection and the Theory of the Firm. *Yale Economic Essays 4*: 225-272.

Winter, S.G. (1975): Optimization and Evolution in the Theory of the Firm. In Day, R.H. & T. Groves (1975): *Adaptive Economic Models*. New York: Academic Press.

Winter, S. (1982): An Essay on the Theory of Production. In S.H Hymans (ed.) (1982): *Economics and the World Around It.* Michigan University of Michigan Press.

Winter, S.G. (1986): The Research Program of the Behavioral Theory of the Firm: Orthodox Critique and Evolutionary Perspectives. In B. Gilad & S. Kaish (eds.) (1986): *Handbook of Behavioral Economics, Vol. A: Behavioral Microeconomics.* Greenwich: JAI Press.

Winter, S.G. (1987): Adaptive Behavior and Economic Theory. In *Hogarth, R.M. & M.W. Reder (1987).*

Witt, U. (1987a): *Individualistische Grundlage der Evolutorischen Ökonomik.* Tübingen: J.C.B. Mohr.

Witt, U. (1987b): How Transaction Rights Are Shaped to Channel Innovativeness. *Journal of Institutional and Theoretical Economics 143:* 180-195.

Witt, U. (1993): Turning Austrian Economics Into an Evolutionary Theory. In *B. Caldwell & S. Böhm (1993).*

About the Author

Nicolai J. Foss was born in 1964 and earned his master's degree in economics from Copenhagen University, and his Ph.D. from Copenhagen Business School, where he is currently employed as assistant professor. His professional honors include the Tietgen Prize and the Zeuthen Prize. In addition to the history of economic doctrines, his research interests include organizational economics and strategic management. Nicolai J. Foss has published in Review of Political Economy, Journal of Evolutionary Economics, Managerial and Decision Economics, Journal of Economic Issues, Review of Austrian Economics, Journal of Social and Evolutionary Systems, Rivista Internazionale di Scienze Sociali, Revue d'Economie Industrielle and other journals.